Changing the Faces of Mathematics

Perspectives on Latinos

Series Editor

Walter G. Secada
University of Wisconsin—Madison
Madison, Wisconsin

Editors

Luis Ortiz-Franco
Chapman University
Orange, California

Norma G. Hernandez
University of Texas at El Paso
El Paso, Texas

Yolanda De La Cruz
Arizona State University West
Phoenix, Arizona

National Council of Teachers of Mathematics
Reston, Virginia

ISBN 0-87353-464-6

Printed in the United States of America

Contents

PREFACE vii

INTRODUCTION 1

PART 1
SOCIOEDUCATIONAL
ISSUES

1. Understanding the Needs of Latino Students in
   Reform-Oriented Mathematics Classrooms 5
   Judit N. Moschkovich
   TERC, Cambridge, Massachusetts

2. Latinos, Income, and Mathematics Achievement: Beating the Odds 13
   Luis Ortiz-Franco
   Chapman University, Orange, California

PART 2
LANGUAGE ISSUES

3. Isn't English a Trip? 21
   José Franco
   EQUALS, University of California at Berkeley, Berkeley, California

4. Spanish-English Language Issues in the Mathematics Classroom 23
   Pilar Ron
   Seville, Spain

5. Adapting Mathematics Instruction for English-Language Learners:
   The Language-Concept Connection 35
   Leslie Garrison
   San Diego State University—Imperial Valley Campus, Calexico, California

   Jill Kerper Mora
   San Diego State University—Imperial Valley Campus, Calexico, California

6. The Mathematics–Bilingual-Education Connection: Two Lessons 49
   Norma G. Hernandez
   University of Texas at El Paso, El Paso, Texas

7. Mathematizing Children's Stories, Helping Children Solve
   Word Problems, and Supporting Parental Involvement 59
   Ana María Lo Cicero
   Northwestern University, Evanston, Illinois

   Karen C. Fuson
   Northwestern University, Evanston, Illinois

   Martha Allexsaht-Snider
   Northwestern University, Evanston, Illinois

8. Challenging Conventional Wisdom: A Case Study 71

Lena Licón Khisty
University of Illinois at Chicago, Chicago, Illinois

Gabriel Viego
University of Illinois at Chicago, Chicago, Illinois

PART 3
TEACHING-LEARNING AIDS

9. Teachers' and Students' Attitudes toward the Use of
Manipulatives in Two Predominantly Latino School Districts 81

Maria L. Bustamante
East Central Heritage Middle School, San Antonio, Texas

Betty Travis
University of Texas at San Antonio, San Antonio, Texas

10. Portafolio de Matemática: Using Mathematics Portfolios
with Latino Students 85

Leslie Garrison
San Diego State University—Imperial Valley Campus, Calexico, California

PART 4
STAFF DEVELOPMENT

11. Taking On the Challenge of Mathematics for All 99

Richard G. Doty
Spurgeon Intermediate School, Santa Ana, California

Susan Mercer
Spurgeon Intermediate School, Santa Ana, California

Marjorie A. Henningsen
University of Pittsburgh, Pittsburgh, Pennsylvania

12. Staff Development to Foster Latino Students' Success
in Mathematics: Insights from Constructivism 113

Gary Ivory
New Mexico State University, Las Cruces, New Mexico

Dolores R. Chaparro
Ysleta Independent School District, El Paso, Texas

Stanley Ball
University of Texas at El Paso, El Paso, Texas

PART 5
INTERVENTION
PROGRAMS

13. TexPREP and Proyecto Access: Making Mathematics Work
    for Minorities 123
    Julio C. Guillén
    New Jersey City University, Jersey City, New Jersey

    Manuel P. Berriozábal
    University of Texas at San Antonio, San Antonio, Texas

14. The Minority Mathematics and Science Education
    Cooperative (MMSEC) Success Story 133
    Olga M. Ramirez
    University of Texas—Pan American, Edinburg, Texas

    John E. Bernard
    University of Texas—Pan American, Edinburg, Texas

15. A Model of Tutoring That Helps Students Gain Access
    to Mathematical Competence 147
    Yolanda De La Cruz
    Arizona State University West, Phoenix, Arizona

16. There's More to Mathematics than Choosing the Letter *C*:
    The Limitations of Test-Driven Intervention 159
    Milagros M. Seda
    University of Texas at El Paso, El Paso, Texas

    Carmen M. Seda
    Ysleta Independent School District, El Paso, Texas

Preface

The publication of *Changing the Faces of Mathematics: Perspectives on Latinos* has both historical and academic significance. The historical significance lies in the fact that the publication of this book is the first instance in the history of mathematics education that a professional mathematics association has published a book that focuses exclusively on Latinos. The academic significance of this book lies in the fact that fifteen of the sixteen articles in this volume are either authored or coauthored by Latinos. An important implication of this fact is that today there are enough Latino scholars in the mathematics education community to put together a book of this nature, whereas ten or fifteen years ago there were not.

The authors who contributed to this volume have the linguistic, cultural, and professional sensitivity to address the teaching and learning issues affecting Latinos from a non–deficit-theory perspective. This is refreshing, considering that in the past the deficit model was the prevalent framework for interpreting the performance and achievement of Latinos in mathematics. The authors in this volume also demonstrate a sound knowledge of the literature related to both Latinos and non-Latinos that pertains to the topics they address in their articles.

This book is a significant accomplishment for both Latinos and mathematics education; it has profound implications for our mission of providing a quality mathematics education to all students. One of these implications is that the mathematics education community now has a cadre of Latino mathematics teachers and mathematics education researchers who can understand, reflect on, and interpret the experiences of Latino students in the mathematics classroom, whether that experience involves assessment, teaching, or learning. This means that the larger community of mathematics educators can no longer marginalize Latino students in national mathematics assessment, research, or teaching reform efforts on the basis that professionals in our field do not have the expertise to address the impact of the linguistic and cultural variables in the Latino population. This cadre of Latino mathematics educators is a valuable resource in integrating the educational needs of Latinos more fully into the process of reform in mathematics education. It remains to be seen whether the mathematics education community will make wise use of this resource in furthering the goal of quality mathematics education for all.

This book is the result of the commitment of many people. It is one in a series of six proposed volumes addressing issues involved in the teaching and learning of mathematics among ethnic minorities and women. The work of the series' Editorial Board on developing the guidelines for this volume is greatly appreciated.

The editors want to thank the following people who assisted us in reviewing and offering valuable recommendations on some of the manuscripts: Ignacio Alarcon, California State University/Bakersfield; Martha Allexsaht-Snider, Northwestern University; Isali Alsina; Manuel Berriozabal, University of Texas at San Antonio; Roberta Dees; Gary Ivory, New Mexico State University; Judit Moschkovich, TERC; Juan José Perez, University of Texas at Brownsville; James A. Telese, University of Texas at Brownsville; and Raymond Castro, California State University/Sonoma.

We also want to express our thanks and appreciation to the authors of the manuscripts in this volume for their patience throughout the process of producing this book, their willingness to accept the comments of the editors, and most of all, their determination and desire to make a difference in the mathematics education of Latinos. Our appreciation also goes to the editorial and production staff at the NCTM Headquarters Office for turning this collection of manuscripts into a finished book.

Last but not least, we want to express our gratitude to our families for sacrificing our family time together so that we could work on this volume. Their contributions to mathematics education are greatly appreciated.

Introduction

Changing the Faces of Mathematics: Perspectives on Latinos focuses on a number of salient research and practice issues in the teaching and learning of mathematics among the second largest minority group in the United States. This group is referred to as *Hispanics* by governmental and other agencies, but the majority of members of the group call themselves *Latinos*. This introduction explains the distinction between the terms *Hispanic* and *Latino* and presents a general summary of the book.

The Terms *Hispanic* and *Latino*

The population group in the United States referred to as *Hispanics* includes primarily people who trace their origins to Latin America. The largest subgroup is of Mexican origin; many of them refer to themselves as *Chicanos* or *Mexican Americans*. The next largest group is of Puerto Rican ancestry; many of them refer to themselves as *Nuyoricans*. The third largest group is of Cuban descent. The rest of the Hispanic population is of Central American origin (Guatemala, El Salvador, Honduras, etc.) and of South American origin (Colombia, Peru, Chile, Argentina, Bolivia, etc.). Although the people of Latin America are aware that their language (Spanish), their names, and their dominant religion (Catholicism) are cultural elements transplanted from Spain to the New World, they prefer to call themselves *Latinos* rather than *Hispanics*. The term *Latinos* can be viewed as a statement of cultural self-determination, and it should be respected as such by society at large, including the mathematics education community. Hence, the term *Latinos* in the title of this book.

Throughout this volume, the following terms are used. *Latinos* is the plural of *Latino,* and it is a neuter adjective that is, by implication, gender neutral. Thus, the term *Latinos* refers to the entire population without distinctions on the basis of gender, age, or marital status. The term *Latinas,* plural of *Latina,* refers to female members of this group. *Latino* and *Latinos,* when followed by the word *man* or *men,* respectively, refer only to male members of this group.

The dominant religion among Latinos is Catholicism; however, there are Latinos of other religious persuasions, such as Protestants, Mormons, and Jews. The majority of Latinos are of mestizo origin, a mixture of American Indian and European or other ethnic origin (the term *American Indian* is used here to refer to the peoples indigenous to the mainland territories and islands of the New World). Other Latinos are pure American Indian (Maya, Inca, Tarahumara, Zapotec, etc.), whereas others are Asians (Japanese, Chinese, etc.), African Americans, or Europeans (Spanish, French, German, Russian, etc.). Thus, Latinos comprise groups with very diverse national, socioeconomic, cultural, ethnic, and religious backgrounds.

Some Latinos, primarily Chicanos, can claim ancestry in this country dating back to before the Pilgrims arrived at Plymouth Rock; others are more recent arrivals. Thus, a first generation Latino immigrant is a person who is born in a Latin American country and who immigrates to the United States. A second-generation Latino immigrant is a person who is born in the United States and whose parents are first-generation immigrants. A third- or subsequent-generation Latino immigrant is a person who is born in the United States and whose parents are second- or subsequent-generation immigrants. The language differences among Latino students that are addressed in some of the articles in this book are rooted in the immigrant generation to which the students belong. Also, some of the studies cited in the articles are considered to be intergenerational because they include in their population sample subjects from two or more immigrant generations.

Latinos are the fastest-growing population group in the United States. This population is concentrated in Arizona, California, Colorado, Texas, Florida, Illinois, and New York. Latinos, however, can be found in many other states, including Alaska and Hawaii. Today there are about twenty-two million people in this group; it is estimated that by the year 2010, or earlier, Latinos will be the largest minority group in this country. By that time, it is projected that in some states, such as California, the largest student population group in grades K–12 will be Latino. These projections have profound implications for research and practice in the teaching and learning of mathematics, given the linguistic and cultural diversity of this emerging group. To give an example, today 89 percent of Latino adults in the United States speak Spanish at home, even though they may speak English outside the home. This cultural factor has major implications for mathematics instruction in the grades K–3 classroom.

Summary of This Book

This volume is divided into five parts: "Socioeducational Issues," "Language Issues," "Teaching-Learning Aids," "Staff Development," and "Intervention Programs." The categorization of some articles was arbitrary, since their content overlaps several sections. For example, the opening article, by Judit Moschkovich, appears in the "Socioeducational Issues" section, but it also fits well in the category of "Language Issues." Moschkovich discusses social issues and language concerns in the context of research and practice in the mathematics classroom. She also addresses the need to develop assessment programs and instruments to tap the mathematical knowledge of first-generation Latino immigrant students in order to assist schools and school districts in placing these students in appropriate mathematics courses. Her discussion of these and other issues reflects a deep understanding of the mathematics education needs of this population.

The second article in the opening section, by Luis Ortiz-Franco, shows that the mathematics achievement of Latinos increased over the twenty-year period between 1972 and 1992 while at the same time their family income levels decreased in absolute and comparative terms compared with those of the majority non-Latino white population. This finding questions the theoretical models and conclusions that postulate a positive correlation between family income and mathematics achievement. However, the author suggests that Latino parents' involvement in their children's education and a higher level of parent education might have contributed more strongly than income to their children's increase in mathematics achievement. It is not possible to determine the cause of the results on the basis of the data analyzed, since the study was nonexperimental. Ortiz-Franco also points out that many teachers' low expectations of, and negative social attitudes toward, their Latino students are serious obstacles to their students' mathematics achievement. Both Moschkovich and Ortiz-Franco also touch on topics concerning teaching and learning in the mathematics classroom.

The second part, "Language Issues," addresses research and practice topics related to bilingualism in mathematics education. José Franco opens this section in a poetic form that captures the difference in the uses and meanings of the same words in everyday vocabulary and in the mathematics register and the resulting difficulties that this difference creates for students who are in the process of learning English as a second language.

In the second article, Pilar Ron discusses in more depth the issues touched on by Franco, and she gives specific attention to the implications of bilingualism in the mathematics classroom. She comments in the context of both theory and practice on issues that arise when grades K–3 bilingual children try to learn verbal mathematical problem solving. Her discussion makes it evident that bilingual teachers who want to improve the English language skills of their students play at once the triple role of language experts, translators, and mathematics teachers. Schools seldom meet the professional needs of teachers of bilingual students, Ron says, which prevents those teachers from providing a sound education to their students.

The next article, by Leslie Garrison and Jill Kerper Mora, discusses, in the context of classroom instruction, the connection between learning a language and learning mathematical concepts. In their discussion they touch on instructional techniques, graphic and symbolic representations in mathematics, and the relationship between language and concept development. They conclude that it is both a comfort and a challenge to teachers to realize that effective mathematics instruction has much in common with effective second-language learning. That theme is also broached by Norma Hernandez in her illustration of mathematics lessons in a bilingual classroom. She argues that the learning of mathematics concepts can be facilitated in a bilingual English-Spanish classroom when the importance of the language of mathematics is emphasized in both languages. She vividly illustrates that process by applying the dialectical method to the teaching of new mathematics concepts to Latino students' learning of English.

Ana Lo Cicero, Karen Fuson, and Martha Allexsaht-Snider also address language in the learning of mathematics, in the context of mathematizing the life stories of children. Their article illustrates that Latino children in grades 1–3 spontaneously use the problem-solving processes described by Polya in *How to Solve It,* including engagement in metacognitive behavior, as they solve mathematical problems that they create from their own life experiences. The authors also emphasize home-and-school integration in mathematics education by highlighting the importance of involving parents in their children's learning of mathematics.

Closing the "Language Issues" section, Lena Khisty and Gabriel Viego hypothesize that mathematics pedagogy among Latinos has been difficult to change, perhaps because most mathematics teachers cannot easily implement the type of learning experiences advocated in the mathematics-reform movement. They argue that teachers are unable to provide such reformed learning experiences because they themselves have never experienced them. However, the authors also discuss the successful pedagogical techniques of a teacher in an urban fifth-grade mathematics classroom and claim that this teacher's success challenges the deficit theory, the view of Latino children as incapable learners. This successful teacher, according to the authors, creates in her classroom a mathematical cultural context that immerses her students in the social norms, thinking, and practices associated with mathematics.

Part 3, "Teaching and Learning Aids," consists of two articles. The article by Maria Bustamante and Betty Travis provides empirical data about the attitudes of teachers and students toward the use of manipulatives in the mathematics classroom in a Texas school district. Although the study reports that both students and teachers expressed a positive attitude toward the use of manipulatives, the authors observed significant gender differences in the students' responses.

Leslie Garrison discusses the use of portfolios to assess the learning of mathematics and English by students who have recently immigrated. The author explains how student portfolios can be used to determine whether the students' learning is in line with the NCTM *Standards* as well as to assess and evaluate the effectiveness of the school's mathematics program. One of Garrison's conclusions is that special attention needs to be paid to the linguistic differences in the student population by allowing students to write in their primary language when appropriate.

In part 4, "Staff Development," the article by Richard Doty, Susan Mercer, and Marjorie Henningsen includes topics on staff and curriculum development and on language issues in the teaching of mathematics. This article is a product of a collaboration between classroom teachers and university-based staff and is based on the experiences of the Quantitative Understanding Amplifying Student Achievement and Reasoning project in a middle school having a predominantly bilingual student population. The successful experiences related in the article also challenge the deficit theory of the learning of mathematics by minority students. The article illustrates the need for a multidimensional approach, including staff development and changes in curriculum and instructional practices, to improve the mathematics achievement of Latinos.

The article by Gary Ivory, Delores Chaparro, and Stanley Ball is an example of a collaboration between university-based researchers and public school personnel in empirical studies applying theoretical constructs (constructivist theory in this instance) in staff development to improve the mathematics achievement of students. One result of this collaboration was that at the end of the study, the investigators began to question the effectiveness of some of the traditional mathematics-teaching methods. Their experience increased their confidence that new teaching methods, such as those advocated by the current mathematics education reform movement, will foster students' understanding and self-reliance as problem solvers.

Both large-scale and small-scale attempts to improve the mathematics achievement of Latino students through learning activities outside the regular classroom setting are related in the last part, "Intervention Programs." The first article, by Manuel Berriozabal and Julio Guillen, discusses the history and success of the oldest mathematics intervention program targeting Latinos in the United States. This program evolved from a local effort, San Antonio PREP, to a statewide model, the Texas Prefreshman Engineering Program (TexPREP); this model is being duplicated in other parts of the country by Proyecto Access. TexPREP has received many awards from private and public organizations, including the Presidential Award for Excellence in Science, Mathematics, and Engineering Mentoring, for its success in increasing the number of Latinos pursuing mathematics-based careers.

Olga Ramirez and John Bernard discuss the evolution of a local intervention program in south Texas, the Minority Mathematics and Science Education Cooperative, designed to improve the mathematics and science achievement of minority students through staff development and home-and-school activities. Among other topics, the authors describe the excitement of parents with limited formal education when they learn new science and mathematics concepts in programs organized by the school. We also learn in this article about the dynamics of personal interaction and individual change among school personnel as the program evolved.

In an article about the After-School Mathematics Tutoring (ASMT) Program, a mathematics tutoring project in the Midwest, Yolanda De La Cruz claims that by operating on the affective domain, that is, by nurturing self-confidence, teachers can induce positive changes in students' attitudes toward academic learning and thereby improve their mathematics achievement. The author discusses the development of those attitude changes through a tutoring model that she developed on the basis of her experiences in the ASMT Program. The author shares with us in vivid detail the process involved in the tutoring program, as well as the personal struggles of the participants.

The last article in this section, by Milagros Seda and Carmen Seda, closes this volume. This essay presents another example of a collaboration between university staff and classroom practitioners in addressing mathematics education issues. The article raises many issues affecting the experience of Latino students in mathematics education, among them language and cultural differences between the students and the assessment instruments used to gauge their mathematical knowledge. The authors point out that Latino students are often taught by people who do not have an adequate academic preparation in mathematics and that the mathematics instruction that they receive is often product rather than process oriented.

Understanding the Needs of Latino Students in Reform-Oriented Mathematics Classrooms 1

Judit N. Moschkovich

Curriculum guidelines and research in mathematics education have outlined the characteristics of reform-oriented mathematics classrooms (National Council of Teachers of Mathematics [NCTM] 1989). These characteristics include an increased emphasis on communication and collaborative work. It is important in designing classroom instruction for Latino students to consider how these two new emphases—a focus on mathematical discourse and new forms of student participation—might intersect with the needs of Latino students and affect their experiences in the mathematics classroom.

First, a clarification: The labels *Latino, Hispanic,* and *Spanish-speaking* may be useful as general descriptors for a population of students. However, these labels can obscure crucial distinctions, such as whether a student is a recent immigrant or a native of the United States (Ogbu 1991) and important differences, such as linguistic diversity in the use of Spanish and English (Garcia and Gonzalez 1995). For example, students labeled as Latino can differ in length of residence in the United States, language proficiency in English, language proficiency in Spanish, prior school experience, and socioeconomic status. Students labeled as Mexican Americans, the largest group of Latinos in the United States (Garcia and Gonzalez 1995), differ in where they were born—in the United States or in Mexico; where they live—in an urban or rural area; which languages they speak; their parents' occupation, income, education, and languages; and how many generations their families have been in the United States (Sánchez 1983).

These differences mean that the needs of Latino students are both diverse and specific to individual students. Consider, for example, the following contrasting situations: A student who is a recent arrival, has missed three years of school in her home country, and is orally fluent in Spanish but not proficient in writing or reading will have very different needs in the mathematics classroom from those of a student who is a recent arrival, has not missed any school in her home country, and has completed a year of algebra in Spanish. These two students in turn have different needs from those of a student who immigrated to the United States several years ago, has some proficiency in Spanish, and has had only one or two years of mathematics classes in Spanish or from those of a student who was born in the United States and whose schooling experience has been entirely in English.

Within this diversity, Latino students still share some common needs with other "minority" students. As part of the minority student population, Latino students need access to curricula, instruction, and teachers that have proved to be effective in

This work was supported in part by the National Science Foundation through a Research Planning Grant and by the National Academy of Education through a Spencer Postdoctoral Fellowship at the Institute for Research on Learning. The opinions expressed do not necessarily reflect the views of these organizations. The author would like to thank Julia Aguirre, Betsy Brenner, Lena Licón Khisty, and several anonymous reviewers for their comments on a previous draft of this chapter.

supporting the success of minority students. The general characteristics of such environments are that the curricula provide "abundant and diverse opportunities for speaking, listening, reading, and writing" and that instruction "encourage students to take risks, construct meaning, and seek reinterpretations of knowledge within compatible social contexts" (Garcia and Gonzalez 1995, p. 424).

Some of the characteristics of teachers who have been documented as being successful with minority students are (*a*) a high commitment to their students' academic success and to student-home communication, (*b*) high expectations for all students, (*c*) the autonomy to change curriculum and instruction to meet the specific needs of their students, and (*d*) a rejection of models of their students as intellectually disadvantaged (Garcia and Gonzalez 1995).

Latino students who are English-language learners share academic and assessment needs with other non-Latino English-language learners. The following example illustrates the importance of considering whether students who are learning English are being placed in mathematics classrooms according to their proficiency in English or their proficiency in mathematics.

While observing a mainstream ninth-grade mathematics classroom, I noticed that two Spanish-dominant Latino students were not participating in the lesson on graphing parabolas. When I asked them (in Spanish) if they were having a problem, they told me they had already studied this material the previous year in their native country. They also said that they felt discouraged because in their view they were falling behind by repeating material they already knew. These two students, like other English-language learners in similar circumstances, might have benefited from a more accurate assessment of their academic knowledge that might lead to a more appropriate study program.

This example is not an isolated incident but reflects a common situation in which English-language learners receive differential treatment because of inappropriate assessment of their skills (Losey 1995). Placing students in mathematics classrooms solely on the basis of English proficiency can lead to the repetition of mathematics content that English-language learners may have already studied, and this repetition can lead to decreased engagement in classroom activities. For placement to be more effective, English-language learners should be assessed on a diversity of skills in a number of different contexts (Losey 1995). For example, written placement tests can be supplemented by other sources of information, such as interviews with the students.

A NEW EMPHASIS ON MATHEMATICAL DISCOURSE

Mathematics curriculum and teaching standards have come to reflect a model of mathematics learning that emphasizes discourse and communication (NCTM 1989). As mathematics classrooms shift from a focus on primarily silent and individual activities (Cazden 1986; Stodolsky 1988) to more verbal and social ones (Cobb, Wood, and Yackel 1993; Flores, Sowder, Philipp, and Schapelle 1996), Latino students are facing new challenges and developing new needs. In reform-oriented mathematics classrooms, students are no longer grappling mainly with acquiring technical vocabulary, developing comprehension skills to read and understand mathematics textbooks, or solving standard word problems. Instead, students are now expected to participate in both verbal and written mathematical discourse practices (Gee 1992), such as explaining solution processes, describing conjectures, proving conclusions, and presenting arguments.

This new emphasis on mathematical discourse will probably change the nature of all students' experiences in the mathematics classroom by increasing oral activities and decreasing activities involving solitary text comprehension. However, it is not clear how this new emphasis might affect Latino students in particular or how classroom instruction can support the development of their mathematical discourse.

On the one hand, the increased expectation for Latino students who are English-language learners to participate in public conversations might increase the possibilities that these students will be assessed as deficient in mathematics because of their developing oral language skills. In contrast, prior to this new emphasis, English-language learners could have appeared more mathematically competent while they worked silently at their desks on a worksheet. On the other hand, this change might also provide more opportunities for English-language learners to participate in purposeful and contextual conversations with other speakers, creating an environment that can support both language and conceptual development.

Recommendations for mathematics instruction for English-language learners have contibuted to teaching practices by describing how instruction can directly address interference between a student's native language and English or between systems of representation in different countries, such as the different use of commas and periods to denote place value. However, many of the current guidelines for mathematics instruction for English-language learners give a limited view of learning mathematics and do not address the new emphasis on mathematical discourse. Instructional recommendations have tended to focus on English-language learners' understanding of word problems, comprehension of written mathematical texts, or vocabulary development (Dale and Cuevas 1987; MacGregor and Moore 1992; Olivares 1996; Rubenstein 1996). However, since Latino students will be expected to discuss, argue, and communicate about mathematics (Brenner 1994), research studies now need to consider these new demands and document how they affect this student population.

A more comprehensive empirical research base is needed to guide the design of classroom mathematics instruction for Latino students who are learning English. Despite the steadily increasing population of American students, estimated to be five million, who are classified as limited in English proficiency (one million of these in California, a large percent of them Latinos), little research has addressed these students' needs in mathematics classrooms. Although several studies have focused on the difficulties faced by Latino students in learning mathematics (Cuevas 1984; Cuevas, Mann, and McClung 1986; Mestre 1982, 1988; Mestre and Gerace 1982; Mestre, Gerace, and Lockhead 1982; Spanos, Rhodes, Dale, and Crandall 1988), these studies examined students solving traditional word problems, understanding individual vocabulary terms, or translating from English to mathematical symbols. It seems difficult to connect these findings about traditional word problems to the design of lessons in which students are expected to write and talk about their solutions to open-ended problems, present written or oral arguments for or against conjectures, and defend their conclusions about a mathematical situation.

Although several current studies have focused on discourse in monolingual mathematics and science classrooms (Cobb, Wood, and Yackel 1993; Lemke 1990; Pimm 1987; Pirie 1991; Richards 1991), researchers have only recently begun to consider conversations in language-minority classrooms (Brenner 1994; Khisty 1995; Khisty, McLeod, and Bertilson 1990; Rosebery, Warren, and Conant 1992; Thornburg and Karp 1992). This developing body of research reflects current models of learning and teaching mathematics, in which mathematical discourse is seen as an integral aspect of learning mathematics.

The design of teaching environments for this population of students would be facilitated by developing—

- a deeper understanding of classroom mathematical discourse in general;
- descriptions of how learning mathematics in two languages involves more than acquiring technical vocabulary or translating word problems;
- examples of the resources bilingual students bring to the mathematics classroom.

Research on student learning and recommendations for teaching mathematics to English-language learners that emphasize the obstacles Latino students face when learning mathematics risk presenting a deficiency model (Garcia and Gonzalez 1995; Gonzalez 1995) of these students. Instead, instruction in mathematical communication needs to consider not only the obstacles students face but also the resources these students use to communicate mathematically.

Research is needed that describes the resources Latino students use in these new classroom situations. Investigations also need to consider aspects of mathematical discourse beyond vocabulary and text comprehension, such as the discourse practices for presenting mathematical conjectures and arguments. Only then can principled classroom recommendations be developed that address the actual needs of Latino students in reforming mathematics classrooms.

In general, as mathematics classroom activities require more oral communication, the needs of Latino students will vary depending on their previous experiences with school mathematical discourse in either English or Spanish and their proficiency in those languages. One important consideration is that a student's overall proficiency in one language does not necessarily reflect proficiency in *mathematical discourse* in that language. For example, a student may be proficient in nonmathematical English but not as proficient in mathematical discourse in English.

Students will also have different language proficiencies in different areas of mathematics. For example, some students who may be proficient in Spanish in one topic, such as percents, may not be proficient in Spanish in another context, such as algebra, because they have not had classroom experiences in Spanish in that subject.

Students will benefit from Spanish translations, written or oral, in various ways. For some, translations can support the understanding of the mathematics concepts, whereas for others, translations can support the development of language proficiency in Spanish. In general, if a student has studied mathematics in Spanish and is a proficient reader in that language, written translations of the material can be useful for developing mathematical concepts and building on the student's previous knowledge. For students who have had little or no experience in a mathematics classroom in Spanish, written translations of the materials will be useful in supporting the development of Spanish proficiency and literacy, but translations may not necessarily clarify the mathematics concepts.

An important consideration is that mathematical conversations involve much more than vocabulary (Halliday 1978; Pimm 1987). Thus, a student who may be less proficient in one language in the vocabulary of a specific topic in mathematics—for example, algebra—may be proficient in another aspect of mathematical discourse, such as presenting clear arguments. Although students may benefit from having access to mathematical vocabulary in Spanish, students use Spanish in mathematical conversations in ways that go beyond vocabulary (Moschkovich 1996a, 1996b).

Sometimes Latino students may present explanations first in one language and then in the other or use a combination of Spanish and English to construct an argument (Moschkovich 1996b). Frequently, these explanations reflect important conceptual knowledge that might not have been evident if the student had been limited to using only one language. Classroom activities can support conceptual development by allowing for flexible language use during mathematical conversations between students and in whole-class discussions.

NEW FORMS OF STUDENT PARTICIPATION

The NCTM *Curriculum and Evaluation Standards for School Mathematics* (the *Standards*) (1989) also calls for new forms of classroom participation. The *Standards* recommends a shift from teacher presentation and individual student seatwork to a diversity of forms for student participation in classroom activities. Students are expected to work in pairs or small groups, participate in whole-class discussions, and make presentations to the class. It is not clear how these proposed forms of student participation will affect Latino students in particular, and no research studies have explored the impact of these new forms of participation.

Two important questions that research on student participation in mathematics classrooms will need to address are (1) how these new forms of participation do or do not reflect Latino students' previous experiences in school or the participation structures (Au 1980) in their homes and (2) how these forms of participation affect Latino students' academic achievement in mathematics.

Although research has described participation structures in the home cultures of other populations, such as native Hawaiian students (Au 1980) and Navaho students (Vogt, Jordan, and Tharp 1987) and how differences in participation structures affect classroom interactions, it is important to note that research specifically addressing the needs of Latino students does not provide a clear basis for generalizations. Even for Mexican Americans, the largest Latino subgroup, generalizations about culturally appropriate instruction do not follow easily from the results of research studies of home environments.

For example, a review of recent studies comparing Mexican American and Anglo home interactions (Losey 1995) found that these studies had not examined a natural setting, used a natural task, or described important differences such as participants' income, social class, or education. Similarly, many of the studies comparing styles of interaction at school and at home had not fully examined each of these settings or considered differences in socioeconomic levels or ethnicity.

It is also difficult to make generalizations about cooperative learning. Although cooperative learning is thought to be appropriate for language minority children in general (Kagan 1986), this recommendation is based on psychological experiments rather than on classroom-based research relating cooperative learning in mathematics classrooms specifically to academic achievement for Latino students. Although studies of successful classroom environments for Mexican Americans conclude that collaborative learning, among other classroom characteristics, can "enhance classroom interaction, and ultimately, student success" (Losey 1995, p. 312), this claim is not yet supported by data on mathematics learning.

Moreover, because these studies usually focused on literacy and language development and did not address mathematics instruction or conceptual development in mathematics, it does not seem appropriate to go from these general suggestions to specific recommendations for organizing the participation of Latino students in mathematics classrooms. More empirical research is needed that explores these questions and that specifically relates mathematics instruction and forms of participation to students' conceptual learning in mathematics.

CONSIDERATIONS FOR DESIGNING INSTRUCTION

Even though at this point it seems difficult to make generalizations about Latino students' needs in reform-oriented mathematics classrooms, the following are some important considerations that can guide the design of mathematics instruction for these students: (1) honor the diversity of Latino students' experiences, (2) know the students and their experiences, (3) avoid deficit models, and (4) provide opportunities for mathematical discussions.

Honor the Diversity of Latino Students' Experiences

One reason to avoid generalizations about the needs of Latino students is that culture is a complex phenomenon. González (1995) decries approaches that "have relegated notions of culture to observable surface markers of folklore, assuming that all members of a particular group share a normative, bounded, and integrated view of their own culture" (p. 237). She presents the view that we cannot assume cultural uniformity or a simple set of shared practices for *any* cultural group (González 1995, p. 237):

> The households from which students emerge are intersected by multiple mediated constructs that can belie a harmonious and homogeneous set of cultural practices, and we cannot assume cultural uniformity as a canon of knowledge that simply has to be transmitted transgenerationally.

Latino students come from diverse cultural groups and have varied experiences. It is difficult to make recommendations about the needs of Latino students in mathematics classrooms that would accurately reflect the experiences of a student from a remote Andean village, a student from a bustling Latin American city, a student from a Southwest border town in the United States, and a student from an Afro-Caribbean island. Although these students will have some shared experiences, such as some relationship to the use of Spanish, there will also be many differences among these students' experiences, either at home or in school. Both the differences and commonalties among Latino students should be kept in mind when designing mathematics instruction.

Know the Students

González goes on to suggest that "approaches to culture that take into account multiple perspectives can reorient educators to consider the everyday lived experieces of their students" (González 1995, p. 237). The best way to determine what are culturally appropriate classroom-participation structures is to get to know the students and their communities (González 1995; González et al. 1995; Moll et al. 1992). For example, decisions about the instructional needs of Latino students should be made on the basis of specific information about the students' previous experiences in mathematics classrooms. It is important to talk explicitly with students about the ways in which they participated in previous mathematics classrooms and how those ways may be the same as, or different from, the ways in which they are expected to participate in their present classroom.

Avoid Deficit Models

Latino students have been characterized by a deficit model in which their failure in schools and on standardized tests is related to their culture and home environment (González 1995). Latino students share with other English-language learners an experience of instruction that has often focused on "language genres, behavior patterns, motivations, attitudes, and expectations that are either unacknowledged by the schools or seen as developmental deficits that must be 'remediated' or proscribed before learning can begin (Garcia and Gonzalez 1995, p. 422).

In designing mathematics instruction for Latino students, we need to move from deficit models of these students to frameworks that value the resources that they bring to the mathematics classroom. Recent work provides examples of frameworks for viewing Latino students or their households as the source of cognitive and social resources rather than as the source of obstacles and deficiencies (González 1995; González et al. 1995; Moll et al. 1992; Moschkovich 1996b).

Provide Opportunities for Mathematical Discussions

The new emphasis on mathematical discourse and the new forms of student participation point to the need for Latino students to have the opportunity to engage in mathematical discussions with their peers, with their teacher, and with their whole class. Mathematical discussions can be defined as "purposeful talk on a mathematical subject in which there are genuine pupil contributions and interactions" (Pirie 1991, p. 143).

Students need opportunities to use the language of mathematics not only to read textbooks, translate algebra word problems into equations, or carry out computations but also to pose mathematical questions, describe the solutions to problems, explain and justify their solutions, present arguments for or against conjectures, and defend their generalizations.

REFERENCES

Au, Kathryn H. "Participation Structures in Reading Lessons: Analysis of a Culturally Appropriate Instructional Event." *Anthropology and Education Quarterly* 11, no. 2 (1980): 91–115.

Brenner, Mary E. "A Communication Framework for Mathematics: Exemplary Instruction for Culturally and Linguistically Diverse Students." In *Language and Learning: Educating Linguistically Diverse Students,* edited by Beverly McLeod, pp. 233–67. Albany, N.Y.: State University of New York, 1994.

Cazden, Courtney B. "Classroom Discourse." In *Handbook of Research on Teaching,* edited by M. C. Wittrock, pp. 123–55. New York: Macmillan, 1986.

Cobb, Paul, Terry Wood, and Erna Yackel. "Discourse, Mathematical Thinking, and Classroom Practice." In *Contexts for Learning: Sociocultural Dynamics in Children's Development,* edited by Ellice Forman, Norris Minick, and C. Addison Stone, pp. 91–119. New York: Oxford University Press, 1993.

Cuevas, Gilbert J., Philip Mann, and Rose Marie McClung. "The Effects of a Language Process Approach on the Mathematics Achievement of First, Third, and Fifth Graders." Paper presented at the annual meeting of the American Educational Research Association, San Francisco, April 1986.

Cuevas, Gilberto J. "Mathematics Learning in English as Second Language." *Journal for Research in Mathematics Education* 15 (March 1984): 134–44.

Dale, Theresa C., and Gilberto J. Cuevas. "Integrating Language and Mathematics Learning." In *ESL through Content Area Instruction: Mathematics, Science, and Social Studies,* edited by JoAnn Crandall, pp. 9–54. Englewood Cliffs, N.J.: Prentice Hall, 1987.

Flores, Alfinio, Judith T. Sowder, Randolph A. Philipp, and Bonnie P. Schapelle. "Orchestrating, Promoting, and Enhancing Mathematical Discourse in the Middle Grades: A Case Study." In *Providing a Foundation for Teaching Middle School Mathematics,* edited by Judith T. Sowder, pp. 275–99. Albany, N.Y.: State University of New York Press, 1996.

Garcia, Eugene E., and René Gonzalez. "Issues in Systemic Reform for Culturally and Linguistically Diverse Students." *Teachers College Record* 96, no. 3 (1995): 418–31.

Gee, James P. *The Social Mind: Language, Ideology, and Social Practice.* New York: Bergin & Garvey, 1992.

González, Norma. "Processual Approaches to Multicultural Education." *Journal of Applied Behavioral Science* 31, no. 2 (1995): 234–44.

González, Norma, Luis C. Moll, Martha F. Tenery, Anna Rivera, Patricia Rendon, Raquel Gonzales, and Cathy Amanti. "Funds of Knowledge for Teaching in Latino Households." *Urban Education* 29, no. 4 (1995): 443–70.

Halliday, Michael A. K. "Sociolinguistics Aspects of Mathematical Education." In *The Social Interpretation of Language and Meaning,* edited by Michael Halliday, pp. 195–204. London: University Park Press, 1978.

Kagan, Spencer. "Cooperative Learning and Sociocultural Factors in Schooling." In *Beyond Language: Social and Cultural Factors in Schooling Language Minority Students,* edited by the Bilingual Education Office, pp. 231–98. Los Angeles: California State University—Los Angeles, Evaluation, Dissemination, and Assessment Center, 1986.

Khisty, Lena Licón. "Making Inequality: Issues of Language and Meanings in Mathematics Teaching with Hispanic Students." In *New Directions for Equity in Mathematics Education,* edited by Walter G. Secada, Elizabeth Fennema, and Lisa Byrd Adajian, pp. 279–97. New York: Cambridge University Press, 1995.

Khisty, Lena Licón, Douglas B. McLeod, and Kathryn Bertilson. "Speaking Mathematically in Bilingual Classrooms: An Exploratory Study of Teacher Discourse." In *Proceedings of the Fourteenth International Conference for the Psychology of Mathematics Education,* vol. 3, edited by George Booker, Paul Cobb, and Teresa N. de Mendicuti, pp. 105–12. Mexico City: Consejo Nacional de Ciencia y Tecnología, 1990.

Lemke, Jay K. *Talking Science: Language, Learning, and Values.* Norwood, N.J.: Ablex Publishing Corp., 1990.

Losey, Kay M. "Mexican American Students and Classroom Interaction: An Overview and Critique." *Review of Educational Research* 65, no. 3 (1995): 283–318.

MacGregor, Mollie, and Robert Moore. *Teaching Mathematics in the Multicultural Classroom.* Melbourne, Victoria, Australia: University of Melbourne Institute of Education, 1992.

Mestre, José. "Just How Important Are Language Skills in Mathematical Problem Solving?" In *Proceedings of the Fourth Annual Meeting of the North American Chapter of the Psychology of Mathematics Education,* edited by Sigrid Wagner, pp. 126–32. Athens, Ga.: University of Georgia, Department of Mathematics, 1982.

———. "The Role of Language Comprehension in Mathematics and Problem Solving." In *Linguistic and Cultural Influences on Learning Mathematics,* edited by Rodney Cocking and José Mestre, pp. 201–20. Hillsdale, N.J.: Lawrence Erlbaum Associates, 1988.

Mestre, José, and William Gerace. "A Study of the Algebra Acquisition of Hispanic and Anglo Ninth Graders: Research Findings Relevant to Teacher Training and Classroom Practice." *Journal of the National Association for Bilingual Education* 10 (1982): 137–67.

Mestre, José, William Gerace, and Jack Lockhead. "The Interdependence of Language and Translational Math Skills among Bilingual Hispanic Engineering Students." *Journal of Research in Science Teaching* 19, no. 5 (1982): 399–410.

Moll, Luis, Cathy Amanti, Deborah Neff, and Norma González. "Funds of Knowledge for Teaching: Using a Qualitative Approach to Connect Homes and Classrooms." *Theory into Practice* 31, no. 2 (Spring 1992): 132–41.

Moschkovich, Judit N. "Learning Mathematics in Two Languages." In *Proceedings of the Twentieth Annual Meeting of the International Group for the Psychology of Mathematics Education,* vol. 4, edited by Luis Puig and Angel Gutierrez, pp. 27–35. Spain: Universitat de Valencia, 1996b.

———. "Moving Up and Getting Steeper: Negotiating Shared Descriptions of Linear Graphs." *Journal of the Learning Sciences* 5, no. 3 (1996a): 239–77.

National Council of Teachers of Mathematics. *Curriculum and Evaluation Standards for School Mathematics.* Reston, Va.: National Council of Teachers of Mathematics, 1989.

Ogbu, John U. "Immigrant and Involuntary Minorities in Comparative Perspective." In *Minority Status and Schooling: A Comparative Study of Immigrant and Involuntary Minorities,* edited by Margaret Gibson and John Ogbu, pp. 3–36. New York: Garland Publishing, 1991.

Olivares, Rafael A. "Communication in Mathematics for Students with Limited English Proficiency." In *Communication in Mathematics, K–12 and Beyond,* 1996 Yearbook of the National Council of Teachers of Mathematics, edited by Portia C. Elliott, pp. 219–30. Reston, Va.: National Council of Teachers of Mathematics, 1996.

Pimm, David. *Speaking Mathematically: Communication in Mathematics Classrooms.* London: Routledge, 1987.

Pirie, Susan. "Peer Discussion in the Context of Mathematical Problem Solving." In *Language in Mathematical Education: Research and Practice,* edited by Kevin Durkin and Beatrice Shire, pp. 143–61. Philadelphia: Open University Press, 1991.

Richards, John. "Mathematical Discussions." In *Radical Constructivism in Mathematics Education,* edited by Ernst von Glasersfeld, pp. 13–51. Dordrecht, Netherlands: Kluwer Academic Publishers, 1991.

Roseberry, Ann, Beth Warren, and Faith Conant. "Appropriating Scientific Discourse: Findings from Language Minority Classrooms." *Journal of the Learning of Sciences* 2, no. 1 (1992): 61–94.

Rubenstein, Rheta. "Strategies to Support the Learning of the Language of Mathematics." In *Communication in Mathematics, K–12 and Beyond,* 1996 Yearbook of the National Council of Teachers of Mathematics, edited by Portia C. Elliott, pp. 214–18. Reston, Va.: National Council of Teachers of Mathematics, 1996.

Sánchez, Rosaura. *Chicano Discourse: Socio-Historic Perspectives.* Rowley, Mass.: Newbury House, 1983.

Spanos, George, Nancy C. Rhodes, Theresa C. Dale, and JoAnn Crandall. "Linguistic Features of Mathematical Problem Solving: Insights and Applications." In *Linguistic and Cultural Influences on Learning Mathematics,* edited by Rodney Cocking and José P. Mestre, pp. 221–40. Hillsdale, N.J.: Lawrence Erlbaum Associates, 1988.

Stodolsky, Susan S. *The Subject Matters: Classroom Activity in Math and Social Studies.* Chicago: University of Chicago Press, 1988.

Thornburg, Devin G., and Karen S. Karp. *Resituating Mathematics and Science Instruction for Language Different Students.* Paper presented at the meeting of the American Educational Association, San Francisco, April 1992.

Vogt, Lynn, Cathy Jordan, and Roland Tharp. "Explaining School Failure, Producing School Success: Two Cases." *Anthropology and Education Quarterly* 18, no. 4 (1987): 276–86.

Latinos, Income, and Mathematics Achievement
Beating the Odds

2

Luis Ortiz-Franco

This article discusses data about Latinos, mathematics achievement, and income over the twenty-year period from 1972 to 1992.

It is important for mathematics educators, teachers, and researchers to be informed about the relationship between mathematics achievement and economic indicators among the various student populations in order to gain a better understanding of those populations. Although much research has been conducted on the relationship between income level and mathematics achievement among the majority white student population, no comparable research is available on Latino students.

White (1982) reviewed more than one hundred studies addressing the non-Latino student population and found that the correlation between mathematics achievement and socioeconomic status (SES) was .20 when students were the unit of analysis, and the correlation was .70 when the school was the unit of analysis. Secada (1992, p. 635), in a review of the literature on mathematics achievement and race, social class, ethnicity, and language, concluded that in general a steady increase in achievement can be expected when SES increases.

According to Mullis, Dossey, Owen, and Phillips (1993, p. 91), countless studies have found that the differences in the mathematics achievement of various student populations (African American, American Indian, Asian, Latino, and white) surveyed in 1992 by the National Assessment of Educational Progress (NAEP) are related to socioeconomic background. Zaslavsky (1994, p. 59) presented data from the 1992 SAT showing that individuals from families with higher income levels attained higher mathematics scores than individuals from families with lower income levels.

These patterns outlined in the literature provide the foundation on which most educators base their expectations about mathematics achievement and income. In particular, most educators expect that the mathematics achievement of students from lower income levels improves only as their socioeconomic condition improves. However, as we shall see, the results from empirical studies investigating the question of mathematics achievement and income among Latinos, or specific subgroups of Latinos, are inconclusive at best and sometimes indicate the opposite—that mathematics achievement by Latino students improves even as their economic condition worsens.

For example, Anderson (1969) conducted an intergenerational study and reported a positive correlation between SES and performance on mathematics achievement among three generations of Chicano (a Latino of Mexican descent living in the United States) students in El Paso, Texas. In a landmark review of the empirical literature on mathematics education, Begle (1979, p. 95) said that there was slight evidence showing that the more Chicanos depart from their native culture and move toward the middle-class culture of the United States, the better their achievement in mathematics. In contrast, Buriel and Cardoza (1988) reported that SES was completely unrelated to mathematics achievement among three generations of Chicano students.

13

From Begle's observation, as well as from the data presented for the general U.S. population discussed above, we might conclude that, for example, as Chicanos or Latinos move further down from the middle class, their achievement in mathematics should remain static or decrease. Although Begle did not elaborate on what he meant by the middle-class culture of the United States, for purposes of this paper, we focus on the economic aspect of social class and define the middle class as that group of people whose family income is at or near the national median, the vast majority of whom are whites.

The purpose of this article is to present data covering a twenty-year period that relate income to mathematics achievement among Latinos. First, observations from the studies cited above serve as points of reference from which to judge the data presented. Subsequently, a discussion outlines plausible interpretations of the data from the perspectives of research and teaching. Finally, conclusions concerning the data close the article.

LATINOS, INCOME, AND MATHEMATICS ACHIEVEMENT

In this section, we present data covering a twenty-year period on family income, poverty rates, and mathematics achievement for the general Latino population.

Income of Latinos

Tienda (1995) examined U.S. Census data related to the distribution of income in the United States over the twenty-year period from 1972 to 1992 and compiled the following results: The median family income in 1972 for non-Latino whites was $36 952; for Latino families, the median income was $25 858, 30 percent below that of whites. In 1992, the corresponding figures were $40 421 for whites and $23 901 for Latinos, a whopping 41 percent difference (p. 408). Thus, between 1972 and 1992, the median family income of Latinos declined in absolute dollars, and they moved further away from the middle class as well.

Poverty Rates of Latinos

Tienda (1995) found that the poverty rate of Latinos under eighteen years of age, precisely the age group most likely to be in school, increased from 28.8 percent in 1977 to 39.9 percent in 1992 and that of whites under eighteen years increased from 11.6 percent to 16.9 percent during the same period (p. 409). Consequently, as the National Center for Educational Statistics (NCES) has observed, relative to whites, Latino children have a greater likelihood of living in poverty (NCES 1995a, p. 6).

Mathematics Achievement of Latinos

From the data on Latino family income given above and from the pattern of positive correlation between SES and mathematics achievement discussed in the introduction to this article, the logical conclusion is that the mathematics achievement of Latinos should have remained static or should have declined in comparison with that of whites for the two decades between 1972 and 1992. However, the actual data on Latinos' income presented above and on mathematics achievement do not support this conclusion (NCES 1995a, p. 58).

For nine-year-olds in 1973, the average mathematics-proficiency score for whites was 225 and for Latinos, 202—a 23-point difference. In 1992, the respective proficiency levels were 235 for whites and 212 for Latinos, still a 23-point difference. Thus, the mathematics-achievement gap between Latino and white nine-year-olds remained unchanged despite the economic decline experienced by Latino children in that twenty-year period.

For thirteen-year-olds in 1973, the corresponding scores were 274 for whites and 239 for Latinos, a 35-point difference. In 1992, the difference was 20 points—279 for whites and 259 for Latinos. Hence, this group of Latino students improved their achievement in mathematics in comparison with their white counterparts even though they moved further away economically from the middle class during that time period.

In the seventeen-year-old population, the mathematics-proficiency score for whites in 1973 was 310 and for Latinos, 277—a gap of 33 points. In 1992 that gap decreased to 20 points; the respective scores were 312 for whites and 292 for Latinos. As in the thirteen-year-old age group, the mathematics achievement of Latinos in the seventeen-year-old group improved relative to that of whites even though the income for Latinos moved further below the national median.

Thus, neither Begle's observation nor the expectations of most educators about the mathematics achievement of Latinos in relation to their economic standing are confirmed by the available data. However, although Latinos closed to some extent the overall mathematics-achievement gap between themselves and white students in the twenty-year period, the gap remains unacceptably wide.

Now let us shift our attention from a comparative perspective to a focus on Latinos only and on types of mathematical skills. Evidence indicates that Latinos have made more progress at the computational level, the lowest level of mathematical skills, than at the higher, multistep, complex problem-solving level (see, e.g., Johnson [1989, pp. 135 and 137]; Secada [1992, p. 629]; and Silver, Smith, and Nelson [1995, pp. 17 and 20]). For instance, 78 percent of seventeen-year-old Latino students performed at or above the "proficient" level in numerical operations and beginning problem solving in 1978; by 1992, the percent of such students performing at that level increased to 94 (NCES 1995b, p. 43).

Similarly, in the area of moderately complex procedures and reasoning skills, only 23 percent of seventeen-year-old Latinos performed at or above the proficient level in 1978, whereas 39 percent did so in 1992. However, in the area of multistep, complex problem-solving skills in both 1978 and 1992, an alarmingly low, and static, 1 percent of the Latino students performed at or above the proficient level (NCES 1995b, p. 43).

DISCUSSION

To recapitulate, in this study we have observed that over a twenty-year period, 1972–92, Latino students improved their level of mathematics achievement even as their general family income level decreased and the percent of school-aged youth in poverty in this population group increased. These findings are at variance with the expected pattern of improvement in mathematics achievement corresponding to improvement in income.

The comments in this section seek to explain why the findings in this article are at variance with previous studies investigating the relationship between income and mathematics achievement in the grades K–12 Latino student population. The discussion addresses this concern from the perspectives of research and practice. Concerning research, we will identify differences in methodological approaches between previous inquiries and the present one that may explain the inconsistencies in the results. Regarding practice, we will attempt to explain the present results from the perspective of factors involving policy, curriculum, instruction, and the involvement of parents in their children's education.

Research

The comments that follow will be limited to comparing the data in this article with the data in Anderson (1969) and Buriel and Cardoza (1988) because they are the only two studies cited in the introduction of this article that used empirical data in the analysis of the relationship between mathematics achievement and a socioeconomic index specific to Latino students.

Although the family-income and mathematics-achievement data analyzed in this article were derived from published sources based on survey and census information, the database could be considered longitudinal because it covered a twenty-year period. Moreover, because the surveys involved national population samples, we can safely assume that Latinos from different immigrant generations responded to the surveys. Thus, the data analyzed in this article can be considered to be both longitudinal and intergenerational. However, although Anderson and Buriel and Cardoza did include an intergenerational aspect in their studies, they did not include longitudinal data in their analyses.

Other differences between those two studies and the present one concern the economic indexes used in the studies. In this study, we used actual income information provided by the U.S. Census, whereas Anderson and Buriel and Cardoza used a combination of parents' educational-attainment level, parents' occupation, and family income to determine the SES of the students. Moreover, in this article, we did not consider various levels of the income factor (low, medium, and high) within the Latino population as both the Anderson and the Buriel and Cardoza investigations did with the SES data.

Consequently, we were not able to conduct either a correlational or other statistical analysis between levels of income and mathematics achievement within the population under study. Had we included such types of analyses in this article, it is plausible that we might have found a positive relationship between the two variables for the levels of family income within the Latino population and a negative correlation for the general family income level.

Another difference between those two studies and this study is that the data used here pertain to the general Latino population, whereas the data analyzed by Anderson and by Buriel and Cardoza focused only on Chicanos. It would be interesting to find out if we would get parallel results for the different subgroups in the Latino population.

An additional difference between this study and the other two investigations involves the method used to measure mathematics achievement. In the other two studies, the investigators used commercially available standardized mathematics achievement tests, whereas in this study we used mathematics data reported by the NCES.

These four methodological differences—(1) in the length of time over which the studies were conducted, (2) in the ranges of economic levels within the population, (3) in the diversity of the population sample, and (4) in the mathematics-achievement assessment instrument—may explain why in this analysis we observed a pattern in the relationship between general family income and mathematics achievement in the Latino population that is different from that observed in previous studies on this topic.

It is possible that such factors as parental involvement in the education of the children, the parents' educational attainment, the conditions of the schools the students attend, and some variables involving teachers might have had an influence on the mathematics achievement of Latino students. These and other variables are discussed below as possible explanations of the findings in this article.

Practice

In this section, we discuss some aspects of parents, schools, and teachers that provide a context in which to judge the gains made by Latinos in mathematics achievement between 1972 and 1992.

Parents

In 1995, the NCES reported that the involvement of Latino parents in their children's education was equal to, and in some respects greater than, that of white parents despite the enormous differences in the levels of educational attainment and family income between the two groups of parents. For instance, in 1994, 60 percent of Latino adults twenty-five to twenty-nine years old had the equivalent of a high school education, compared with 86 percent of their white counterparts. Yet similar percents of Latino and white students had parents who checked their homework (NCES 1995a, pp. 9, 244). Moreover, Latino eighth graders were more likely than their white counterparts to report that their parents had limited their television viewing and that their parents had visited their classes (NCES 1995a, p. 9). Thus, Latino parents are important partners in the education of Latino youth. Perhaps their parental practices have contributed to improving the achievement of their children in mathematics.

Another parental characteristic that might have contributed to that achievement gain could have been the improved educational-attainment level of the general Latino population over the twenty-year period in question. For instance, 47.6 percent of Latinos twenty-five to twenty-nine years old had completed high school in 1972, but by 1992, 60.9 percent had done so. Moreover, for the same age bracket, 7.8 percent had completed four or more years of college in 1972, whereas in 1992 that percent increased to 15.6 (NCES 1995a, pp. 244, 246).

The Condition of Schools and the Learning Environment

Latino seniors in 1992 were more likely than white seniors to report that disruptions by other students interfered with their learning, that fights often occurred between different ethnic groups, that they did not feel safe at school, and that there were many gangs at school (NCES 1995a, pp. 9, 12–13). These social conditions very likely create a stressful learning environment for Latinos in the schools.

When we put in this school context the gains in mathematics achievement made by Latinos, we can conclude that many Latino students are able to overcome unfavorable school environments. Moreover, when we include the stress created in the family by declining family income, we can infer that many Latino students show a high level of academic resilience (see Gonzalez and Padilla [1997] for additional information on the academic resilience of Latino high school students).

Furthermore, when schools are categorized on the basis of students' average academic performance, the following rates of Latino students were attending the bottom one-third of the schools in 1992: 57 percent of fourth graders, 58 percent of eighth graders, and 52 percent of twelfth graders (Mullis, Dossey, Owen, and Phillips 1993, p. 153). Furthermore, a disproportionate number of Latino students in secondary schools are assigned to nonacademic tracks and are thereby forced to study an unchallenging mathematics curriculum (Oakes 1990, p. vii).

As has been amply documented elsewhere (see, e.g., Frankenstein [1995, p. 165], Oakes [1990, pp. ix–xi, 79], and Tate [1995, passim]), the central bureaucracies in school districts allocate more and better resources to schools attended by white middle-class and upper-class students than to schools attended by low-income students and ethnic minorities. Both teachers and students are the victims of these policies that contribute to creating unequal educational and learning opportunities for students and poor working conditions for teachers.

Under these circumstances, only an organized home-school-community alliance among parents, mathematics teachers and other mathematics educators, and community leaders can change the status quo in education. Consequently, if the current mathematics education reform movement advocating an increased emphasis on applications, mathematical reasoning, problem solving, and the use of technology in the teaching of mathematics is to succeed for all students, mathematics educators (researchers, teachers, and others), parents, and community leaders must form the base for an effective coalition to bring about a fair allocation of resources to all schools. If we fail to accomplish such a reallocation of resources, the improvement in the mathematics-achievement index of Latinos will continue to be very slow, as evidenced by the data on mathematics achievement for the last twenty years. In fact, the latest NAEP data indicate that between 1992 and 1996, Latino students improved their average index in mathematics achievement by 4 points at the fourth-grade and eighth-grade levels and by 3 points at the twelfth-grade level (Reese, Miller, Mazzo, and Dossey 1997, p. 33).

Teachers

The pattern of Latino students' achieving higher levels of improvement in lower-level mathematical skills, such as computation, than in higher-level skills, such as multistep, complex problem solving, reflects the nature of the mathematics instruction that Latinos have received in the schools. Cole and Griffin (1987, pp. 4–5), Frankenstein (1995), and Oakes (1990, p. 101) assert that schools serving minority children tend to put more emphasis on drilling the basics than on teaching the higher-level skills that are needed to excel in mathematics.

Latino students learn what they are taught. Hence, they would learn the higher-order skills of mathematical reasoning and multistep problem solving if teachers emphasized those skills in their classroom teaching, as shown by the results of several studies: (1) Villaseñor and Kepner (1993) with elementary school children, (2) the QUASAR project (see, e.g., Silver and Lane [1995]) with middle school students, and (3) the successes in high school of Jaime Escalante and Ben Jimenez (see, e.g., Matthews [1988]).

Teachers are the key to improving the quality of mathematics education that students receive. Many teachers over the years have consistently tried to provide a quality mathematics education to their Latino students, notwithstanding the poor institutional support provided to them by school bureaucracies. Latino students have been able to improve their achievement in mathematics in large part because of those teachers.

Conversely, many teachers of Latino students have racist views and attitudes and low expectations for their students (see, e.g., Apple [1992, p. 419], Heid and Jump [1993, p. 161], Oakes [1990, p. 101], Silver, Smith, and Nelson [1995, p. 20], Thompson and Jakucyn [1993, p.175], and Zaslavsky [1996, p. 7]). Some of those teachers purposefully adopt or advocate practices designed to diminish the students' self-confidence and to make it very frustrating for students to succeed.

For example, at a mathematics education conference held in California in December 1996, a white teacher related the following anecdote. In the school in California where she works, some teachers, on seeing their Latino students do well in the teacher-generated mathematics tests, have suggested increasing the difficulty level of the tests in order to make it impossible for the Latino students to pass the tests. Those teachers, however, do not recommend improving the quality of either instruction or the mathematics curriculum to make it possible for their students to succeed in the more difficult tests that the teachers advocate. Clearly, those practices are educationally irresponsible and are very likely a manifestation of the racist tendencies of the teachers involved.

We urge and challenge teachers to rid themselves, through introspection, reflection, and intense personal engagement, of negative views toward their Latino students. There are successful mathematics education reform programs around the country, such as the Mathematics Renaissance project in California (see Acquarelli and Mumme [1996]) and the Mathematics Education Equity Leadership (MEEL) project in New York City (see Peterson and Barnes [1996]), that are designed to help teachers confront the issues of equity, class, gender, race, and discrimination in mathematics education.

The experiences of those projects demonstrate that initially the participating teachers are highly uncomfortable with confronting issues of equity but after their participation in a series of emotionally intense sessions, their attitudes, beliefs, and classroom practices change and their students' mathematics achievement improves as well. It is difficult to change the negative attitudes and beliefs about equity issues that have been ingrained in us as part of our sociocultural upbringing. Although these issues are emotionally charged, teachers' negative attitudes and beliefs about Latino students can be changed. Once their views are changed, they can effectively contribute to furthering the mathematics education of their Latino students.

Given the inadequate educational resources, poor school learning environments, and negative social attitudes on the part of some teachers, we need to devote more energy and professional attention to teaching Latino students applications, mathematical reasoning, and multistep and complex problem solving. They are eager and ready to learn, and their parents are ready to assist us in this task.

Are we mathematics educators up to the challenge? As the well-known Latino leader, Cesar Chavez, always said, "Sí se puede!" ("Yes, it can be done!"). The results of the study by Villaseñor and Kepner and the experiences of the QUASAR project and Jaime Escalante and Ben Jimenez have demonstrated that this objective is achievable.

SUMMING UP

The data discussed in this article about the mathematics achievement and income of Latinos from 1972 to 1992 reveals the following salient facts: (1) the mathematics achievement level of Latino students increased, (2) during the same period, their family median income level decreased significantly when compared with the national median for whites, and (3) the poverty rate among the school-aged population increased dramatically over the same period of time. These three factors offer compelling evidence that for the general Latino population, there is a negative correlation between declining income and mathematics achievement. However, because no similar data are available for specific subpopulations of Latino groups (Chicanos, Puerto Ricans, Cubans, Salvadorans, Guatemalans, etc.), we are unable to say whether the same pattern applies to those groups.

It was also observed that the educational-attainment level of Latinos between twenty-five and twenty-nine years of age increased significantly during the same period (1972–92) and that Latino parents were very involved in their children's education. It is quite possible that these family characteristics had a stronger influence than income on the mathematics achievement of Latino students.

It was also noted that the gains that Latinos have made are at the computational level and that their performance in applications, reasoning, and multistep, complex problem solving needs to be improved. Teachers of Latino students are urged to put increased emphasis on the latter skills in their classroom teaching.

Moreover, it is recommended that a coalition of mathematics educators, teachers, parents, and community leaders be formed to bring about a more equitable distribution of resources to schools attended by Latino students.

REFERENCES

Acquarelli, Kris, and Judith Mumme. "A Renaissance in Mathematics Education Reform." *Phi Delta Kappan* (March 1996): 478–84.

Anderson, James G. *Factors Affecting Achievement among Mexican-Americans in a Metropolitan Context.* Final Report, Mathematics Education Program, Southwest Educational Development Laboratory. Las Cruces, N.M.: New Mexico State University, 1969.

Apple, Michael W. "Do the Standards Go Far Enough? Power, Policy, and Practice in Mathematics Education." *Journal for Research in Mathematics Education* 23 (November 1992): 412–31.

Begle, E. G. *Critical Variables in Mathematics Education: Findings from a Survey of the Empirical Literature.* Washington, D.C.: Mathematical Association of America and National Council of Teachers of Mathematics, 1979.

Buriel, Raymond, and Desdemona Cardoza. "Sociocultural Correlates of Achievement among Three Generations of Mexican American High School Seniors." *American Educational Research Journal* 25 (Summer 1988): 177–92.

Cole, Michael, and Peg Griffin. *Contextual Factors in Education.* Madison, Wis.: Wisconsin Center for Educational Research, University of Wisconsin, 1987.

Frankenstein, Marilyn. "Equity in Mathematics Education: Class in the World Outside the Class." In *New Directions for Equity in Mathematics Education,* edited by Walter G. Secada, Elizabeth Fennema, and Lisa Byrd Adajian, pp. 165–90. New York: Cambridge University Press, 1995.

Gonzalez, Rosemary, and Amado Padilla. "The Academic Resilience of Mexican American High School Students." *Hispanic Journal of Behavioral Sciences* 19, no. 3 (1997): 301–17.

Heid, Camilla A., and Theresa L. Jump. "Females, Minorities, and the Physically Handicapped in Mathematics and Science: A Model Program." In *Reaching All Students with Mathematics,* edited by Gilbert Cuevas and Mark Driscoll, pp. 159–73. Reston, Va.: National Council of Teachers of Mathematics, 1993.

Johnson, Martin L. "Minority Differences in Mathematics." In *Results from the Fourth Mathematics Assessment of the National Assessment of Educational Progress,* edited by Mary Montgomery Lindquist, pp. 135–48. Reston, Va.: National Council of Teachers of Mathematics, 1989.

Matthews, Jay. *The Best Teacher in America.* New York: Henry Holt & Co., 1988.

Mullis, Ina V. S., John A. Dossey, Eugene H. Owen, and Gary W. Phillips. *NAEP 1992: Mathematics Report Card for the Nation and the States.* Washington, D.C.: U.S. Department of Education, National Center for Educational Statistics, 1993.

Oakes, Jeannie. *Multiplying Inequalities: The Effects of Race, Social Class, and Tracking on Opportunities to Learn Mathematics and Science.* Santa Monica, Calif.: Rand Corporation, 1990.

Peterson, Penelope, and Carol Barnes. "Learning Together: The Challenge of Mathematics, Equity, and Leadership." *Phi Delta Kappan* (March 1996): 485–91.

Reese, Clyde M., Karen E. Miller, John Mazzo, and John A. Dossey. *NAEP 1996: Mathematics Report Card for the Nation and the States.* Washington, D.C.: U.S. Department of Education, National Center for Educational Statistics, 1997.

Secada, Walter G. "Race, Ethnicity, Social Cass, Language, and Achievement in Mathematics." In *Handbook of Research on Mathematics Teaching and Learning,* edited by Douglas A. Grouws, pp. 623–60. New York.: Macmillan Publishing Co., 1992.

Silver, Edward A., and Suzanne Lane. "Can Instructional Reform in Urban Middle Schools Help Students Narrow the Mathematical Performance Gap? Some Evidence from the QUASAR Project." *Research in Middle Level Education* 18, no. 2 (1995): 49–70.

Silver, Edward A., Margaret Schwan Smith, and Barbara Scott Nelson. "The QUASAR Project: Equity Concerns Meet Mathematics Education Reform in the Middle School." In *New Directions for Equity in Mathematics Education,* edited by Walter G. Secada, Elizabeth Fennema, and Lisa Byrd Adajian, pp. 9–56. New York.: Cambridge University Press, 1995.

Tate, William. "Economics, Equity, and the National Mathematics Assessment: Are We Creating a National Toll Road?" In *New Directions for Equity in Mathematics Education,* edited by Walter G. Secada, Elizabeth Fennema, and Lisa Byrd Adajian, pp. 191–206. New York, N.Y.: Cambridge University Press, 1995.

Thompson, Denisse R., and Natalie Jakucyn. "Helping Inner-City Girls Succeed: The METRO Achievement Program." In *Reaching All Students with Mathematics,* edited by Gilbert Cuevas and Mark Driscoll, pp. 175–96. Reston, Va.: National Council of Teachers of Mathematics, 1993.

Tienda, Marta. "Latinos and the American Pie: Can Latinos Achieve Economic Parity?" *Hispanic Journal of Behavioral Sciences* 17, no. 4 (1995), 403–29.

U.S. Department of Education. National Center for Educational Statistics. *The Condition of Education 1995.* Washington, D.C.: U.S. Department of Education, Office of Educational Research and Improvement, 1995a.

————. *Mini-Digest of Education Statistics 1995.* Washington, D.C.: U.S. Department of Education, Office of Educational Research and Improvement, 1995b.

Villaseñor, Albert, Jr., and Henry S. Kepner, Jr. "Arithmetic from a Problem-Solving Perspective: An Urban Implementation." *Journal for Research in Mathematics Education* 24 (January 1993): 62–69.

White, Karl R. "The Relation between Socioeconomic Status and Academic Achievement." *Psychological Bulletin* 91 (May 1982): 461–81.

Zaslavsky, Claudia. *Fear of Math: How to Get Over It and Get On with Your Life.* New Brunswick, N.J.: Rutgers University Press, 1994.

————. *The Multicultural Math Classroom: Bringing In the World.* Portsmouth, N.H.: Heinemann, 1996.

Isn't English a Trip?

José Franco

Isn't English a trip?

Every day while I sit in class
and wait for Mrs. Jones to call on me,
she writes on the **chalkboard**
but calls it a **blackboard**
and yet—
I look at a **greenboard.**

And when reading time rolls around,
It's hard to understand why the word **Nike**
is not pronounced like **bike,**
or **hike,**
or **Mike.**

Mrs. Jones always gives us these rules.
I remember the one about
"when two vowels go walking,
the first one does the talking
and the second one does the walking."

And guess what!

It works with a word like *beans.*
There are two vowels—
e does the talking
and *a* does the walking.

Sort of like my sister and me—
she does all the talking and I do all the walking.

BUT
then they break the rules.

What about words like
choose
or **eight**
or **feather?**
There are two vowels walking.
So which one is the talker and
which one is the walker?

I thought it would be easier
when math class started.
Because that's just about numbers,
and circles,
and things like that,
right?

Was I in for a surprise!

When Mrs. Jones started talking about **addition,**
she used the word **plus**
like 2 **plus** 2 equals 4.
Sounds good to me.
But last week she mentioned the word **combine,**
and she said that meant **addition,** too.

All right …

On Monday we were doing some math problems.

(Oh man! I had a hard time reading—
TOO MANY WORDS!
I didn't understand them all,
but my buddy Julio helped me out.
Now I owe him one,
but that's another story.)

Anyway …
We were doing our math problems.
I read the problem
and it said the herd of elephants was **increased by** three.
Julio and his cousin Julia told me that **increased by**
means **addition** also.

"What, Mrs. Jones?
Could you please repeat your question?
What's the sum of all the elephants?"

Hmmmmm
What did Julia tell me **sum** meant?
Is that the same as **some,**
like "when **some** of the kids tease me"?

"Sorry, Mrs. Jones.
I don't know what the **sum** is."

(Actually I don't know what that word means.)

Oh well—
I hope tomorrow I have a better day.
Right now
I have to catch up with my friend Herb.
I just learned in science class today
that in the word *herb,*
the *h* is silent.
I need to apologize to Erb for saying his name wrong.
Isn't English a trip?!

Spanish-English Language Issues in the Mathematics Classroom 4

Pilar Ron

The role of language in the mathematics classroom has become increasingly important in the current trend toward mathematics reform. Children are encouraged to reflect on their mathematical solutions and verbalize their explanations. It is not that language was not important before but rather than the new emphasis is an acknowledgment of the important role of language in mathematics education.

Language is so pervasive in our everyday lives that we tend to take it for granted. Since we all learn language effortlessly, we may assume that we and our children have acquired a higher level of language skills than we actually have. This pervasive attitude toward language has resulted in two serious misconceptions that affect how we deal with language issues in both the monolingual and bilingual mathematics classroom.

The language of mathematics (i.e., the language we use to talk about mathematics and to express mathematical concepts) is often assumed to be an intrinsic part of our everyday language. Under this assumption, we fall into the misconception of considering the language of mathematics to be as easily acquired as everyday language is. Furthermore, we assume that everyday language reflects mathematical symbolic language in a straightforward manner. Although we recognize that certain words and phrases (such as *horizontal* and *vertical, subtract, difference,* etc.) are a specialized vocabulary that the child needs to learn, we may assume that the language we use to make those words meaningful are a part of the child's everyday language.

Constructing meaning in mathematics through the use of language (i.e., using the language of mathematics) goes beyond explaining a mathematical term in simpler words. We sometimes fail to recognize that learning the language of mathematics is a process that takes time and effort. The fact that children (or adults) can use language to communicate does not automatically mean that they know how to use it to construct meaning in mathematics.

If we cannot take for granted what it means to know the language of mathematics in just one language, matters get more complicated when we consider bilingualism and mathematics. After all, what does it really mean to be bilingual? It is rare for a bilingual person to be equally strong in both languages, whatever they may be, in all aspects of his or her life. Usually bilingual persons have learned certain topics in only one of the languages spoken, and for those topics they lack the necessary vocabulary and fluency in the other language.

When we think about the mathematics classroom, we are faced with a second misconception about language, namely, that if a person is bilingual, he or she automatically knows the language of mathematics in both languages. Bilingual teachers may sometimes be unprepared to teach the language of mathematics (and therefore the mathematical concepts that that language expresses) for the simple reason that they lack that specialized language in the language or languages in which they teach.

The research reported in this paper was supported in part by the National Science Foundation (NSF) under grant no. RED 935373 and in part by the Spencer Foundation. The opinions expressed in this chapter are those of the author and do not necessarily reflect the views of NSF or of the Spencer Foundation.

The language issues discussed in this paper concentrate on the grades K–3 classroom. The elementary school classroom offers unique insights for the study of language in the mathematics classroom for several reasons. First, children of elementary school age are still learning how to use and manipulate language. Second, children are first exposed to the language of mathematics at this educational level. For these reasons, therefore, these grade levels are the crucial place to begin to study how the language of mathematics emerges. At this point, the language of mathematics is simple enough that its relationship with the everyday language can easily be explored in a way that is much more difficult when the language of mathematics becomes more complex.

The analysis of the language of the mathematics classroom proposed here arises from three sources: (1) extensive experience in a Spanish-English bilingual elementary school classroom for three years while I participated in a research project focused on helping children learn word problems, (2) experience in translating a large collection of word problems as a resource for teachers, and (3) extensive work in tutorial sessions with young children to determine the major difficulties that children have with particular word problems.

THE LANGUAGE OF THE MATHEMATICS CLASSROOM

With the current worldwide trend of mathematics reform, language is becoming as important in mathematics—and rightfully so—as it is in language arts. Mathematics reform curricula put a great deal of emphasis on having children explore, explain, reflect, reason, and communicate. The goal is to have children become proficient at analytical reasoning, not just at calculation. All this exploring, explaining, reflecting, and reasoning is communicated through language.

When children enter the school system, they enter a new world in which the rules of the game are different from those they have been using to that point. They are expected to sit still and listen, pay attention to their teacher and classmates, and speak or be silent when asked to. Along with learning new social skills, they have to learn how to use language in a different way.

The language of the classroom has very specific norms that differ from the way we use language in our everyday lives. For instance, in the classroom, turn-taking decisions (e.g., when it is permissible to take a turn in the conversation or to talk or interrupt) are as highly structured in the classroom as the introduction of a topic and of the purpose of the discourse, which is usually initiated by the teacher with the direct or indirect goal of teaching and learning (Gawned 1990).

If the language used in the classroom is a subset of the everyday language but governed by different rules of discourse, the language of mathematics is usually thought of as a subset of the language of the classroom. For instance, in the circular model proposed in Gawned (1990), different aspects of the language of mathematics are part of the language of the classroom, which is in turn part of the "real world" language.

Models like this obscure the fact that the language of mathematics differs from the everyday language in a very important aspect: the language of mathematics is not acquired effortlessly and naturally through social interaction but rather learned and taught in school as a separate register and often as a consciously memorized vocabulary. A *register* is the specific, sometimes specialized, vocabulary and expressions associated with certain domains. In the example of mathematics, we do not go through our daily life saying things like "Oh, I already have these two items on my shopping list, so I have to subtract two from the list of items I need to buy," even if that is exactly what we do by crossing them off our list. The word *subtract* does not form part of the language of most five- or six-year-olds, even if they have an emerging model of that mathematical concept, before they are introduced to it in school.

In this sense, mathematical terms are not items of everyday language, even though mathematical operations are part of our everyday lives.

We do, however, use everyday language to build up the mathematical concepts and the language we use to express them. Doing so is especially important if we are trying to make the mathematical concepts meaningful. The use of language in the mathematics classroom is best described as a process of language learning with four separated stages of language development, as illustrated in figure 4.1.

Symbolic Language	**Symbolic Language**
Symbolic written language and its oral counterpart (learned and taught)	$15 + x = 22.$ "Fifteen plus x equals twenty-two."
↑	↑
The Language of Mathematics Problem Solving	**The Language of Mathematics Problem Solving**
The mathematical register— language used to verbalize mathematical concepts and to talk about them (learned and taught)	I have \$15. I have to add some amount to the number of dollars I already have, 15, to get the total amount of money I need to buy the doll, \$22.
↑	↑
Mathematized-Situation Language	**Mathematized-Situation Language**
Everyday language in which mathematical relations are made more relevant (mostly acquired naturally with some learned and taught terms)	I want to buy a doll that costs \$22. I have already saved \$15. I still need to save some more money before I can buy the doll. How many dollars do I still have to save?
↑	↑
Everyday Language	**Everyday Language**
Language acquired through social interaction (acquired naturally)	*Said:* I have been saving some money because I want to buy a Barbie doll. I have already got \$15 from my grandma and uncle. I still need some more money. *Known but left unsaid:* The Barbie doll costs \$22, for instance.
(a) Language in the mathematics classroom	(b) Language in the mathematics classroom: an example

Fig. 4.1

In figure 4.1, the path toward symbolic mathematical language starts with the everyday language. Everyday language, the language the child has when she or he enters school, is used to create a mathematized-situation language in which mathematical relations are made more relevant. The mathematized language is basically a manipulation of the everyday language, and as such it shares many of its characteristics.

However, the mathematized language expresses relations that are not necessary or important in the everyday language. For instance, although the relation "having more" is easily expressed in the everyday language, the relation "having more than" is not; to express that relation we use mathematized language. At this step, the language, is very similar to the everyday language, but the mathematical nature of the concepts in question becomes more relevant.

Consider, for instance, a situation in which a child is saving up money to buy a toy. Everyday language can be vague and ambiguous. In everyday language, we may not say how much the toy costs or how much money the child has already saved. In the mathematized situation language, the elements that are mathematically relevant—the amount needed to buy the toy, the amount already saved, and the relationship between the two amounts—are made explicit. In the elementary school, word problems are the best example of mathematized-situation language.

The mathematized-situation language is used in turn to build up the language of mathematics and the language of mathematics problem solving, the language in which mathematical concepts are expressed. This is the language in which the mathematical register is expressed; such language is learned, not casually acquired or picked up. The language of mathematics loses the ambiguity found in everyday language.

Mathematical terms that are common in the everyday language are redefined according to the mathematical properties of the construction or concept they express. For instance, what we call a circle in the everyday language may be redefined in mathematical terms as a circle, an ellipse, or an oval region or as none of the above, for example, a convex region. In the example of the child saving up to buy a toy, the mathematized-situation language is interpreted and "translated" into a problem-solving statement.

Ultimately, the language of mathematics is "translated" into the mathematical language of symbols and equations in written and spoken language. This is the most abstract level of language development and the one that most clearly requires conscious learning.

At each successive stage, the language is not so much absorbed naturally in normal use but becomes more consciously learned and the mathematical nature of the register becomes more relevant (see fig. 4.1). While building up this language, the child is constructing the meaning and concepts that that language is used to represent. The child is going from the informal, spontaneous mathematical concepts of the everyday language to the formal concepts of the language of mathematics (Vygotsky 1986). The mathematized language is the link between the two types of concepts, and the concepts expressed in this language can therefore be considered as "referenced" concepts, where the mathematics is still intimately linked to the everyday language of the child (Fuson et al. 1995).

The most important aspect of this model of the language of mathematics is that the everyday language the child brings from home along with the mathematized language the child is exposed to in class is the foundation of the language of mathematics. Without a strong development of the child's language skills, the language of mathematics can become meaningless.

Going from the everyday language, which is by nature vague and ambiguous, to the mathematical language, which is precise and unambiguous, can result in errors that generally stem from the misconception that mathematical symbolic language directly represents natural language and vice versa. Take, for example, Oscar, a first grader from El Salvador, who attends a Spanish-English speaking bilingual class in an inner-city school in Chicago.

In Oscar's classroom, children were expected to write in their mathematics journals every day. On a particular day, Oscar shared his journal entry which he read as follows:

Drawn on the blackboard	O O O O + O O O O
Written on the blackboard	$4 + 4 + 8 =$
Spoken	*"4 más 4 más, 8"* (4 plus 4 more, 8)

Oscar used the mathematical plus symbol (read in Spanish as *más*) to represent both the symbolic language term *más* (plus) and the everyday language term *más* (more) and therefore produced an incorrect equation. Oscar was, however, familiar enough with simple equations to know that he had to include the equals symbol, which he did by adding it at the end. Note that his rendering of the mathematical expression *4 más 4 más 8* lacks a verb when compared to the more accurate form *4 más 4 más* son *8* (4 plus 4 more *are* 8).

Translating from natural language, be it the everyday language or the language of mathematics, to a symbolic mathematical expression is not easy even for adults. When translating the mathematized-situation expression "there are six times as many students as professors" into the symbolic language of equations, even university engineering students incorrectly used the equation $6S = P$ (where S is the number of students and P the number of professors) instead of the correct $S = 6P$ (Rosnick and Clement [1980]; Clement, Lochhead, and Monk [1981]; Kaput and Clement [1979]; and Rosnick [1981]).

That common mistake seems to come from incorrectly interpreting the equals symbol to mean "for every" (Cocking and Chipman 1988). Furthermore, the students are confusing the equation for a problem in which the situation is represented by "for every six students there is one professor" with the solution equation for a problem in which the equality between the two quantities is established, that is "the number of students equals six times the number of professors" (see also Fuson, Carroll, and Landis [1996] for more details on this topic).

THE BILINGUAL CLASSROOM

If dealing with one single language can produce such a complex system, it stands to reason that the system can get more complicated when two or more languages come into play. Whatever the ultimate reason, language-minority students lag behind monolingual students in their mathematics achievement, especially on word problems, in which language and mathematics are more intricately linked (Macnamara 1967; Cummins 1979, 1981; Cocking and Chipman 1988; Mestre 1988).

Bilingualism is sometimes used to refer to different degrees of competence in two languages. This is particularly true when taking into account the language of mathematics, since that language is largely taught in school and not usually acquired outside school. A bilingual person may have attained different degrees of bilingualism in the language of mathematics, as shown in figure 4.2.

In the example of a bilingual person, we have to take into account not only the knowledge, or lack thereof, of the language of mathematics in both the dominant language (L1) and the weaker language (L2) but also the degree of transference between the languages. For instance, a student may know how to count to ten in both English and Spanish and not be able to immediately translate the word for a number from English to Spanish, or vice versa.

Bilingual adults will usually be proficient in translating from the everyday language to symbolic mathematical language in the language in which they were schooled (the dominant language, or L1). The same cannot be said, however, for the weaker language, L2. In the second language, their mathematical knowledge could be sketchy. Although a bilingual adult will have a strong everyday language in L2, the mathematized-situation language may not be as well developed as in the dominant language. The knowledge of the language of mathematics problem solving and of symbolic language could be even weaker. To acquire true bilingualism in mathematics, a person has to study mathematics in both languages.

In the example of a Spanish-speaking child in the United States, the picture becomes more complex because the child still has to learn all the stages of the language of mathematics in the language used in school. A Spanish-dominant child who is being taught in English may have the added difficulty of constructing the language of mathematics on a weak base of the everyday language in English. A teacher in this instance would have to provide more opportunities to improve and develop the child's second language in school.

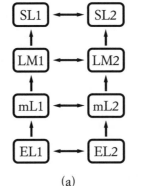

(a)
Bilingual adult with mathematics bilinguality (has studied mathematics in L1 and L2)

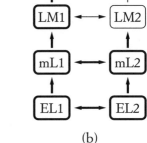

(b)
Bilingual adult with mathematics monolinguality (has studied mathematics in L1 and learned some of the mathematical register for L2)

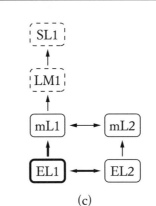

(c)
Bilingual child schooled in L1

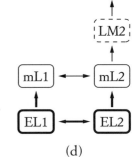

(d)
Bilingual child schooled in L2 (eventually L2 will become the dominant language)

SL = symbolic language
LM = language of mathematics
mL = mathematized-situation language
EL = everyday language
L1 = dominant language
L2 = weaker language

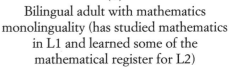

- - - - Weak, inconsistent, incomplete

―――― Stronger but still incomplete; some inconsistencies

━━━━ Strongly established (for that age group)

Fig. 4.2. Degrees of bilingualism and the language of mathematics

These different degrees of bilingualism can give rise to very different problems. A child may have a strong everyday language in his or her dominant language, for instance, Spanish, and a weaker everyday language in a second language, say, English, but he or she may still be schooled in the weaker language, English. That child may well have an everyday language in the weaker language that lacks even the most common elements of the mathematics register. Such an example is Dora, a bilingual, English-dominant third grader in an inner-city school in Chicago.

She attends an English-speaking class, but both English and Spanish are spoken at her home. She has volunteered to help in an after-school tutoring program and is working with two Spanish-speaking first graders. When working on word problems, she asks to use English, her dominant language. Because her students do not speak English, she is given the problems in both English and Spanish—English so that she can understand the problems and Spanish so that her students can understand them, too. After a short while, she asks if she can read the problems in Spanish but say the numbers in English. Although she has no problem using her everyday Spanish to communicate, she does not know all the number words in Spanish.

Even when a child learns the language of mathematics in both the dominant language, for instance, Spanish, and in the weaker language, English, the transfer, or translation, from one language to the other is not automatic. Carola is a Spanish-speaking third grader who attends an English-speaking class. When she is being interviewed on a variety of mathematical tasks, the interviewer offers her a choice of language to use and she chooses Spanish. Although Spanish is her dominant everyday language, she has an imperfect transference of the language of mathematics between the two languages. As illustrated below, English is progressively becoming her dominant language in the language of mathematics.

> *Interviewer: ¿Cuántos son 9 más 6?* (How much is 9 plus 6?)
>
> *Carola:* ¿Cuál es más—*plus or minus?* (What is *más*—plus or minus?)

In some instances, the transference can also produce errors in L1 that have their origin in errors in L2. Take the example of Freddy. As a Spanish-speaking kindergartner in a bilingual English-Spanish classroom, Freddy could easily count from 1 to 10 in both languages. However, if asked to translate a number from one language to the other, Freddy would have to count in the other language until that number was reached. He could not translate directly from L1 to L2, or vice versa.

When he moved on to first grade, Freddy was in a Spanish-speaking classroom. Although classified as one of the more advanced children in his class, he had trouble counting to 100. When asked to count by tens, he would very often make the typical English mistake of using the teen numbers instead of the decade numbers from 30 onward.

> *Freddy: Diez, veinte, trece, catorce, quince, dieciseis, diecisiete, dieciocho, diecinueve, veinte* (10, 20, 13, 14, 15, 16, 17, 18, 19, 20)

This mistake has a phonological basis in English because *thirteen* and *thirty* are very close in pronunciation from the perspective of Spanish speakers. In Spanish, teen numbers, however, are not similar in pronunciation to decade numbers; for instance, consider *trece* (thirteen) and *treinta* (thirty). Freddy's error in English can be explained only if we posit an L2 interference in the meaning of the numbers.

This interdependence of L1 and L2 at each stage of the development from the everyday language to the mathematical symbolic language is particularly important if we consider that in most bilingual programs in the United States, bilingual children are taught for a number of years in their dominant language before they are mainstreamed into English-speaking classes. Proficiency in the everyday language in L1 and L2 does not necessarily mean that mainstreaming is going to be successful unless the students attain a similar degree of proficiency in the language of mathematics in both languages.

WHAT CAN THE GRADES K–3 TEACHER DO?

The connection between language and mathematics for bilinguals, and even for monolinguals, has been recognized for a long time (Knight and Hargis [1977]; Morris [1975]; Cummins [1979, 1981]; Mestre [1988, 1989]; Cuevas [1984]; Saxe

[1988]; Spanos et al. [1988]; Khisty [1995], among others). Language issues in the elementary school classroom come across most clearly in solving word problems.

Word problems are a crucial element of mathematics instruction in the primary grades because they are used for developing analytical reasoning skills that children will need later on for algebra. Most of those problems, however, depict artificial situations that attempt to recreate real-world situations through language. In this sense, they must be considered primarily as texts that have to be interpreted and secondarily as problems that have to be solved.

In the primary grades, solving mathematical word problems often requires language learning before the child can interpret the problem and solve it. Children must go through a number of steps that are intimately connected to the different levels of development in the language of mathematics.

First, children have to understand the language in the word problem. Second, they have to interpret the mathematical relations in the problem so that they can understand what unknown quantity the problem asks about. Third, they have to find a way to identify that unknown quantity. That is, the children have to figure out how to make use of the mathematical relations to find a mathematical solution to the problem. At times, the children may be asked to go one step further and translate that solution procedure to the abstract symbols of a mathematical equation.

Language plays an important role at each of these three steps. All children enter school with an everyday language, or more than one such language if they are bilingual, that has not been formally taught but rather has been acquired effortlessly through social interaction before entering school. A teacher has to use the language that the child brings to the school to construct a mathematized language in which mathematical relations are made more relevant. That is the birthing ground from which the language of mathematics will emerge.

Teachers are then confronted with an enormous task: to teach the children the language before they can teach them the mathematics. To teach the language, teachers have to be able to manipulate it, to play with it; for the bilingual teacher that task can be overwhelming. We have to consider again the misconception of what it means to be bilingual in the mathematical domain. Mathematical concepts are abstractions that transfer from language to language.

For instance, if one grasps the concept of multiplication in L1, then one also grasps the concept of multiplication in L2. What may be missing is the language of multiplication in L2. For that reason, a Spanish-English bilingual teacher who has been schooled primarily in English can encounter a number of difficulties when teaching in Spanish. Those difficulties can hinder the learning process in the mathematics classroom.

For example, teachers may lack the appropriate mathematics register in the bilingual students' dominant language, and may even lack the necessary resources, such as appropriate textbooks, that could provide that register. Furthermore, teachers may not be able to exploit the linguistics characteristics of the children's dominant language or may not be aware of the language aspects that may confuse the children.

Even if a teacher is completely bilingual in the mathematics domain and therefore has all the elements of the mathematized language and the language of mathematics in both languages, that by itself does not guarantee academic success for the students. After all, just using the Spanish term for a mathematical concept does not ensure that the children are going to immediately understand that concept. Children have to experience mathematics before they can understand mathematics. Part of that experience comes from experimenting with language.

Children need to be involved in producing language, both oral and written; in understanding the meaning of language; and in taking advantage of the flexibility of language. Part of a teacher's job, then, is to ensure that children are exposed to multiple ways of expressing the same mathematical concept whenever the language allows for multiple expressions. A child with extensive experience with the mathematized language is better prepared to deal with the language of mathematics and the mathematical concepts conveyed by that language than a child who lacks such experience (see Fuson, Hudson and Ron [forthcoming] and Lo Cicero and Fuson [1996] for ways to implement this language exploration in the teaching of word problems in the elementary school classroom).

Experience with mathematized language will greatly enhance a child's ability to interpret and solve a word problem correctly. In a sense, this means that children have to learn new applications for language. A teacher must then involve students in language experimentation, that is, exposing the children to mathematized language so that the language of mathematics and the concepts expressed by it are more accessible to the children.

What exactly do we mean by language experimentation? Let's take, for instance, a word problem involving a comparison. The comparison situation represented in figure 4.3 can be expressed in multiple ways, such as orally and graphically.

Everyday Language:
Rosa has seven peanuts.
Joshua has five peanuts.

Everyday Language:
Rosa tiene siete cacahuates.
Joshua teine cinco.

Mathematized-Situation Language:
Rosa has more peanuts than Joshua.
    How many more?
Joshua has fewer peanuts than Rosa.
    How many fewer?
How many extra peanuts does Rosa have?

How many peanuts extra does Rosa have?
How many peanuts does Rosa have to eat to
    have as many as Joshua?
How many peanuts does Rosa have to eat to
    have the same number of peanuts that
    Joshua has?
How many peanuts does Joshua have to buy
    to have as many as Rosa?
How many peanuts does Joshua have to buy
    to have the same number of peanuts that
    Rosa has?
How many more peanuts does Rosa have
    than Joshua?
How many fewer peanuts does Joshua have
    than Rosa?

Mathematized-Situation Language:
Rosa tiene más cacahuates que Joshua.
    ¿Cuántos más?
Joshua tiene menos cacahuates que Rosa.
    ¿Cuántos menos?
¿Cuántos cacahuates más que Joshua tiene
    Rosa?
¿Cuántos cacahuates extra tiene Rosa?
¿Cuántos cacahuates de más tiene Rosa?
¿Cuántos cacahuates le sobran a Rosa?
¿Cuántos cacahuates de menos tiene
    Joshua?
¿Cuántos cacahuates menos que Rosa tiene
    Joshua?
¿Cuántos cacahuates le faltan a Joshua?
¿Cuántos cacahuates tiene que comerse
    Rosa para tener tantos como Joshua?
¿Cuántos cacahuates tiene que comerse
    Rosa para tener la misma cantidad que
    tiene Joshua?
¿Cuántos cacahuates más tiene que comprar
    Joshua para tener tantos como Rosa?
¿Cuántos cacahuates más tiene que comprar
    Joshua para tener la misma cantidad que
    tiene Rosa?

**The Language of Mathematics
    Problem Solving:**
What is the difference between Joshua's
    peanuts and Rosa's?
If we compare Joshua's and Rosa's peanuts,
    who has more? How many more?

How many more peanuts does Joshua need
    to catch up to Rosa?

**The Language of Mathematics
    Problem Solving:**
¿Cuál es la diferencia entre los cacahuates
    que tiene Joshua y los que tiene Rosa?
Si comparamos los cacahuates de Rosa y los
    de Joshua, ¿quién tiene más?, ¿cuántos
    más?
¿Cuántos cacahuates necesita quitarle
    Joshua a Rosa para que los dos tengan la
    misma cantidad?

Fig. 4.3. Exploring language: an example from matching word problems

Children can be asked to "say" the problem in one way, then in a different way, and so on. In classrooms where both English and Spanish are spoken, the aim should be not a literal translation of the problem into the other language, since some expressions have no clear equivalent in the other language, but rather different ways to express the same situation in both languages. In a word problem involving a comparison, a teacher could explore alternatives similar to those shown in figure 4.3. The sentences in this example are not translations but different ways to express the same comparison situation in the two languages.

After children have experimented with the language of comparison, they should be able to interpret these problems correctly. In addition, this experimentation, along with a graphic representation of the problem, allows a child to posit possible solution procedures for the problem of "how many more peanuts does Joshua need to catch up to Rosa?"

CONCLUSION

It is important to understand that language issues in the monolingual classroom offer insights into the bilingual situation. A bilingual child who is being schooled in a language other than his or her dominant language will face more linguistic challenges than those experienced by the monolingual student who speaks the language of instruction. A weak everyday and mathematized language can result in increased difficulty in learning the language of mathematics and therefore in the child's mathematical ability. Bilingual children may need more opportunities to explore the languages involved for the simple reasons that (*a*) they are using more than one everyday or mathematized language and (*b*) the transference between L1 and L2 is not automatic.

In situations like these, a teacher who wants to improve language skills among her students is forced to take on the role of language expert and sometimes even of translator. It is clear that bilingual teachers have professional needs that go beyond the need of good materials published in the language of instruction. Those professional needs must be met in order to enable those teachers to prepare their students better for academic success. In particular, bilingual teachers need to have access to (*a*) a knowledge base about the linguistic characteristics of the language(s) of the classroom that may facilitate or hinder mathematics understanding; (*b*) techniques for using the mathematized language, which is the building block that links the everyday language to the language of mathematics; and (*c*) knowledge about cultural practices and issues that may affect the understanding of mathematics.

The model proposed in this article has an important consequence for bilingual teachers or teacher's aides who lack bilinguality in mathematics. Given that the language of mathematics is learned mostly in school and not acquired naturally, a teacher who does not have this specialized register needs to make a conscious effort to learn it. The mathematical concepts that the teacher already understands will transfer from one language to the other. The "new" learned language will enhance the teacher's ability to teach bilingual children.

REFERENCES

Clement, John, Jack Lochhead, and G. Monk. "Translation Difficulties in Learning Mathematics." *American Mathematical Monthly* 88 (1981): 286–90.

Cocking, Rodney, and Susan Chipman. "Conceptual Issues Related to Mathematics Achievement of Language Minority Children." In *Linguistic and Cultural Influences on Learning Mathematics,* edited by Rodney Cocking and José Mestre, pp. 17–46. Hillsdale, N.J.: Lawrence Erlbaum Associates, 1988.

Cuevas, Gilberto J. "Mathematics Learning in English as a Second Language." *Journal for Research in Mathematics Education* 15 (March 1984): 134–44.

Cummins, Jim. *Bilingualism and Language Minority Children.* Toronto, Ontario: Ontario Institute for Studies in Education Press, 1981.

———. "Linguistic Interdependence and the Educational Development of Bilingual Children." *Review of Educational Research* 49, no. 2 (1979): 222–51.

Fuson, Karen, William Carroll, and Judith Landis. "Levels in Conceptualizing and Solving Addition/ Subtraction Compare Word Problems." *Cognition and Instruction* 14, no. 3 (1996): 345–71.

Fuson, Karen, Kristin Hudson, and Pilar Ron. "Phases of Classroom Mathematical Problem-Solving Activity: The PCMPA Framework for Supporting Algebraic Thinking in Primary School Classrooms." In *Employing Children's Natural Powers to Build Algebraic Reasoning in the Context of Elementary Mathematics,* edited by James Kaput, forthcoming.

Fuson, Karen, Liliana Zecker, Ana Lo Cicero, and Pilar Ron. "El Mercado in Latino Primary Classrooms: A Fruitful Narrative Theme for the Development of Children's Conceptual Mathematics." Paper presented at the annual meeting of the American Educational Research Association, San Francisco, April 1995.

Gawned, Sue. "The Emerging Model of the Language of Mathematics." In *Language in Mathematics,* edited by Jennie Brickmore-Brand, pp. 27–42. Portsmouth, NH: Heinemann, 1990.

Kaput, James, and John Clement. Letter to the editor. *Journal of Children's Mathematical Behavior* 2, no. 2 (1979): 208.

Khisty, Lena Licón. "Making Inequality: Issues of Language and Meanings in Mathematics Teaching with Hispanic Students." In *New Directions for Equity in Mathematics Education,* edited by Walter G. Secada, Elizabeth Fennema, and Lisa Byrd Adajian, pp. 279–97. New York: Cambridge University Press, 1995.

Knight, Lester, and Charles Hargis. "Math Language Ability: Its Relationship to Reading in Math." *Language Arts* 54, no. 4 (1977): 423–28.

Lo Cicero, Ana, and Karen Fuson. "Making a Difference in Latino Children's Math Learning: Listening to Children, Mathematizing Their Stories, and Supporting Parents." Unpublished. 1996.

Macnamara, John. *Bilingualism in Primary Education.* Edinburgh: Edinburgh University Press, 1967.

Mestre, José. "Hispanic and Anglo Students' Misconceptions in Mathematics." Charleston, W. Va.: ERIC Clearninghouse on Rural Education and Small Schools, 1989. (*ERIC Digest:* no. EDO-RC-89-9)

———. "The Role of Language Comprehension in Mathematics and Problem Solving." In *Linguistic and Cultural Influences on Learning Mathematics,* edited by Rodney Cocking and José Mestre, pp. 201–20. Hillsdale, N.J.: Lawrence Erlbaum Associates, 1988.

Morris, Robert. "Linguistic Problems Encountered by Contemporary Curriculum Development Projects in Mathematics." In *Interactions between Linguistics and Mathematics Education: Final Report of the Symposium Sponsored by UNESCO, CEDO, and ICMI, Nairobi, Kenya, September 1–11, 1974* (ED-74/CONF. 808), pp. 25–58. Paris: United Nations Educational, Scientific and Cultural Organization, 1975.

Rosnick, Peter. "Some Misconceptions concerning the Concept of Variable." *Mathematics Teacher* 74 (September 1981): 418–20, 450.

Rosnick, Peter, and John Clement. "Learning without Understanding: The Effect of Tutoring Strategies on Algebra Misconceptions." *Journal of Mathematics Behavior* 3, no. 1 (1980): 3–27.

Saxe, George. "Linking Language with Mathematics Achievement." In *Linguistic and Cultural Influences on Learning Mathematics,* edited by Rodney Cocking and José Mestre, pp. 47–62. Hillsdale, N.J.: Lawrence Erlbaum Associates, 1988.

Spanos, George, Nancy Rhodes, Theresa C. Dale, and JoAnn Crandall. "Linguistic Features of Mathematical Problem Solving: Insights and Applications." In *Linguistic and Cultural Influences on Learning Mathematics,* edited by Rodney Cocking and José Mestre, pp. 221–40. Hillsdale, N.J.: Lawrence Erlbaum Associates, 1988.

Vygotsky, Lev A. *Thought and Language.* Translated by Alex Kozulin. Cambridge, Mass.: MIT Press, 1986.

Adapting Mathematics Instruction for English-Language Learners
The Language-Concept Connection

5

Leslie Garrison
Jill Kerper Mora

Statistics on mathematics achievement show that Latinos are significantly under-represented in all scientific and engineering careers in direct proportion to the amount of mathematics required for a particular job (Secada 1992; National Research Council 1989). A factor in the low levels of achievement among Latino students may be the misconception among educators that since mathematics uses symbols, it is therefore "culture free" and ideal for instructing students who are still learning the English language, or "English-language learners" (California Department of Education 1990). This misconception ignores the vital role of language in the development of mathematical concepts. Mathematics power is rooted in a strong conceptual understanding of mathematics, and this conceptual base is best developed through concrete experiences and language (National Council of Teachers of Mathematics [NCTM] 1989).

The relationship between language proficiency and mathematics achievement has been documented by researchers such as De Avila and Duncan (1981), who found that the low achievement in mathematics of Latino English-language learners (ELL) can be attributed to low levels of English proficiency. A lack of understanding about the role of language in mathematics instruction has led either to unreasonably high expectations for English-language learners' achievement in situations in which they receive no linguistic support or to lowered expectations that deny equal access to mathematical skills and reasoning (Secada 1992). The dilemma faced by the mathematics teacher of English-language learners is this: How should mathematics be taught to make a meaningful and powerful curriculum accessible to English-language learners?

Concept development occurs naturally when all students are fluent in the language of instruction, whether that be English, Spanish, or another language. However, many classrooms contain students at various levels of English proficiency, and teachers are faced with the challenge of covering new concepts in a language all students can understand. Many instructional strategies aim at making instruction accessible. According to the research in psycholinguistic development and learning, one of the key elements in teaching second-language learners is what Krashen (1981) terms *comprehensible input.* This is a construct developed to describe language that is understandable and meaningful under optimal conditions. Krashen explains this theory in instructional terms with the formula $i + 1$, where instruction (i), in order to be comprehensible and promote second-language fluency must be one level more complex than the second-language proficiency of the student. This allows for the language to be understood while also challenging the learners to increase their second-language proficiency. Comprehensible input is provided in school contexts through certain planned strategies, including the use of concrete contextual referents and the lack of restriction on the use of the students' primary language. The principle of $i + 1$ is the basis for what is termed Specially Designed Academic Instruction in English (SDAIE), also called *sheltered English instruction,* advocated for English-language learners (Díaz-Rico and Weed 1995). Sheltered instruction includes a set of strategies used to adapt content-area material for English-language learners.

The formula $i + 1$ was originally developed to describe the effective instruction of ELL students. The formula refers to instruction that is just one level of linguistic complexity beyond students' current level of understanding. The principle of $i + 1$ applies across curricular areas, since effective instruction is based on advancing students from their current level of understanding to the next level of complexity. This developmental process is also advocated in mathematics instruction.

The National Council of Teachers of Mathematics (NCTM) advocates an incremental developmental process in mathematics instruction in *Curriculum and Evaluation Standards for School Mathematics* (1989). These standards offer guidance on how to construct a conceptual understanding of mathematics by urging teachers to begin each new concept with concrete examples and experiences. The curriculum should then provide opportunities for students to make connections among concrete experiences, semiconcrete graphical depiction, abstract symbolic representations, verbal language, and written expression to develop a thorough understanding of the new concept.

Martorella (1986) describes concepts as categories into which knowledge and experiences are grouped or classified. This process of classification and integration is ongoing, and the learner is constantly sorting, relating, and extending conceptual categories. Concepts can range from the simple to the very complex and from concrete to abstract.

Concept development can be the primary goal in mathematics classrooms where all students are proficient in the language of instruction. However, in linguistically diverse classrooms, teachers must also consider the linguistic complexity of the language used in instruction and the language proficiency of the students in order to provide comprehensible input. If new concepts are introduced in an unfamiliar language, students must struggle with two unknowns: the language and the concept. This dual challenge of unknowns makes learning formidable (De Avila 1984).

The field of mathematics requires students to think in terms of concepts, abstract ideas, and symbols. Roe, Stoodt, and Burns (1987) describe mathematics as a highly compressed form of communication in which a single symbol may represent several words or relationships. For example, the equals sign (=) represents the concept of equality and the "greater than or equal to" symbol ($\geq$) simultaneously depicts the concepts of relative numerical value and equality.

In addition, terms in mathematics such as *count, odd,* or *times* may have a definition that is different from their meaning in everyday conversation. These polysemous terms can cause confusion among English-language learners because the students must discern the specialized meaning of common terms in a mathematical context. Since most English language learners first encounter the word *odd* as meaning unusual or different, when they hear a number referred to as odd, they may assume that something about the number is incorrect. The point of the teacher's presentation is often lost while students grapple to make sense of both new vocabulary and words with multiple meanings. Mathematics teachers must therefore consider both the linguistic and conceptual complexity of the language of instruction when designing lessons.

THE LANGUAGE-CONCEPT CONNECTION: AN INSTRUCTIONAL MODEL

The theoretical foundations for English-language instructional models are based on the relationship between the language of instruction and the development of concepts and skills. Cummins (1984) documented research from five different sources that supports the theory that there is a common underlying language proficiency in bilingual students that facilitates a transfer of learning between a student's first and second language.

This transfer of learning takes place when a certain "threshold" of proficiency is attained in the second language and when concepts and cognitive skills are firmly established. The data from studies of immigrant students' acquisition of academic skills and English and from successful bilingual programs in many countries indicate that although language-minority students develop a relatively high level of English proficiency in basic communication, the ability to understand and perform in academic settings, where language is more abstract and complex, develops at a much slower rate. Most English-language learners are unlikely to attain this proficiency in academic language until the later grades of elementary school (Cummins 1981).

Legarreta-Marcaida (1981) describes the preview-review technique as a strategy in which new learning is initally introduced and explained in the students' native language and later presented and reinforced in the second language by focusing on the new labels and vocabulary used to describe the previously established concepts. The purpose of this instructional strategy is twofold: (1) to ensure comprehensible input for English-language learners and (2) to establish skills and concepts soundly in order to facilitate the transfer of learning from the first to the second language as students acquire the necessary second-language proficiency.

The basic principle underlying the different strategies for bilingual instruction can be summarized as follows: *To teach an unknown concept, use the known language; to teach an unknown language, use a known concept.* The relationship between language and concept development to ensure comprehensible input for instruction is represented in table 5.1.

Table 5.1
The Language-Concept Connection

Domain	Language	Concept	Learning
A	Unknown	Unknown	Limited learning opportunity; modify instruction
B	Known	Unknown	Concept development
C	Unknown	Known	Language development
D	Known	Known	Concept and language mastery; advance to next conceptual or linguistic level

Domain A: Unknown Language, Unknown Concept

When a student understands neither the language of instruction nor the concept presented, learning opportunities are limited. For example, when a new concept such as place value is introduced to a student who has little command of the language of instruction, the student may confuse numbers such as fourteen and forty or eighteen and eighty because they sound very similar in English. While the student is trying to determine what number the teacher said and to translate it into the primary language, he or she misses the explanation that the 4 represents four groups of ten and 0 indicates that there are no additional units to include. As a result, it is unlikely that the student will either master the concept or advance linguistically through this lesson. On the contrary, he or she may experience frustration that further impedes understanding. The following scenario further illustrates this situation in Domain A.

Domain A in the Classroom

Ms. A., who teaches a linguistically diverse classroom of third graders, is starting a unit on multiplication. She is explaining that multiplication is actually repeated addition. Enrique, a monolingual Spanish-speaking student, sits and carefully watches what Ms. A. is doing. Her animated gestures give few clues about the topic of the lecture. After a few minutes, Enrique's attention drifts and he starts playing with his pencil. Ms. A. concludes her instruction and hands out a worksheet for the students to complete. Eager to finish his work, Enrique attempts the first problem but quickly gets frustrated and stops, sits, and waits because he has understood neither the language nor the concept presented.

To revisit the $i + 1$ theory, language is learned most rapidly when presented at a level at which the student understands most of what is being said and needs to determine only a limited number of words from the context. When too much new vocabulary is presented, the student loses the thread of the conversation, and the level of comprehension plummets. For the student to comprehend and learn, instructional modifications must be made.

Students will not persist in trying to make sense of instruction when, despite their best efforts, they cannot comprehend the input. Therefore, instruction in the "unknown language, unknown concept" domain must be modified and adapted so that it is comprehensible to the student. At this juncture, the teacher must decide whether to go through known language to develop concepts (Domain B, see below) or whether to go through known concepts to develop language (Domain C, see below). The decision is based on such factors as the goals of instruction, the possibility of teaching in the students' primary language, and the ability of the teacher to modify the linguistic and conceptual input in the second language.

Domain B: Known Language, Unknown Concept

In bilingual education classrooms where instruction is provided in the primary language, basic concepts are developed in the language familiar to the students. When the language of instruction is removed as an obstacle to learning concepts, teachers can focus instruction on the systemic development of conceptual knowledge. This concept development occurs naturally when all students are fluent in the language of instruction, whether that be English, Spanish, or another language. Teachers planning to work in Domain B must first determine whether students are fluent in the academic language of their primary language. Some students whose primary language is Spanish may be very fluent in conversational Spanish because they learned the language at home and are fully capable of communicating in Spanish. However, fluency in conversational Spanish does not equate to fluency in the underlying vocabulary and concepts of academic Spanish. For example, a lesson covering the concept of using data to make predictions might ask students to perform stock market predictions on the basis of the percentage of growth in certain stocks over a period of time. If all students in the class are fluent Spanish speakers, the teacher might give instructions in Spanish using the term *porcentaje* (percentage). This lesson will be in Domain B (Known Language, Unknown Skill) only for the bilingual students who already understand the underlying concept of pecentage. Even those students who recognize the term *porcentaje* may not understand the concept or know how percentages are derived. Therefore, teachers must determine that students understand the underlying concepts of a lesson before a new concept or skill can be successfully introduced through the primary language.

Mathematics has the unique advantage of being able to employ a variety of modalities for instruction. Beyond verbal language, ideas can be expressed through graphical depiction, symbolic representations, and the manipulation of concrete objects. Each of these other modes of presentation has the distinct advantage of being relatively independent of any particular spoken language, which allows new mathematical concepts to be successfully introduced to English-language learners.

If material is presented verbally, English-language learners benefit when the rate of speech is slowed, important terms are defined, and syntactic structures are simplified by using shortened, regularly patterned sentences. Visuals, schematic drawings, and demonstrations also boost the comprehension of verbally presented material. Gonzales (1994) describes these strategies of "sheltered instruction" as a synthesis of the components of quality teaching with the principles of language acquisition. In the sheltered environment, the teacher's task is to use the principles of second-language learning to build on the background knowledge students have acquired in their native language. The following example illustrates a possible instance of this situation in the classroom.

Domain B in the Classroom

Mr. B. teaches in a bilingual classroom where most students receive instruction in Spanish. Before he introduces the concept of multiplication, Mr. B. reviews the foundation concepts and vocabulary in both Spanish and English to ensure that the students understand. The students brainstorm items that come in groups, such as six packs of sodas, five sticks of gum in a package, twelve eggs in a dozen, and so forth. A table of the items is written, in both English and Spanish, on chart paper and then expanded to show how many items are included in one group, two groups, and three groups. Students are placed in teams and complete a similar chart that tells how many eyes, noses, and fingers are represented on their team. As a culminating activity, each student explains in his or her mathematics journal, in either Spanish or English, how the answers to the team chart were determined.

Domain C: Unknown Language, Known Concept

Once the conceptual foundation has been established in English-language learners, concepts can be used as a vehicle for learning English. When students are familiar with the topic used in an English-language lesson, they can better anticipate what is going to be said and more readily determine words from the context. Instruction of this type is used in transition and English-as-a-second-language (ESL) classrooms, where the primary goal is to develop skills in English.

Students who already have a strong conceptual base in the subject matter can focus on learning the new vocabulary, phonology, and syntax of their second language to express or explain already familiar concepts. Students who lack a conceptual base, however, often struggle in an immersion program because of the complexities of developing mathematical concepts presented in an unfamiliar language.

Teachers whose students are of mixed English-language abilities can use Domain C (Unknown Language, Known Concept) instruction as a reinforcement and follow-up to Domain B (Known Language, Unknown Concept) instruction. For example, after students have started developing a conceptual understanding of the lesson through instruction in the known or familiar language, the English vocabulary to support the lesson is introduced. Doing so puts the new material at a comprehensible level and focuses on the language-development aspects of learning while solidifying the conceptual learning base. To ensure that students have mastered a concept, mastery should be assessed in the students' dominant language or language of preference. Portfolios are a valuable tool in assessing the level of understanding of mathematical concepts, especially with English-language learners. (See "Portafolio de Matemática" in this volume.)

Occasionally, instruction is provided in the opposite order by first teaching the supporting English terms and then constructing the concept. This sequencing is not usually recommended by experts in either mathematics or bilingual education, since language and vocabulary are difficult to comprehend and retain without an understanding of the concepts they represent. Therefore, first developing a concept of place value through the use of manipulatives, graphic depiction, and so forth aids in learning the accompanying vocabulary. This condition is depicted in the following scenario.

Domain C in the Classroom

Mr. C. teaches a beginning ESL class to adults at the local community center. His students are recent immigrants who received their basic education in languages other than English. The focus of today's lesson is to teach the meaning of more, most and fewer, fewest as well as the supporting vocabulary word *cube.* Students arrange their desks in a circle, and each student is given several small cubes. Mr. C. picks up one cube and states, "This is a *cube.* What is this called?" Julia replies, "A *cube.*" Mr. C. picks up two additional cubes and says, "I have three *cubes.* Juan, how many *cubes* do you have?" Juan responds, and several other students also tell the number of cubes they have.

Mr. C. moves to two adjacent students. Norma has five *cubes* and Alicia has three *cubes.* Norma has *more cubes* than Alicia. Pedro has *more cubes* than Ivan. Who has *more cubes* than Tran?"

Comparisons are made between several other pairs of students, and then the students are encouraged to make additional comparisons. A similar format is followed for *most, fewer,* and *fewest.* Students are able to infer the meaning of the words through relating the repeated concrete examples to the already established concepts of *cube, more, most, few,* and *fewest.*

Domain D: Known Language, Known Concept

The domain of known concepts and known language provides a venue for review and evaluation. When the students have mastered both the language and the concepts presented in the curriculum, the students should be given an opportunity to demonstrate their competence. When assessing students' learning, special care must be taken to ensure that the student has command of the language used to communicate mastery. If the students do not control the language enough to express their thinking clearly and precisely, the teacher will not be able to discern whether poor performance in mathematics has a conceptual or a linguistic root. To address this problem, a series of evaluation alternatives appropriate for English-language learners is described toward the end of this paper.

Domain D in the Classroom

Ms. D. teaches mathematics to a linguistically diverse group of eighth graders. She starts the preparation for an upcoming examination on measurement with a review of the vocabulary used throughout the unit. Images depicting important vocabulary words as well as Spanish translations adorn much of the room. At the conclusion of the vocabulary review, students are given two objects—one a cylinder, the other a rock—and asked to work in groups to determine the volume of each.

The groups quickly start into action, each talking in a mixture of English and Spanish, depending on the language ability of the members. The students practice using mathematical language and review newly learned concepts in measurements as they set about solving the problems at hand. Near the end of the period, Ms. D. asks for the groups to report on their findings to the whole class. The other groups listen, question, challenge, and learn from their peers and Ms. D.'s comments.

Finally, the students are asked to write the definition of *volume,* in either English or Spanish, and give examples of how volume is important in real-life situations. Although most classroom instruction and classwork are completed in English as a measure to increase fluency in English, tests given to measure concept mastery can be completed in English or Spanish.

HOW TO MAKE INPUT COMPREHENSIBLE

Language-minority students can understand mathematics instruction if the concepts and operations are presented using techniques that make the concepts comprehensible to the students. Appropriate instruction requires additional language and academic support through specialized teaching strategies and attention to the students' particular linguistic and academic needs (Díaz-Rico and Weed 1995). Teachers need not be fluent in the students' first language to be successful in teaching English-language learners. However, a knowledge of the basic principles of second-language learning and sound teaching practices, along with a commitment to modifying instructional strategies, will produce increased academic growth in second-language students.

Teaching Vocabulary

The close relationship between vocabulary and concept development was established by researchers working with hearing-impaired students. They discovered that concepts were more difficult to develop and retain in students who have restricted vocabularies (Bracken and Cato 1986). This research further establishes a rationale for why mathematics teachers should fully develop concepts through concrete experiences and systematically teach accompanying vocabulary to assist in the comprehension and retention of concepts in mathematics. Words are labels for thoughts, ideas, concepts, and thinking, and vocabulary is central to concept formation, understanding, and articulation.

Both concepts and vocabulary are acquired and refined gradually (Roe, Stoodt, and Burns 1987). A mathematics teacher cannot assume that English-language learners understand the meaning of words simply because they can pronounce them or use them in coherent sentences. Identifying words with the concepts they label implies both familiarity with the word and the association of ideas with the linguistic form.

As English-language learners make the transition from primary language into English instruction, the English equivalents for the mathematical terms they learned in their primary language might not be covered in the upcoming lessons, creating gaps in their English vocabulary that are irregular and unpredictable. Therefore, mathematics teachers should review or preview all essential vocabulary at the beginning of a lesson or unit, especially when English-language learners are in the class. New mathematical vocabulary in the second language, however, is most effectively introduced after students have established the concepts the vocabulary words represent so that they learn the new "label" for the known concept.

Using Manipulatives

Relating new vocabulary to tangible objects is one of the basic premises of second-language instruction. Words are easier to remember when students can see and touch the objects they represent while repeatedly hearing and saying the new words. Mathematics manipulatives provide excellent opportunities for this type of vocabulary development. A sample list of concepts and the associated vocabulary that can be built using mathematics manipulatives is shown in table 5.2.

The close link between words and mathematical concepts can be seen by the listing shown in table 5.2. Each of the terms represents both an English word and a universal concept. For example, *greater than* represents the English terminology to describe comparative number or size. *Greater than* is also a universal concept that is present in all languages. Once the concept of greater than has been established, students do not need to relearn the concept in English; they need only to learn the English label for the previously established concept. Therefore, vocabulary must be learned in each new language, but concepts, once mastered, do not need to be retaught (Cummins 1984).

Building Context

English-language learners communicate more readily when the conversation takes place in a known context. A familiar context helps the listener limit the likely topics of conversation and better anticipate what the speaker is going to say. For example,

Table 5.2
Concepts, Manipulatives, and Vocabulary

Concept	Manipulative	Vocabulary
Measurement	Ruler, yardstick	Inch, foot, yard
Relationships	Tangrams, attribute blocks	Larger, smaller More, less Greater than, less than Same, different Curve, straight Above, below, next to Big, bigger, biggest
Critical attributes	Tangrams, attribute blocks	Width, height, length Circle, triangle, square Color Edge, side, corner, vertex

English-language learners will find familiar cues to help them anticipate and understand what a clerk is asking in a store or a teller is saying at the bank because in either situation, the conversations tend to follow a predictable pattern.

The same principle applies in mathematics instruction. Context helps students both understand problems and evaluate the reasonableness of their responses. New mathematics curricula use this principle by building lessons around a central theme that is developed over weeks or months. Mathematics problems are extracted from situations that arise as the unit unfolds. This type of curriculum benefits English-language learners because they have time to understand the context of the lessons, relate the context to previous experiences, anticipate the types of problems that might be asked, and develop the necessary vocabulary to comprehend the topics and communicate their thinking. Developing the context also helps all students understand the reasonableness of their responses. Each of these aspects helps English-language learners develop and demonstrate their full mathematics potential.

Working in Groups

Student work groups provide opportunities for students to develop both listening and speaking skills in English and to increase mathematical understanding. Most learners of a second language are hesitant to speak in front of the whole class; however, they will speak freely in a small group. Small-group settings afford all students greater opportunities to express their ideas, and they give bilingual students important practice in both receptive and expressive English. Student work groups are also a valuable teaching tool, since students who did not fully understand the lesson presented will have access to peer guides and interpreters as they proceed through the assignment.

The interaction in a small group also fosters concept development as students receive input from peers, explain their reasoning, get feedback from others, and refine their thinking on the basis of additional information. This process allows students to internalize the ideas presented and come to a fuller understanding of the concepts taught in the lesson (Kirsner and Bethell 1992).

ALTERNATIVE RESPONSE OPTIONS

For students to demonstrate competence, they should respond about a known concept using a known language. If students lack control of the language, they will not be able to express their understanding of a concept clearly. The fortunate aspect of mathematics instruction is that a variety of response options, or "languages," is available, so students who have difficulty expressing their thinking in English can use other modes of communication while they are developing English-language skills. The "languages" available to express mathematical ideas include written responses (in either the primary or the secondary language), graphical representations, and mathematical symbols. By employing a variety of response options, teachers can optimize the opportunity for English-language learners to express their mathematical thinking.

Developing Written Responses

The difficulty of expressing ideas in a secondary language can be mitigated by having students write their responses in the language of greatest fluency. During this writing process, the language difficulty is lessened and the students are able to concentrate on concept and thought development. If the teacher is unable to read the response, the students can translate their writing. During the translation stage, the students need to concentrate only on language, since their thinking has already been recorded. Teachers can also use other students or aides to help with the translation.

An illustration of how students can answer more completely in their primary language can be seen in Janet's work (see figs. 5.1 and 5.2). After a lesson on determining the area of a triangle, the students in Janet's class were asked to explain the process in English. Since Janet was a recent immigrant, her English was very limited, and her response provided little information about her understanding of the concept (fig. 5.1). Janet's teacher asked her to do the problem again, answering in Spanish (fig. 5.2). This response gives a much greater insight into her grasp of the concept.

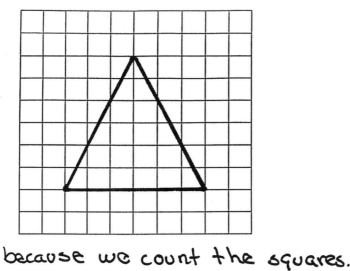

because we count the squares.

Fig. 5.1. Janet's incomplete response in English gives little information about her understanding of the concept of the area of a triangle.

Writing is the most advanced linguistic skill, the most difficult to learn, and therefore usually the last skill mastered by second-language learners (Díaz-Rico and Weed 1995). Speech provides English-language learners with an easier vehicle to communicate because they can use gestures, voice intonation, and both verbal and nonverbal cues from the listener to aid communication. Mathematics students who have a verbal command of English but do not supply complete written responses should be provided the opportunity to exhibit their mathematical competence orally. They can do so both formally, as in a test, or informally while they are working on a problem in groups.

Writing and speaking are both important tools to help students develop mathematical reasoning, but students who have yet to master these skills in English need to have other response options while their English-language ability is being developed.

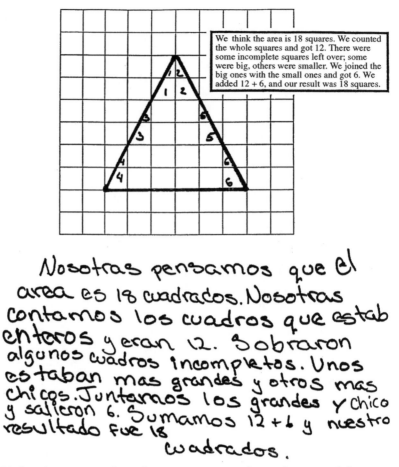

We think the area is 18 squares. We counted the whole squares and got 12. There were some incomplete squares left over; some were big, others were smaller. We joined the big ones with the small ones and got 6. We added 12 + 6, and our result was 18 squares.

Nosotras pensamos que el area es 18 cuadrados. Nosotras contamos los cuadros que estab enteros y eran 12. Sobraron algunos cuadros incompletos. Unos estaban mas grandes y otros mas chicos. Juntamos los grandes y chico y salieron 6. Sumamos 12 + 6 y nuestro resultado fue 18 cuadrados.

Fig. 5.2. Janet's response in Spanish gives a greater insight into her grasp of the concept of the area of a triangle.

Using Graphical Representations

Demonstration

Demonstrating a concept is an important means of communicating mathematical thinking. When teachers tell students, "Show me," students must use the available manipulatives or tools to demonstrate the concept. These props can support the developing English-language skills of students by decreasing the amount of language needed to communicate effectively. Encouraging students to use manipulatives or other tools to demonstrate their thinking will both stimulate their intellect and facilitate communication.

Graphical Depiction

Many mathematical concepts can be represented more clearly through drawings than through words. The concept of multiplication, for example, can be shown pictorially more easily than it can be described verbally or in writing. Since graphical representations require few, if any, words, they represent an excellent vehicle for English-language learners to explain concepts. The student work in figure 5.3 is an excellent example of how multiplication can be represented graphically and in words.

The fifth-grade student whose work is illustrated in figure 5.3 is making the transition into English instruction and learning to express thoughts in her second language. By graphically representing the concept as well as practicing the accompanying vocabulary (*times, sets, groups, circles*), she is able to better demonstrate an understanding of the material. The visual, conceptual, and vocabulary-building elements in this lesson from *Math by All Means* (Burns 1991) make the unit exceptionally well suited for teaching and assessing English-language learners.

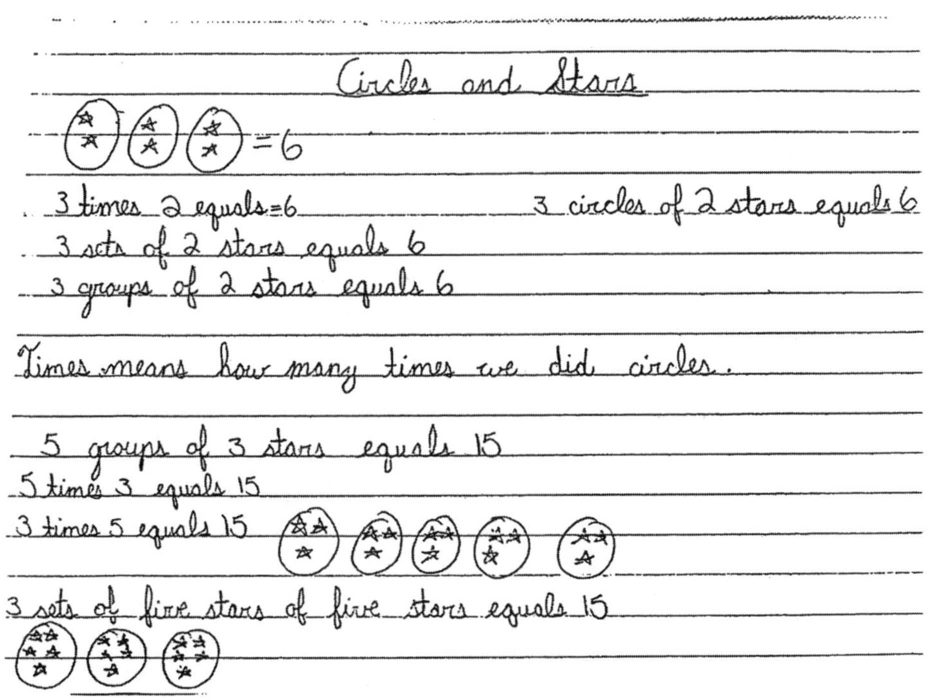

Fig. 5.3. A graphical and verbal explanation of multiplication

In addition to helping English-language learners, graphics are important tools for all students to represent their mathematical thinking. Their use helps students to visualize ideas and relationships and develop a fuller understanding of underlying concepts. All students should be encouraged to represent responses using graphical depiction, whenever appropriate, but these evaluative procedures are especially important for students with limited language proficiency.

Symbolic Representation

Numbers are tools used to represent mathematical thought symbolically. This symbolic representation is more abstract and therefore more difficult to learn than such concrete representations as manipulatives or drawings. The *Curriculum and Evaluation Standards for School Mathematics* (NCTM 1989) states that symbolic representations are best learned after concepts have been developed.

Many countries in the world use the Arabic system of numeration, making symbols nearly universal in mathematics. Symbol universality across languages, however, can also encourage teachers to move too quickly to the symbolic expressions before the conceptual foundation has been built. Students' ability to manipulate symbols without the proper conceptual foundation limits their progress into higher mathematics, since conceptual understanding is the basis for advanced mathematics.

Johnson (1991) describes this relationship between what is known linguistically and what is known conceptually as *logological knowledge.* Once a concept is firmly established through language, the knowledge can become language free as a cognitive structure. This process allows the transfer and application of knowledge in abstract reasoning and noncontextualized situations, which are foundational skills for advanced mathematics. Students who have built a conceptual understanding in their primary language can quickly communicate in the symbolic language of mathematics. However, if students lack a conceptual foundation, one must be developed before they are expected to communicate using the abstract symbolic language. When mathematical learning has been carefully developed over time with a solid base, which can be demonstrated by the students' ability to describe a concept or process in the language they know best, as Janet did, English-language learners will be ready to master more-complex mathematics with full understanding and long-term retention.

45

CONCLUSION

It is both a comfort and a challenge to teachers to realize that effective mathematics instruction has much in common with effective second-language teaching. The formula for providing comprehensible input for English-language learners and the strategies used to build mathematical concepts are parallel in their potential for maximizing learning in that they both work on the principle of teaching the unknown from the known. An essential element in making mathematics instruction accessible to English-language learners is careful planning. When teachers analyze the complexity of the concepts being taught and plan a step-by-step development of these concepts along with their corresponding linguistic labels or descriptions, students will benefit through advances in both mathematics and language learning.

The emphasis placed on intellectual development in mathematics by NCTM's *Curriculum and Evaluation Standards for School Mathematics* (1989) requires that mathematics educators work hand in hand with language educators to ensure a positive interaction of language and cognitive factors as students learn to manipulate complex concepts in increasingly sophisticated linguistic forms. We need not use revolutionary new strategies or invent a new curriculum. We have only to reinforce effective practices by raising teachers' awareness of the concept-language connection.

REFERENCES

Bracken, Bruce A., and Linda A. Cato. "Rate of Conceptual Development among Deaf Preschool and Primary Children As Compared to a Matched Group of Non–Hearing Impaired Children." *Psychology in the Schools* 23, no. 1 (1986): 95–99.

Burns, Marilyn. *Math by All Means: Multiplication.* Sausalito, Calif.: Math Solutions Publications, 1991.

California Department of Education. *Bilingual Education Handbook: Designing Instruction of LEP Students.* Sacramento, Calif.: California Department of Education, 1990.

Cummins, Jim. *Bilingualism and Special Education: Issues in Assessment and Pedagogy.* San Diego, Calif.: College-Hill Press, 1984.

———. "The Role of Primary Language Development in Promoting Education Success for Language Minority Students." In *Schooling and Language Minority Students: A Theoretical Framework,* edited by David P. Dolson and Guillermo Lopez, pp. 3–49. Sacramento, Calif.: California Department of Education, 1981.

De Avila, Edward A. "Language Proficiency: Confusion, Paradoxes, and a Few Admonitions to Psychologists, Educators, Linguists, and Others Developing Assessment Procedures for Language Minority Students." In *Placement Procedures in Bilingual Education: Education and Policy Issues,* edited by Charlene Rivera, pp. 19–30. Avon, England: Multilingual Matters, Ltd., 1984.

De Avila, Edward A., and S. E. Duncan. *A Convergent Approach to Oral Language Assessment: Theoretical and Technical Specification of Language Assessment Scales (LAS) Form A.* San Rafael, Calif.: Linguametrics, 1981.

Díaz-Rico, Lynne T., and Kathryn Z. Weed. *The Cross-Cultural Language and Academic Development Handbook.* Boston: Allyn & Bacon, 1995.

Gonzales, Linda N. *Sheltered Instruction Handbook.* Carlsbad, Calif.: Gonzales & Gonzales, 1994.

Johnson, Janice. "Constructive Processes in Bilingualism and Their Cognitive Growth Effects." In *Language Processing in Bilingual Children,* edited by Ellen Bialystok, pp. 193–221. Cambridge: Cambridge University Press, 1991.

Kirsner, Steven A., and Sandra Bethell. *Creating a Flexible and Responsive Learning Environment for General Mathematics Students.* Research Report 92-7. East Lansing, Mich.: National Center for Research on Teacher Learning, 1992.

Krashen, Stephen. *Second Language Acquisition and Second Language Learning.* London: Pergamon Press, 1981.

Legarreta-Marcaida, Dorothy. "Effective Use of the Primary Language in the Classroom." In *Schooling and Language Minority Students: A Theoretical Framework,* edited by David P. Dolson and Guillermo Lopez, pp. 83–116. Sacramento, Calif.: California Department of Education, 1981.

Martorella, Peter H. "Teaching Concepts." In *Classroom Teaching Skills,* 3rd ed., edited by James M. Cooper, pp. 181–223. Lexington, Mass.: D.C. Heath & Co., 1986.

National Council of Teachers of Mathematics. *Curriculum and Evaluation Standards for School Mathematics.* Reston, Va.: National Council of Teacher of Mathematics, 1989.

National Research Council. Mathematical Sciences Education Board. *Everybody Counts: A Report to the Nation on the Future of Mathematics Education.* Washington, D.C.: National Academy Press, 1989.

Roe, Betty D., Barbara D. Stoodt, and Paul C. Burns. *Secondary School Reading Instruction: The Content Areas.* Boston: Houghton Mifflin Co., 1987.

Secada, Walter. "Evaluating the Mathematics Education of Limited English Proficient Students in a Time of Educational Change." *Focus on Evaluation and Measurement,* 1992. (ERIC Document Reproduction Service no. ED 349 828)

Terrell, Tracy. "The Natural Approach in Bilingual Education." In *Schooling and Language Minority Students: A Theoretical Framework,* edited by David P. Dolson and Guillermo Lopez, pp. 117–46. Sacramento, Calif.: California Department of Education, 1981.

The Mathematics-Bilingual-Education Connection
Two Lessons

6

Norma G. Hernandez

For at least thirty years, accounts of mathematics achievement have consistently reported a marked difference between the achievement of Latino (also labeled *Chicano* and *Hispanic*) students and the majority group (Hernandez 1973; De La Cruz 1992). Recent studies, however, suggest the existence of specific factors related to this disproportionality that if addressed, could lead to a change in Latinos' mathematics achievement. One factor linked with the lack of progress in increasing achievement is related to school processes that perpetuate deficiencies.

A shift in research paradigms suggests that institutional deficits contribute to the observed lack of achievement. Early research studies assumed that cognitive deficits and cultural and linguistic deficits, or both, contributed significantly to this under-achievement (Hernandez 1973). Current research, however, assumes that "there is a process of school failure that involves inadequate or inappropriate instructional decisions that de facto handicap poor and ethnic minority students" (Khisty 1995, p. 280). This recent paradigm provides a basis for this discussion.

If we assume, as Khisty (1995, p. 282) does, that (1) the teacher has to model desired cognitive behavior, (2) learning is most effective in the child's primary language, and (3) everyday language must be used to communicate mathematical ideas that have unique meanings and structures that may be different from those of ordinary language, then we create an additive instructional environment. An additive environment validates and empowers the child through her or his language, culture, talents, and skills to understand and use mathematics. A subtractive environment, however, denies the importance of the student's language and thus disables the child linguistically; that is, it denies the child an opportunity to talk about mathematics—to develop and negotiate its meanings.

USING SPANISH TO FACILITATE AN IDEA

I suggest in this discussion that learning mathematics can be facilitated in a bilingual mathematics class when the importance of the language of mathematics is emphasized. A natural emphasis on examining one mathematical idea by using two languages, one of which is familiar, establishes a bilingual connection with the mathematical concept. For example, in examining a mathematical idea using two languages, one of which is familiar, the student is able to establish a connection between the familiar language and the mathematical idea while simultaneously making a connection between the familiar language and the new language, thus making a bilingual connection. Furthermore, the familiar language, Spanish in this instance, identified as a valid language that can be used to enhance mathematical understanding.

The two lessons described below consisted of giving students an appropriate series of examples using manipulatives as models to develop several concepts. These examples were labeled with mathematical terms in both English and Spanish whenever possible. The students were then to infer the nature of the concept by noticing the attributes of the model associated with the new terms.

The objective was to help students develop new mathematical notions through a bilingual approach. This procedure consisted of the students' physical manipulation of items in a given sequence, pattern, or model that was associated with the mathematical term in English or Spanish or both, which, when connected to the model, produced a new, mathematical cognitive structure, or concept. In other words, a manipulation or a model associated with new terms in both languages in a motivating, supportive environment generated the new mathematical construct.

Furthermore, developing a mathematical idea through the use of two *similar words*, one of which is already a part of the student's underlying cognitive framework, gives the student a *second* method to increase his or her memory of verbal descriptions and definitions. The objective is to help the child construct a vivid experience to define and label the new concept. The familiar word contributes to the vividness of the experience.

Mathematical notions can be learned partly in school and partly outside of school. If the two environments are made to overlap as much as possible, the learning of concepts is facilitated. When a mismatch occurs, however, care must be taken to help students see that certain understandings developed in the home may not be the same as those used in school. The two lessons that follow demonstrate a classroom environment in which a bilingual approach is used to facilitate the learning of mathematics.

At times the lesson described may be more teacher directed than a more "politically correct" lesson might be. Kessler and Quinn (1987) suggest that a more teacher-centered approach may be necessary to structure and manage the activities to ensure that each student has access to second-language input and, I would add, interaction.

Teachers who work in elementary schools with a large Latino population are often assigned to either a bilingual English-Spanish classroom or to a monolingual English classroom composed of bilingual students who are "transitioning" into English and are expected to be able to receive instruction solely in English. Teachers in both situations often ask me, "What strategies can we use to help our students increase their mathematics achievement?" or a related question, "How can we help them understand mathematical concepts?"

My response to them is usually in the form of two questions:

1. Do you consider the language (not special mathematical terms) you use to be of importance in helping students construct and learn new concepts?

2. Do you emphasize the importance of the language of mathematics in your lessons? In other words, do you use familiar Spanish words to help them understand a new mathematical concept? (It is assumed that teachers at the early grades are, generally speaking, bilingual in English and Spanish.)

The two following lessons describe an effort to demonstrate the importance of using familiar language to facilitate learning mathematics, as implied in the two questions posed above.

One Lesson

During a third-grade bilingual mathematics lesson, students were to develop concepts of measurement of length and weight; they were to estimate and then measure the circumference or length of objects, as appropriate. The estimates were to be recorded and compared with the actual measurements. Since it was close to Thanksgiving, the objects to be measured and weighed were squash and small pumpkins.

The third-grade classroom that I was invited to observe and work with had been designated a bilingual classroom. Consequently, the students and the teacher spoke English or Spanish at will. The intent of these classes, however, is that students transition into

English as quickly as possible to prepare them to take the end-of-year achievement test, which is administered solely in English. Therefore, much of the instruction is given in English with Spanish added as needed.

The students in this class worked in groups of four. Each group had one pumpkin, one Italian squash, a metric tape measure, a balance scale, and a piece of butcher paper to record the estimates and the measurements. The word *calabaza,* in Spanish as spoken in Mexico, means both pumpkin and squash.

In the dialogue that follows, *T* represents the teacher and *S* represents a student, not necessarily the same student every time.

> *T:* Students, today we will work with these pumpkins and squash to describe them in different ways. We will also measure them in different ways. Who has some ideas of how to begin?
>
> *S:* We can count the rings on them.
>
> *T:* We can count the rings, or ridges. We say *canales* in Spanish. The word *canales* is like the English word *canals.* We can use it to describe the pumpkins. Counting in English is *contar* in Spanish. Counting tells us how many ridges, or *canales,* we have. All right, select one of the pumpkins, estimate the number of ridges it has, write the number down, then count the ridges, the *canales.* Record the number of ridges your pumpkin has. Was your estimate close?

During this part of the lesson, English and Spanish are used for various reasons: (1) to show that the two languages are equally valued in the mathematics classroom; (2) to recognize and use the students' ideas in the lesson, thus enabling them to develop a sense of confidence about the worth of their expressions in either English or Spanish; and (3) to place a conscious focus on the use of language, Spanish in particular, to learn mathematics—to communicate academic meaning (Dale and Cuevas 1987). The students' language, as shown in this dialogue, has a place in learning mathematics (Cummins 1981).

Furthermore, the use of a few unfamiliar terms may severely retard the students' comprehension of a word problem (Marks, Doctorow, and Wittrock 1974) or in this example, severely hamper their understanding of a concept. Thus, the use of familiar Spanish words within the context of the lesson will aid in the understanding of the new concept.

(The students describe the pumpkins by counting the ridges and reporting the number of ridges for each pumpkin.)

> *T:* What else can we do? *(pause)* Let's work with the squash.
>
> *S:* We can measure how long they are.
>
> *T:* Yes, we can measure their length. How do you say *measure* in Spanish?
>
> *S: Medir.*
>
> *T:* Yes, *medir.* Thank you. What do we do when we measure the length of something? Let's measure the length of this squash, or *calabaza.*
>
> *S:* Put the measuring tape along the side of the squash and look at the tape. The squash is seventeen centimeters long.

The students are asked to contribute knowledge and information to the class. In U.S. schools with a large Latino enrollment, the students who have attended school in Mexico and may have a knowledge of mathematical expressions in Spanish can become a resource for the class in supplying the accepted Spanish mathematics terminology. This contribution again serves to empower the students to use their culturally related abilities.

> *T:* Very good. Now each group can pick a squash, *calabaza,* and estimate and record the estimate of its length. In Spanish we say, *lo largo de le calabaza*—the length of the squash. *(The students estimate and measure the squash.)*

T: Now, let's study two of the words we just used—*measure* and *medir* and *length, lo largo*. Notice the two words *measure* and *medir*. (*The teacher has written the words on word strips and circled the letters* me.)

S: The first two letters are the same.

T: Yes, that can help you remember that *measure* and *medir* mean the same thing. Look at the other two words—*length* and *lo largo*—on the word strips. Who can tell me how they are alike?

S: Both start with the letter *l*.

T: Very good. What else?

S: Largo looks like the word *large*.

In the exchange above the students and the teachers note the similarities of related words. (The roots of the verb *to measure* are found in Middle English and Old French from the Latin *mensurare,* where the *me* is encountered as it is in both modern English and Spanish. The words *large* and *largo* are also derived from Middle English, Old French, and the Latin *largus.*)

The teacher continues to model appropriate cognitive behavior:

T: Very good! Yes, a large thing would probably be long or have a large length. *Largo* means long, but when you say *lo largo (points to the words on a word strip) de la calabaza,* you are talking about the length of the squash.

The teacher poses a problem for the students' consideration—measuring the length of a round object. When the students suggest a solution, the teacher is careful to help them see that a new term is necessary to avoid confusing two related ideas.

T: Let's take turns describing the squash by its length. (*The students describe the length of the squash.*) Now, let's measure the pumpkin. How can we measure the pumpkin? Can we take its length? *¿Podemos medir lo largo de la calabaza? (Long pause)*

S: It's hard to measure the length because you have to go around the side of the pumpkin, but we could go all the way around the pumpkin.

T: Yes, we could measure all the way around the pumpkin. Would that be the length of the pumpkin? (*Pause*) If we go all the way around the pumpkin, we have to call that measurement something else to tell another person that it is not just the length but the length all the way around.

T: Does anyone know the word to use when we measure the distance around something?

S: Circunferencia.

T: Yes. In mathematics the word *circumference* or *circunferencia (points to the word strips)* is used to describe the distance or length around something. How can we measure the circumference, or *circunferencia,* of the pumpkins?

S: Like this. And it's the biggest part of the pumpkin. (*The student places the tape horizontally around the thickest part of the pumpkin as it sits on the desk.*) [Note: We could have discussed the words *horizontal* and *vertical,* but doing so was not considered relevant at this point in the lesson.]

T: That's a good idea. Does anyone have another suggestion?

S: Like this. (*The student places the tape vertically around the pumpkin.*)

T: Which method do you think we should use?

S: Around the top like this! (*measures horizontally*) Because the pumpkin has holes on the top and on the bottom and the tape just kinda skips over them.

S: It's not as long if you measure it like this. (*measures vertically*) (*comments of agreement*)

T: Could we measure it both ways?

S: We could say how fat it is and how tall it is.

T: All right, then, measure the circumference of the pumpkin at the thickest part and then around the top. You can measure it both ways and describe it in two different ways. Estimate, record, and then measure.

The students use informal language to talk about which measurements to use to describe the pumpkins. As the lesson progresses, the students begin to use more formal terms in their second-language interactions.

(After the students have had time to estimate, record, and measure the circumference, they take turns describing the pumpkins.)

T: Let's study two of the words we just used—*circumference* and *circunferencia.* How are they alike?

S: They are the same, except in Spanish the word ends in *ia* and in English there is only an *e.*

T: Very good! What else can you see in the words? *(long pause)* Can anyone see part of a word that is familiar. *(long pause)*

S: Yes! *Circle!* We measured a circle!

T: Very good! The letters *circ* (underscores them on the word strips) are the first letters of the word *circle.* So, what do *circumference* and *circunferencia* mean?

S: Circle!

T: Pumpkins are not exactly in the shape of a circle, but close enough. OK. Circle is a shape, so what is circumference?

S: It's the length around the pumpkin.

T: Very good! When we measured the length around the pumpkin, we used the tape measure and what shape did it form?

S: A circle!

T: What did we call that length?

S: *Circunferencia.*

Again, the teacher is careful to point out that even though *circumference* is used in reference to circles, it is nevertheless a length.

T: Yes, *circumference* or *circunferencia.* In mathematics we use words that help us remember what we are taking about. For example *circ* will help us remember we are measuring the length around circles. Very good. Now we are going to describe the pumpkins in another way. We are going to find out how much the pumpkins weigh. The word *weight* in Spanish is *peso (points to a word strip).*

T: We will use these balances to measure the weight of the pumpkins. A balance has a scale marked on it to help us weigh objects. In Spanish balances are called *basculas,* or *balanzas (points to the word strip for* balanza, *only).* Also, the word *escala* in Spanish is like the word *scale* in English. The two words are alike. Find the scale on your balance. *Encuentra la escala en tu balanza.* (The teacher and I felt that introducing the English word *scale* as used, for example, in the nurse's office would detract from the lesson at this point. We postponed it to a continuation of the lesson on weight.)

T: The word *escala* is like the Spanish word *escalera,* which means stepladder. If you turn your balance up and down like this *(turns one of the balance scales to a vertical position),* then you can see that if you look at the numbers on the scale, it looks like a stepladder. *(The teacher helps the students focus on the scale.)*

T: Each rung, or *escala,* is a step. You can see the scales have steps from one long line on each number to the next number. You can also see that there are smaller steps between the larger steps. The smaller steps between the larger ones do not have numbers.

Next the teacher poses a problem for the students' consideration that requires higher-order thinking. The issue of one curriculum for *all* students suggests that if problem solving is the central focus of the National Council of Teachers of Mathematics (NCTM) (NCTM 1989, p. 23), then it should be the central focus for bilingual students.

T: Why do you think these instruments we are going to use to measure weight are called balances? *(The teacher walks around as students examine the scales to have them note that the lines on the scale show grams; discusses with the students how to weigh the pumpkins; makes suggestions and asks questions so that the students notice the various moving parts of the scales; and names the various parts: the pan* [el platillo], *the arm* [el brazo], *the control rod* [el control], *and the pointer* [el indice o la flecha]*.)*

T: The word *indice* in Spanish is like the word *index* in English. This finger *(holding up an index finger)* is called the *index finger* and is used to … do what?

S: You point with it.

T: Yes, to point to something. We can also call the pointer the *indicator.*

T: What does the word *balance* mean to you? *(long pause)* How many of you know how to ride a bicycle? What do you have to do to ride it and not fall?

The teacher provides a familiar analogy the students can use to visualize balancing. She then extends the idea to the balancing of objects to find their weight. Everyday language can be used with a special mathematical meaning.

S: You have to stayed balanced. You can't go to one side or the other. You have to stay straight.

T: Yes, to ride your bike you have to stay balanced. And that is how we are going to find the weight of these pumpkins; we are going to balance them with this *balanza.*

T: I see most of you putting the pumpkin on the pan and moving the pointer on the scale. Now, who can tell us how to weigh the pumpkins?

At this point students use everyday, familiar language to refer to mathematical objects or terms.

S: You put the pumpkin on the pan and then move this bar, this pointer, until, until … I don't know.

T: That's a good start. Who can go on from there? *(pause)*

S: When you put the pumpkin on the *balanza,* the arm moves to the top of the box. You have to move this pointer real slow until the arm goes down and stops at the bottom of the box.

T: Does everyone agree? *(pause)* Do you want to move the pointer so the arm moves all the way to the bottom of the box? *(pause)* *(the students shake their heads in the negative)* If you don't want the arm control at the top of the box, do you want it at the very bottom?

S: You want it to balance. Maybe we can move the pointer until the arm is in the middle. Uh, you know, when it is balanced.

S: Yes! That's right! You want the weight of the pumpkin to be *balanced* with the weight of the pointer *(other comments of agreement).*

T: What does the pointer tell us? ¿*Que indica el indice?*

S: How much the pumpkin weighs.

T: Where do you read the pointer?

S: There, where the little arrow is pointing to the numbers.

T: Does everyone agree? Someone tell us how you weigh the pumpkins.

The teacher poses a problem for the students' consideration. She wants them to discover that if the arm goes all the way to the bottom, there is no way to determine the pumpkin's weight. She is probing for appropriate suggestions to determine the weight of the object in the pan.

S: You move the pointer slowly until the arm is in the middle of the box because you want to balance it. Then you read the bar where the little arrow points to the number.

T: Very good! Now, estimate the weight of the pumpkin in grams, record your estimate, and then weigh it.

The teachers walks around the room, asking questions *and* offering suggestions.

T: I see that many of you are having trouble writing down the weight of the pumpkin. What is the problem?

S: The pointer is between numbers. I can't tell if it weighs fifty-one or fifty-two grams.

T: Is there another way we can say what the weight is?

S: The weight is between fifty-one and fifty-two grams.

T: Yes, we can say that the weight is less than fifty-two grams but more than fifty-one. In Spanish we would say, "The pumpkin *pesa más que cincuenta y uno gramos pero menos que cincuenta y dos.*"

T: Let's look at our scale. Between the numbers there are some small lines. How many are there? Yes, there are ten. Since each step between numbers is divided into ten equal, smaller steps, each one of these smaller steps is called *one tenth.* Who can tell the class why they are called tenths? *(pause)*

As the lesson progresses, the use of formal mathematical language by the teacher increases. As the students continue to discuss correct procedures, they, too, use the more formal language to express ideas.

S: When we studied fractions we called them *one half* and *one third.*

T: One-half is one part out of how many equal parts? Yes, two equal parts. And one-third? Yes, one-third is one part of three equal parts. If we have ten equal parts, then what do we have?

S: One-tenth.

T: Yes, one-tenth is a fraction, and it is one part of ten equal parts. Who can tell the class what one-tenth is in Spanish?

S: ¿*Un décimo?*

T: Yes, that is right. Each small step is called *un décimo.* Now, let's see how many tenths this pumpkin weighs. From the number fifty-one we count the small lines until we get to the pointer. Count: one, two, three. What does the pumpkin weigh?

S: Fifty-one and three-tenths.

S: We have to say the unit—grams.

T: Very good. We say fifty-one and three-tenths grams. *Pesa cincuenta y uno gramos con tres décimos.* Other groups, please continue weighing your pumpkins now that you know how to read the scale. When you finish, write the weights in order from the least, *lo menos,* to the most, *lo más.* Be sure to compare your estimates with the measured weights to see how well you are learning to estimate weight.

It had not been the intention of the teacher to focus on fractions. As the lesson continued, however, it became obvious that the students were ready to use fractions to make more-precise measurements of the weight of the pumpkins. The opportunity fit the notion of the "teachable moment" as described by Posner (Posner et al. 1982). Since the students had had several lessons on unit fractions, the teacher took advantage of the opportunity and continued with the idea of determining the weight to include tenths.

T: Now that you have learned to read tenths of a gram on the scale, measure the lengths of the *calabazas* and the *circunferencia* of the pumpkins. Look at the measuring tapes. Tell me what you see *(pause).*

S: There are smaller lines between the centimeters. Like the scale. There are ten of them.

T: Yes, there are ten smaller units. What would we call them—each one of them?

S: Décimos. Tenths.

T: OK. Measure the lengths and the circumference to the nearest tenth.

S: Mine is seventeen and seven-tenths. *(The groups report their measurements to the nearest tenth.)*

At this point the lesson ended to give the students time to complete their assigned tasks. A final assignment was for them to summarize what they had learned about finding the length, shape (circular), and weight of the pumpkins. The teacher and I discussed how the use of the root words of the mathematical terms facilitated the learning of the new concepts, especially if the two words were similar in spelling and pronunciation, more so if the words were cognates. (Cognates are words, whether in English or Spanish, that are related by common origin and similar in meaning and spelling.)

The teacher and I noted the appropriateness of the traditional mathematical term that had been selected to name the referent concept (*circle, circumference*). I reported to the teacher that I use this technique with my mathematics methods classes at the university, even though the classes are taught solely in English. (Bilingual Latinos, in general, constitute at least 50 percent of my methods classes. Some of those students become bilingual teachers at the elementary school level.) In a bilingual classroom, however, there is a natural tendency to explain new mathematical terms by focusing on relevant English and Spanish cognates, which makes a vivid connection between the two languages and the mathematical terms.

A Second Lesson

In one of my mathematics methods courses one lesson requires students to construct such geometric figures as two congruent lines, two congruent triangles, and a line perpendicular to a given line, using only a compass and a straightedge. During the time they work in groups, the students who know Spanish are encouraged to state the geometric Spanish terms for geometric figures and such concepts as compass, radius, diameter, and protractor. For example, they will say that *radio, diámetro,* and *transportador* are radius, diameter, and protractor, respectively.

The discussion continues with an examination of the compass. What does it do? In a given geometric construction, for example, the objective is to copy a given line segment, that is, to make two line segments *congruent*. A line segment is *congruent* (*congruente*) to a given line segment by assuming Euclid's notion of superposition; in other words, one line segment is made to fit over the other one. In effect, this is what the compass helps us do.

We can copy a line segment with the compass by placing the metal point on one endpoint of the given line segment and placing the point of the pencil on the other endpoint of the line segment. We can now literally *transport* that line segment to another location on a given line of arbitrary length by superpositioning the transported line segment on the new line. The point of the compass is placed at one predetermined point and the arc drawn by the pencil point intersecting the second line determines the second point. A new line segment has now been determined that is congruent to the given line segment. We say the two lines are *congruent* by superposition. (*Note:* The word *transportador* in Spanish generally refers to a protractor. In class, however, the students choose to use *transportador* to refer to the compass as well as to the protractor. The students know the correct names of the instruments, but the word *transportador* seems to fascinate them because they use it even after they have been corrected.)

Both the idea of *transporting* a given line segment and Euclid's fundamental notion of superposition are used in other constructions. The compass, then, becomes an instrument that transports a line segment to a given location. Many of the students, even those who are monolingual English speakers, begin to refer to the compass as a "transporter" and to the task of constructing congruent angles and other similar tasks as "transporting" line segments. The idea of transporting a line segment then carries over to "transporting" a radius, thus suggesting the conclusion that the radii of a circle are congruent.

SUMMARY

In making a mathematics–bilingual-education connection, the fundamental notion is not that Latinos need mathematics different from that studied by the "majority" students but rather, as Carey et al. (1995) propose, that effective instruction for *all children* must be carried out on the basis of what is known about how children learn with understanding. The role language plays in affecting bilingual children's thinking, the nature and dynamics of discourse about mathematics in a bilingual classroom, and the relevant emotional and motivational factors are related to effective instruction. Instruction that indeed diminishes educational inequities by considering the linguistic factors illustrated in these two lessons must be designed and implemented in order for Latino children to have an opportunity to maximize their learning from instruction.

REFERENCES

Carey, Deborah A., Elizabeth Fennema, Thomas P. Carpenter, and Megan L. Franke. "Equity and Mathematics Education." In *New Directions for Equity in Mathematics Education,* edited by Walter G. Secada, Elizabeth Fennema, and Lisa Byrd Austin, pp. 93–125. New York: Cambridge University Press, 1995.

Cummins, James. "The Role of Primary Language Development in Promoting Educational Success for Language Minority Students." In *Schooling and Language Minority Students: A Theoretical Framework,* edited by David P. Dolson and Guillermo Lopez, pp. 3–50. Sacramento, Calif.: California Department of Education, 1981.

Dale, Teresa C., and Gilbert J. Cuevas. "Integrating Language and Mathematics Learning." In *ESL through Content-Area Instruction: Mathematics, Science, Social Studies,* edited by Jo Ann Crandall, pp. 9–54. Englewood Cliffs, N. J.: Prentice Hall Press, 1987.

De La Cruz, Yolanda. "Strategies for Working with Latino Families in Mathematics." Paper presented at the Asilomar Mathematics Conference, California Mathematics Council—Northern Section, Monterey Peninsula, California, December 1992.

Hernandez, Norma G. "Variables Affecting Achievement of Middle School Mexican-American Students." *Review of Educational Research* 43 (1973): 1–39.

Kessler, Carolyn, and Mary Ellen Quinn. "ESL and Science Learning." In *ESL through Content-Area Instruction: Mathematics, Science, Social Studies,* edited by Jo Ann Crandall, pp. 55–87. Englewood Cliffs, N.J.: Prentice Hall Press, 1987.

Khisty, Lena Licón. "Making Inequality: Issues of Language and Meanings in Mathematics Teaching with Hispanic Students." In *New Directions for Equity in Mathematics Education,* edited by Walter G. Secada, Elizabeth Fennema, and Lisa Byrd Austin, pp. 279–97. New York: Cambridge University Press, 1995.

Marks, Carolyn B., Marlene J. Doctorow, and Milton C. Wittrock. "Word Frequency and Reading Comprehension." *Journal of Educational Research* 67 (February 1974): 259–62.

National Council of Teachers of Mathematics. *Curriculum and Evaluation Standards for School Mathematics.* Reston, Va.: National Council of Teachers of Mathematics, 1989.

Posner, George J., Kenneth A. Strike, Peter W. Hewson, and William A. Gertzog. "Accommodation of Scientific Conception: Toward a Theory of Conceptual Change." *Science Education* 66, no. 2 (1982): 211–27.

Mathematizing Children's Stories, Helping Children Solve Word Problems, and Supporting Parental Involvement

7

Ana María Lo Cicero
Karen C. Fuson
Martha Allexsaht-Snider

In this article, we draw on our experiences in a six-year project (Children's Math Worlds) designed to teach mathematics to first-, second-, and third-grade Latino inner-city children in English- and Spanish-speaking classes. Through those experiences we have learned that it is necessary to interweave elements of mathematics into children's lives in order to make teaching more effective. These approaches have worked with Latino children and with children from other backgrounds who were in our urban classrooms. The recent experiences of teachers using these approaches in other kinds of classrooms, including those in affluent upper-middle-class schools, suggest to us that these approaches are effective with all children.

Given the complex patterns of immigration to the United States from many different countries of the Spanish-speaking Americas, teachers' own life experiences may differ considerably from the life experiences of Latino inner-city children. Many children in a given class or school may emigrate from the same community (one typical pattern in the Chicago area and elsewhere), or children may come from many different places. Finding out about students' lives enables teachers to enact a curriculum that partially unfolds from children's real-life experiences. In the process, mathematics learning and teaching become meaningful, enlightening, involving, empowering, and creative.

USING CHILDREN'S STORIES IN MATHEMATICS CLASS

Eliciting Children's Stories

One way to accomplish the interweaving of mathematics and children's lives is to elicit children's stories of their life experiences. Some children are eager and ready to share their stories. Others are initially too shy to tell them to the whole class, so they draw or write their stories. Eventually, all children participate.

The research reported in this chapter was supported in part by the National Science Foundation (NSF) under Grant no. RED 935373 and in part by the Spencer Foundation. The opinions expressed in this chapter are those of the authors and do not necessarily reflect the views of NSF or of the Spencer Foundation. We wish to thank all the teachers and children with whom we worked and the rest of the Children's Math Worlds team (especially Pilar Ron, Yolanda De La Cruz, Kristin Hudson, and Stephen Smith) for helping us develop and articulate these views and put them into practice.

Asking children to bring photographs from home about a trip the family has taken (or any photographs) opens up great stories and gives teachers insights into their students' lives. Children love to listen to one another's stories. Using their stories as a basis for mathematics work helps children develop their listening skills. Children's stories give some insight into their lives, and consequently, they feel included.

The class becomes alive and dynamic because children usually understand and enjoy the stories told by their peers. Any confusion can be clarified by questions from other children.

Teachers can choose the stories that they think are fruitful to expand mathematically. Stories can be told at other times of the day and returned to and told again (perhaps by another child to emphasize listening and remembering) during mathematics class. Each child's story can be returned to over and over during the year to provide ongoing coherence and inclusion. Mathematical aspects can be expanded. Nonmathematical aspects can be discussed in other subject areas. Children feel very excited and affirmed whenever their story is mentioned in class.

Coconstructing Stories with the Whole Class

The unfolding multiple narratives of children's experiences provide a framework coconstructed by the teacher and children within which teachers relate new mathematical ideas to children's lives and to their common experiences of the shared stories. These processes of coconstruction enable all children to participate in all the stories. The stories and their related mathematics arise from, and belong to, the class members. Using children's stories in these ways develops thinking and creativity and facilitates children's emerging mental, oral, and written competence with language and with mathematics.

The following exchange between Guillermo (*G*) and the teacher (*T*) is an example from one of our Spanish-speaking classes early in the first grade. Adelaida (*A*), José (*J*), and María (*M*) also participated in the conversation.

> *T:* Guillermo, cuéntanos una historia sobre algo que te pasó. (Guillermo, tell us a story about something that happened to you.)
>
> *G:* Iba caminando al parque y el viento me llevó el sombrero y corrí mucho para alcanzarlo. (I was walking to the park, and the wind took my hat away, and I ran a lot to reach it.)
>
> *T:* ¡Qué lindo cuento! ¿Quién puede hacerle una pregunta a Guillermo sobre su cuento? (That's a great story. Who can ask Guillermo a question about his story?)

This story opened up many interesting questions, comments, and discussions about being alone and about different types of hats. Had he brought the sombrero here from Mexico? Was he able to catch it? Opportunities that could be pursued in other subject areas are obvious. Here we concentrate on the teacher's work to mathematize the story with the children, that is, to focus on possible mathematical elements and expand on them.

> *T:* ¿Cuántas cuadras corriste? (How many blocks did you run?)
>
> *G:* Como cinco. ¡Sí, cinco! (About five. Yes, five!)
>
> *T:* Así que cuando corriste dos cuadras, ¿cuántas más tuviste que correr? Contestemos la pregunta mostrando la respuesta con los dedos. Recuerden que así contestamos todas las preguntas, así puedo ver cómo trabajan todos. (So once you had to run two blocks, how many more did you have to run? Let's all answer the question by showing the answer with our fingers. Remember we are answering all questions this way so I can see how all of you work.)
>
> *(Most children show three fingers automatically, but some still need to count and raise each finger instead of showing three fingers.)*

T: ¿Cómo hallaron la respuesta? (How did you get the answer?)

(Three different children show and explain how they got the answer.)

T: Por favor, ven y dibuja en la pizarra las cuadras que corriste. (Please come to the board and draw the blocks you ran.)

(Guillermo draws five line segments on the chalkboard:
_____ _____ _____ _____ _____*)*

T: ¿A quién le gustaría hacerle a Guillermo una pregunta con números? Sí, Adelaida. (Who would like to ask Guillermo questions with numbers? Yes, Adelaida.)

A: Cuando estabas en la cuadra número cuatro, ¿cuántas te faltaban? (When you were on block number four, how many were you missing?) *(Most children show one finger.)*

We find that English-speaking children commonly ask, "How many more to go?" whereas Spanish-speaking children more often use *falta,* "How many are you missing?"

(The teacher asks two different children to explain how they got their answer, and then asks the class to think of other questions.)

T: Escuchemos la pregunta de José. (Let's listen to José's question.)

J: Cuando encontraste el sombrero, ¿cuántas cuadras caminaste hasta el parque? (After you found the hat, how many blocks did you have to walk to go to the park?)

G: Tres. (Three.)

T: ¿Alguna otra pregunta? (Any other questions?) *(The teacher then frames the story for the whole class because she thought that by now some children might not have the whole situation in memory.)* Así que Guillermo corrió cinco cuadras tratando de conseguir su sombrero y caminó tres cuadras para llegar al parque. ¿Quién puede hacer una pregunta sobre esto? (So Guillermo walked five blocks running after his sombrero and three blocks to the park. Who can ask a question about this? *(The teacher here resists the impulse to ask the obvious question herself and turns the story back over to the class.)* Escuchemos a María. (Let's hear María.)

M: ¿Cuántas cuadras corrió y caminó Guillermo? (How many blocks did Guillermo run and walk?)

T: Muy buena pregunta, María. Así que, ¿cuántas cuadras fueron en total? Enséñenme la respuesta con los deditos. (Very good question, María. So, how many blocks were there in all? Show me the answer with your fingers.)

(The teacher has introduced the mathematical term en total. *Most children show eight fingers.)*

The teacher asks three different children to show how they got their answer. She then asks Adelaida to draw the three more blocks on the chalkboard so everyone can see them. She labels the place where the sombrero blew off, the place where it was caught, and the park. She then asks a child to retell Guillermo's story pointing at the "math drawing" of it on the chalkboard.

The next day the teacher writes on the chalkboard a word problem taken from Guillermo's story:

> There are 10 blocks from Guillermo's house to the park. He ran six blocks and walked the rest. How many blocks did he walk?

Later, as the children get used to different kinds of word problems, they can pose many of the mathematics problems that they create by themselves.

Mathematizing Children's Stories

The important features of the process of mathematizing a child's story have been illustrated in our example. A schematic overview of the mathematizing process is shown in figure 7.1. This process can be used for more-complicated kinds of mathematics problems.

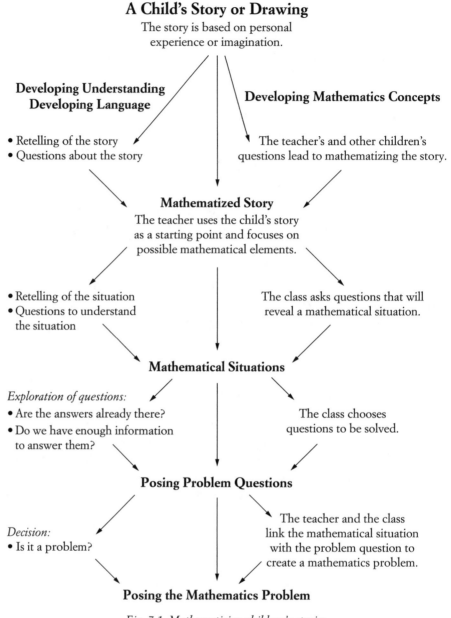

Fig. 7.1. Mathematizing children's stories

We want to emphasize the importance of the involvement of the class in the mathematizing coconstruction process. The steps in this story come from questions asked by other members of the class, which makes the story more of a whole-class narrative. It also gives children experiences in posing questions. Such experiences are important because we have found that early in word-problem solving, asking the question is the most difficult part for children.

The teacher orchestrates the mathematizing coconstruction process by calling on various selected students, by maintaining the clarity of the ongoing situation in the minds of all the children in the class (e.g., by stating the current story), and, when necessary, by guiding the story to mathematical elements that are within the grasp of many children in the class. Sometimes this process flows easily with little input from the teacher. At other times the teacher makes suggestions, especially when she or he needs to introduce a new topic. But we have been surprised at how much can and does arise from the children.

Our work on mathematizing is similar to the process, described by Hornberger (1990) and the Santa Barbara Classroom Discourse Group (1995), of bilingual teachers' building a common classroom experience or classroom culture in the area of literacy. These authors have documented the ways in which teachers and students together construct a community of learners in which children from a variety of backgrounds can find common language and touchstones for making connections with the sometimes unfamiliar world of the school curriculum.

The steps in teacher-guided problem solving are outlined in figure 7.2. Understanding the problem situation has been discussed above in the mathematizing section. After the problem is solved, discussing and explaining some situations have several functions, as discussed below. Using mathematical drawings or other visual supports for problem solving is also very helpful, as we outline below.

Understanding the problem situation

• The students read the problem silently, or the teacher rereads it and emphasizes each step.

• Other students orally reconstruct the problem and retell it in their own words.

• The class discusses what information the problem gives and does not give. (What is it *telling* you? What do you already know?)

• The class discusses what the question is. (What is the problem asking you to solve? What do you wnat to find out?)

Problem solving

• The students solve the problem as a class, alone, in pairs, or in groups.

• The students who finish first can help other students, write how they solved the problem, write a new problem, or explain their solution to someone else who has finished.

Explaining the problem solving

• The teacher chooses two or more different solution strategies to be explained. It saves a lot of time if four or five students have solved the problem at the chalkboard and some of these students are chosen. Each chosen student describes his or her method, thus engaging in self-reflection and communicating understanding to others. (The teacher patiently gives the students time to explain their solution strategies in their own words. She or he may ask other students to help if a student reaches an impass.)

• If a student has not worked at the chalkboard, the teacher needs to draw or write on the chalkboard to summarize the solution each student describes; the teacher may need to further guide a child to a clearer description and demonstration and may need to summarize again so all understand.

Discussing and reviewing the problem solving

• The teacher leads a discussion about the alternative methods. Who else used each method? What is hard or easy about each method? What is good about each? Who might want help to learn one of the methods?

• The teacher reviews the problem and its answer.

Generating problems

• The teacher encourages the students to write their own word problems.

• Some of these problems are read and solved in class or shared with younger students.

• Sometimes the teacher changes the quantities in the problems to make them more challenging.

• The teacher motivates the students to apply some of these problems in their daily life, especially problems about buying and selling in the market.

Note. Sometimes it is useful to concentrate just on certain of these steps. Not every step is necessary every time.

Fig. 7.2. Steps in teacher-guided problem solving

Asking different children to show their solution methods is a way for teachers to find out how individual children are thinking, which permits teachers to tailor future activities to the children's needs. This ongoing process of adaptation can also help the teacher create a balance between the needs of the more-advanced and the less-advanced children in the class. In Guillermo's story, the teacher asked a student to draw the situation on the chalkboard as a support for the less-advanced children and also as a demonstration of the kind of mathematical drawings children would be expected to make to illustrate word problems and story situations. But she worked mainly with finger solutions, which many children could do at least partially.

Giving visual, drawn supports for a mathematical story facilitates the problem-solving discourse about it and serves as a model of problem solving for the children. Later the teacher will ask all the children to make a drawing for a given story. This is a good way for the teacher and other students to understand the children's thinking. It also facilitates children's reflection on their own work and helps them be able to explain their solution methods. Making mathematical drawings allows children to work at their own level.

After a short period of drawing pictures to show a word problem, children begin making drawings using circles, lines, or their own symbols to show the situation. Somewhat later they begin to label the parts of the drawing to relate to the situation, and they highlight the answer by putting a box (square or rectangular) around the label identifying the answer and around the numerical answer. With larger numbers or in measurement problems, the drawings can show the mathematical situation in a more schematic form with labeled numbers. The children also may need to do a calculation rather than count the entities, as they do in drawings with smaller numbers. Some examples of both kinds are given in figure 7.3. Children do not necessarily need to draw problems that are easy for them, but they do draw those that are more difficult. Labeling these drawings is the first step toward algebraic problem solving (for a discussion of the later steps, see Fuson, Hudson, and Ron in press).

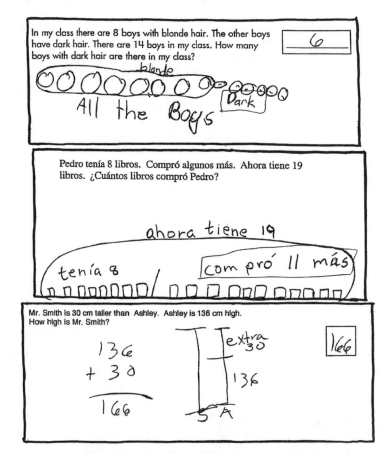

Fig. 7.3. Examples of children's labeled mathematical drawings

The use of visual conceptual supports that show a given mathematical concept is useful to help all children develop an understanding of that concept. This is true at the higher grades as well as at the primary grades, where it is more common. Such visual conceptual supports are especially important for children who are in an English-speaking class but whose English is not fluent.

It is also important that such supports be used during mathematical conversations in class, for example, when children explain how they solved a problem. Frequently, such conversations are merely verbal, with no link to visual supports. Less-advanced children and children who are not fluent in English have difficulties understanding such verbal conversations when they take place in English (Murphy 1997).

It is helpful for the teacher to write numerical symbols and make drawings on the chalkboard as a child describes his or her problem-solving strategy so that all can follow. Even better is to have some children work at the chalkboard while others work at their seats. The teacher can then select two or three of the children at the chalkboard to explain their solution method (over time all children can get a turn to explain). Having the drawings already displayed is much faster than sending a child to the chalkboard to draw a solution after all the children have arrived at an answer.

Children can also illustrate the mathematical quantities in a problem, such as multi-digit numbers or fractions. Such drawings can help them build understandings of these quantities that later can direct their actions on numbers. Figure 7.4 shows an example of such a quantity drawing by Jessica, a first grader. She is showing a problem in which the orange tree had thiry-seven oranges and the pear tree had fifteen pears. The students were to find how many fruits altogether (or how many fruits both trees had).

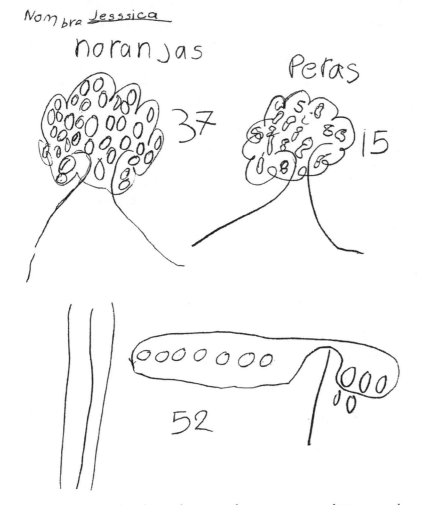

Fig. 7.4. Finding and explaining how many fruits 37 oranges and 15 pears make

Jessica uses a ten-structured representation of ten-sticks (the vertical sticks at the bottom of the drawing) and circles we had developed through extensive activities in class (see Fuson, Smith, and Lo Cicero [1997] and Fuson, Lo Cicero, Hudson, and Smith [1997] for a description). Initially, the children grouped objects in columns of ten. Some classes used penny strips that showed ten pennies on one side and a dime on the back; the strips helped the children organize their columns of ten. The children then drew small circles or dots in columns of ten. After they had used such unitary drawings to count to 100 by tens and ones and write numbers to 100, they began to draw a vertical line through each column of ten circles.

Eventually, whenever individual children were ready, they drew only the ten-stick and not the ten circles that originally composed it. Jessica's drawing shows 3 ten-sticks and 7 ones on the left (37) and 1 ten-stick and 5 ones (15) on the right. She enclosed ten circles to make another ten, so she had 5 tens and 2 ones (52) in total. The children used such drawn ten-sticks and ones to add and subtract.

For subtraction, they opened up a ten-stick or took away part of the ten-stick and drew the leftover circles. The systematic use of drawn conceptual supports linked to the mathematical words and symbols can facilitate students' learning in all areas of mathematics (see Van de Walle [1994] for suggestions in many different areas of mathematics).

FAMILY INVOLVEMENT

Another way of connecting with students is involving their parents in the educational process. Many inner-city Latino parents hold their child's teacher in great esteem. They have high expectations of the influence the teacher will have on their child. Most depend on the teacher to pull their children beyond what they themselves have achieved.

The pace of schooling in this country means that the teachers cannot do it alone. They need the parents' help. Parents need to know that the teacher's expectation is that the child will receive help at home if necessary. However, some (or even many) parents may need some guidance about how to help.

In our experience with parents, some do not initially know how to help effectively, and many—especially those who have had little formal schooling—feel insecure in this role and need encouragement. With reformed curricula, this problem is even worse because the way mathematics is taught may be different from the way the parent learned.

We have developed, and learned from teachers, some ways to communicate effectively with family members (see also Delgado-Gaitan [1990] and Goldenberg and Gallimore [1991]). Through many conversations over the years with many parents, we have found almost all parents eager to support their children's learning, and most can arrange some help. We have found it essential to identify a "math helper" at home to assist the child with mathematics homework.

The helper can be from the extended family: a parent, relative, neighbor, or older sibling; almost all families can identify such a person. Having such a designated helper is useful because the ordinary pressures of family life may result in diffused responsibility. Sometimes only a little help or attention is necessary, and the child can finish independently. Individual attention can give the child confidence as well as improve his or her performance. The teacher can work and communicate with the helper over time to establish a valuable ongoing relationship. See the outline for the math helper in figure 7.5.

It is educationally sound to take a few minutes in class to talk about homework that was done with a mathematics helper. Several children can give very brief reports about such helping (Who helped? With what? When?). Over time, this process gives

Who can be the math helper?
- One or both parents
- An older sibling
- Other relatives
- A neighbor or friend

What can the teacher do?
- Send home a letter asking the parent to identify a math helper
- Provide a mathematics envelope or notebook for communicating back and forth with the math helper
- Organize a family math night to review methods of helping students with mathematics and games for the family or math helpers

What can the math helper do?
- Ask the student to talk about what she or he does in mathematics class
- Help the parent or teacher overcome language and cultural difficulties
- Try to set a particular time and space for working with the child
- Help the child understand the homework but never do it all for the child
- Praise and reinforce any accomplishments; encourage and point to progress over time; share stories of how hard it was for the helper to learn something

When solving a word problem, the math helper can—
- read the problem sentence by sentence, pausing to let the child draw or show with objects what happens in the story;
- ask the child to repeat the story in his or her own words;
- never ask if the problem is a "plus or a minus" problem;
- ask the child to explain why he or she did the problem as he or she did; sometimes such a question is enough for the child to realize that he or she made a mistake;
- guide children by asking questions whenever possible: What is the problem telling you? What is it asking you to solve? What do you know?

When solving numerical problems—
- let the child do as much as possible;
- try to help the child understand the quantities involved (tens and ones, fractions); ask the child to draw the quantities;
- give the least possible help when the child is stuck;
- show or do a step for the child only when necessary.

Fig. 7.5. An outline for the math helper

insight into the children's lives at home, and the students can share stories of success and attention at home. The results of such collaborative efforts at home can also be used as problems for the mathematics class, such as working on a word problem a parent has written with a child.

Figure 7.6 shows an example of a homework assignment done by a first grader with the assistance of a home helper. In this worksheet, we asked the home helper to read the word problem with the child and to have the child make a drawing. It is interesting to note that the helper writes the story for the child, adapting our worksheet story about a park to a new story about the child's own home; the helper has related the word problem we gave to the child's life.

Before the children are asked to seek assistance from the home helper, they must understand and know how to explain what the homework entails. The last five minutes or so of class can be dedicated to a short discussion about the goals, vocabulary, and methods of the assignment. This is essential in order for children to be able to explain the assignment to the helper. Sometimes written communication to the helper from the teacher may facilitate this process.

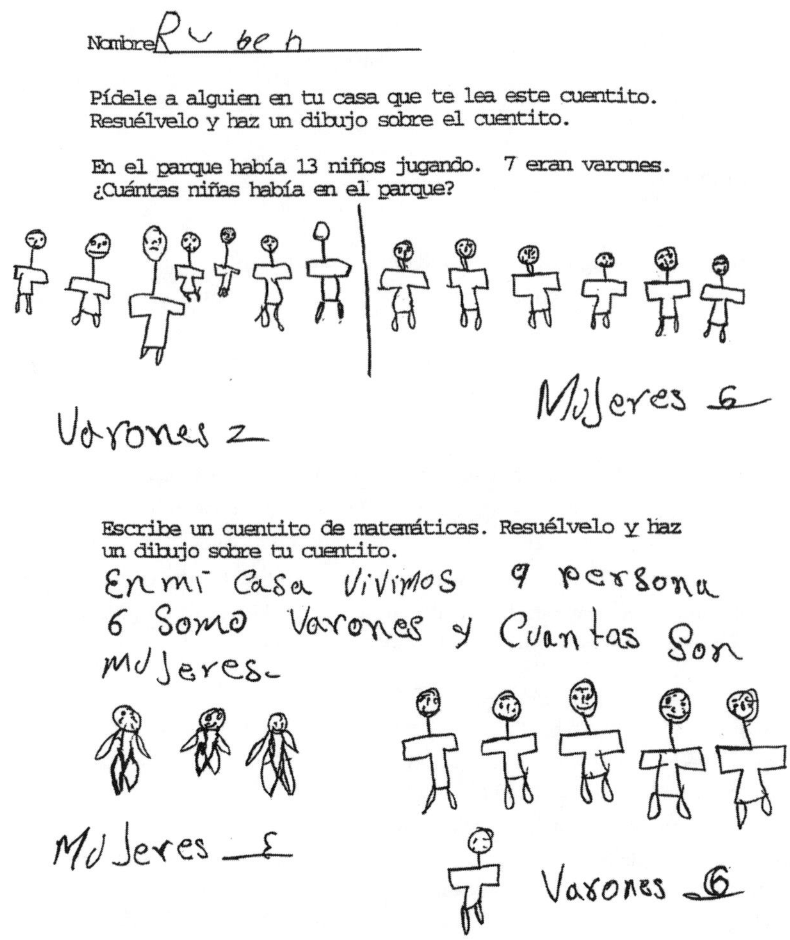

Nombre Ruben

Pídele a alguien en tu casa que te lea este cuentito.
Resuélvelo y haz un dibujo sobre el cuentito.

En el parque había 13 niños jugando. 7 eran varones.
¿Cuántas niñas había en el parque?

Varones 2   Mujeres 6

Escribe un cuentito de matemáticas. Resuélvelo y haz
un dibujo sobre tu cuentito.

En mi casa vivimos 9 persona
6 soma varones y cuantas son
mujeres.

Mujeres _£_   Varones _6_

Fig. 7.6. Homework done with a home helper

In class, we frequently use word problems written by the children at home (some-times we change the quantities to make them more challenging) so that the students get to solve other students' problems. Doing so allows children to see the connection between completing their homework and participating in class discussions using their homework. We are not the only ones to use this approach.

McCaleb (1994) has written about using this kind of approach with Spanish-speaking families to foster literacy and a sense of family-school collaboration in promoting children's success in school. Moll, Amanti, Neff, and Gonzalez (1992) have also writ-ten about teachers who involve parents and community members in sharing "house-hold funds of knowledge" that form the basis of interdisciplinary units of study in all areas of the curriculum.

Since the math helper may speak or read only in Spanish, it is helpful for home-work to be available in Spanish and English for such children. We have found that some children in English-speaking classes refuse to speak Spanish at home (though most continue to understand it), which leads to increasingly less communication between them and family members who speak only Spanish. This problem may be acute for children in Kindergarten through grade 2, some of whom seem to deal with a bilingual life by concentrating their output in one language.

Wong Fillmore (1991) and Pease-Alvarez (1993) have conducted research and written extensively about the problem of language loss among bilingual children. Such a situation is of course very distressing to family members. They can be reas-sured that some children do begin to speak Spanish again when they are older. Continuing to use Spanish with children in activities such as mathematics homework is valuable.

CONCLUSION

The approach we present offers children opportunities to understand mathematical concepts. The emphasis is on the mathematical processes they use rather than the answer they obtain. Before we began our extensive work with word problems, the children in one Spanish-speaking second-grade class solved all types of word problems on an end-of-the-year test by adding. They did not even try to understand the problem situation; they just looked for the numbers and added.

The question teachers hear frequently in a traditional mathematics class—Do I add or subtract?—is equally problematic. Such an approach by a child (e.g., just looking at key words) is especially counterproductive with the more complex problems used in reform mathematics. In these problems, the solution method may be opposite to the situation.

In the following problem, for example, the underlying situation may be subtraction, but the student has to add to find the unknown quantity:

> Juan had some enchiladas on his plate. He ate 4 of them. Now he has 3 enchiladas on his plate. How many enchiladas did he start with?

All children need to be helped to learn that they can solve problems by trying to understand the underlying situation. When they do so, and make their own drawing to show the situation, they can perform quite well on word problems.

The performance of the urban, mostly Latino, first and second graders who used our approach was equivalent to or better than that of samples of middle-class children using traditional textbooks and was even equivalent to that of Japanese and Chinese children on some items (Fuson 1996; Fuson, Smith, and Lo Cicero 1997). Sixty-six percent were at grade level on standardized tests of word-problem solving, and 90 percent were at grade level in computation (Fuson 1996).

A combination of listening to children, mathematizing their stories, using children's labeled mathematical drawings and later labeled number drawings, providing visual conceptual supports for learning mathematical concepts, and eliciting explanations from children about how they solved problems is powerful and helps our children, from Latino and other backgrounds, become successful in mathematics. This approach increases competence in oral and written communication. For the fullest effect, it needs to be complemented by involving families in their children's mathematical learning.

Finally, a vital ingredient for the success of Latino children is high expectations by the teacher and the school. High expectations combined with a teaching and learning environment in which meanings are coconstructed by teachers, students, and parents will greatly increase the success of inner-city Latino children in mathematics.

REFERENCES

Delgado-Gaitan, Concha. *Literacy for Empowerment: The Role of Parents in Children's Education.* New York: Falmer Press, 1990.

Fuson, Karen C. "Latino Children's Construction of Arithmetical Understanding in Urban Classrooms That Support Thinking." Paper presented at the Annual Meeting of the American Educational Research Association, New York, April 1996.

Fuson, Karen C., Kristin Hudson, and Pilar Ron. "Phases of Classroom Mathematical Problem-Solving Activity: The PCMPA Framework for Supporting Algebraic Thinking in Primary School Classrooms." In *Employing Children's Natural Powers to Build Algebraic Reasoning in the Context of Elementary Mathematics,* edited by James Kaput. Mahwah, N.J.: Lawrence Earlbaum Associates, in press.

Fuson, Karen C., Ana María Lo Cicero, Kristin Hudson, and Steven T. Smith. "Snapshots across Two Years in the Life of an Urban Latino Classroom." In *Making Sense: Teaching and Learning Mathematics with Understanding,* edited by James Hiebert, Thomas Carpenter, Elizabeth Fennema, Karen C. Fuson, Diana Wearne, Hanlie Murray, Alwyn Olivier, and Piet Human, pp. 129–60. Portsmouth, N.H.: Hienemann, 1997.

Fuson, Karen C., Steven T. Smith, and Ana María Lo Cicero. "Supporting Latino First Graders' Ten-Structured Thinking in Urban Classrooms." *Journal for Research in Mathematics Education* 28 (December 1997): 738–66.

Goldenberg, Claude, and Ron Gallimore. "Local Knowledge, Research Knowledge, and Educational Change: A Case Study of Early Spanish Reading Improvement." *Educational Researcher* 2, no. 8 (1991): 2–14.

Hornberger, Nancy H. "Creating Successful Learning Contexts for Bilingual Literacy." *Teachers College Record* 92, no. 2 (1990): 212–29.

McCaleb, Sudia P. *Building Communities of Learners: A Collaboration among Teachers, Students, Families, and Community.* New York: St. Martin's Press, 1994.

Moll, Luis C., C. Amanti, D. Neff, and Norma Gonzalez. "Funds of Knowledge for Teaching: Using a Qualitative Approach to Connect Homes and Classrooms." *Theory into Practice* 31, no. 2 (1992): 132–41.

Murphy, Lauren. "Learning and Affective Issues among Higher- and Lower-Achieving Third-Grade Students in Math Reform Classrooms: Perspectives of Children, Parents, and Teachers." Ph. D. diss., Northwestern University, 1997.

Pease-Alvarez, Lucinda. *Moving In and Out of Bilingualism: Investigating Native Language Maintenance and Shift in Mexican-Descent Children.* Research Report 6. Santa Cruz, Calif.: National Center for Research on Cultural Diversity and Second Language Learning, 1993.

Santa Barbara Classroom Discourse Group. "Two Languages, One Community: An Examination of Educational Possibilities." In *Changing Schools for Changing Students: An Anthology of Research on Language Minorities,* edited by Reynaldo Macias and Reyna Garcia, pp. 63–106. Santa Barbara: Linguistic Minority Research Institute, 1995.

Van de Walle, John A. *Elementary School Mathematics: Teaching Developmentally.* 2nd ed. New York: Longman, 1994.

Wells, Gordon, and Gen Ling Chang-Wells. *Constructing Knowledge Together: Classrooms as Centers of Inquiry and Literacy.* Portsmouth, N.H.: Hienemann Educational Books, 1992.

Wong Fillmore, L. "When Learning a Second Language Means Losing the First." *Early Childhood Research Quarterly* 6, (1991): 323–46.

FOR FURTHER READING

Allexsaht-Snider, Martha, and Julian Weissglass. "Promoting Equality in Mathematics Education: Support for Teachers." Unpublished manuscript, 1996. (Photocopy available from CECIMS, University of California at Santa Barbara, Santa Barbara, CA 93106.)

Fuson, Karen C., Ana María Lo Cicero, Pilar Ron, and Liliana Zecker. "El Mercado: A Fruitful Narrative for the Development of Mathematical Thinking in a Latino First- and Second-Grade Classroom." Unpublished manuscript. (For a photocopy, e-mail fuson@nwu.edu.)

Hiebert, James, Thomas Carpenter, Elizabeth Fennema, Karen Fuson, Diana Wearne, Hanlie Murray, Alwyn Olivier, and Piet Human. *Making Sense: Teaching and Learning Mathematics with Understanding.* Portsmouth, N.H.: Hienemann Educational Books, 1997.

———. "Problem Solving as a Basis for Reform in Curriculum and Instruction: The Case of Mathematics." *Educational Researcher* 25, no. 4 (1996): 12–21.

Khisty, Lena Licón. "Making Inequality: Issues of Language and Meanings in Mathematics Teaching with Hispanic Students." In *New Directions for Equity in Mathematics Education,* edited by Walter G. Secada, Elizabeth Fennema, and Lisa Byrd Austin, pp. 279–97. New York: Cambridge University Press, 1995.

Lo Cicero, Ana María, and Elba Cora. "Creating a Classroom of Math Listeners and Discussers." Paper presented at the Annual Meeting of the American Educational Research Association, New York, April 1996.

———. "The Second Mother Advances Children's Mathematical Thinking and Helps Children Learn from and Help Each Other." Paper presented at the Annual Meeting of the American Educational Research Association, Chicago, March 1997.

Lo Cicero, Ana María, and Kristin Hudson. "The Arts as Pathways to Mathematical Thinking in Urban Elementary Schools." Paper presented at the Annual Meeting of the American Educational Research Association, Chicago, March 1997.

Ron, Pilar. "My Family Taught Me This Way." In *The Teaching and Learning of Algorithms in School Mathematics,* 1998 Yearbook of the National Council of Teachers of Mathematics, edited by Lorna J. Morrow, pp. 115–19. Reston, Va.: National Council of Teachers of Mathematics, 1998.

Smith, Steven, and Patti Sugiyama. "Creating an Environment for Children's Explaining, Helping, and Sustained Complex Learning." Paper presented at the Annual Meeting of the American Educational Research Association, Chicago, March 1997.

Challenging Conventional Wisdom

A Case Study

8

Lena Licón Khisty
Gabriel Viego

During the last thirty years or more a mythology has developed regarding educational "problem" children or those who are poor or from ethnic or linguistic minorities. The myths pertain to why among these children there are such persistent patterns of general underachievement and underrepresentation in the "professional" subjects such as mathematics, science, and other closely associated fields. The myths have generated a conventional wisdom (Knapp and Shields 1991) that seemingly everyone accepts. Ask any teacher (or for that matter, any person on the street) why Latino—and Native American and African American—students fail in school, and she or he readily responds with such reasons as lack of parental support, poor neighborhoods, poor language abilities, and impoverished school facilities.

Indeed, a quick glance at the country's demographics reveals a large proportion of Latinos living in poverty in inner-city neighborhoods or in rural agricultural centers, where we are more likely to find inferior school facilities and where families are more challenged to make economic ends meet. However, these are political "disadvantages" (Moll 1991). Unfortunately, these disadvantages, along with what some consider more individual "deficits" such as limited English proficiency, form the core of a deficit model that permeates educational thinking and policy. But do these conditions or this model really explain why Latinos have the highest dropout rate, with 50 percent of students not completing high school (National Council of La Raza 1988)? Could it be that our conventional wisdom has led us into a self-fulfilling prophecy that binds us to business as usual and blinds us to alternatives?

In this discussion, we present a teacher who seemingly has challenged conventional wisdom in all its forms. In her fifth-grade class in a poor, urban school, all thirty or more of the Latino children—including those identified as having learning disabilities—are "smart" in mathematics. She repeats her success year after year. How does she do it? We would like to begin to answer this question by highlighting some of the characteristics of her teaching that seem to make her effective. We begin the discussion with some background to the challenge we present. We follow with a description of the important elements of our teacher's pedagogy and then conclude with some thoughts about the future directions for reform.

THE OLD PROBLEM THAT WILL NOT CHANGE

The idea that educators have preconceived notions about their minority students that can be biased and that can influence instructional decisions in ways that are detrimental

The research reported here was supported in part by grant no. 2-1-21072 from the Great Cities Faculty Seed Fund, University of Illinois at Chicago. Any opinions, conclusions, or recommendations are those of the authors and do not necessarily reflect those of the agency.

to students is not new (see, e.g., Licón [1979] and Brophy and Good [1986]). Conversely, many researchers have offered arguments and even examples of outstanding teaching of Latinos that challenge our assumptions of what students can do; however, these examples have come primarily from the area of literacy instruction (e.g., Diaz, Moll, and Mehan [1986]; Vogt, Jordan, and Tharp [1987]; Gutierrez and Meyer [1995]) examples relate to a different content and the conclusions of the investigations (i.e., educational results for Latinos can be different) have not transferred to the teaching of mathematics.

Anyon (1980) and Oakes (1990) have long pointed out that schooling in general, and mathematics instruction for minority students in particular, have been overwhelmingly characterized by low-level learning experiences, a differentiated curriculum, and ability grouping. Such organizational factors severely limit how and what students learn. Therefore, it is little wonder that Latinos do not do well academically. More recently Grubb (1995, p. 20) echoes Anyon and Oakes by pointing out that "The dominant approach to teaching—called by such terms as 'skills and drills,' 'teacher-centered instruction,' 'top-down approaches,' 'skills development,'" … does not address complex competencies, and thus is fraught with problems that ultimately disadvantage students.

Moll and Diaz (1987, p. 302) offered the following for consideration:

> Although student characteristics certainly matter, when the same children are shown to succeed under modified instructional arrangements it becomes clear that the problems these working-class children face in school must be viewed primarily as a consequence of institutional arrangements that constrain children and teachers by not capitalizing fully on their talents, resources, and skills…. [T]his conclusion is pedagogically optimistic because it suggests that just as academic failure is socially organized, academic success can be socially arranged.

Still, in the majority of classrooms across the country, the instructional arrangements that are used with Latinos, particularly in mathematics, have remained the same: low level, remedial, and oriented toward decontextualized skills (Grubb 1995). The conventional wisdom for teaching mathematics to Latinos has been resistant to change in spite of reform activities and examples from research.

Why has mathematical pedagogy for Latinos been difficult to change? One possible reason is that most teachers, including Latino teachers themselves, cannot easily implement a type of pedagogy and reformed learning experiences in mathematics that they have never experienced. To reform pedagogy to meet new visions of what it means to do and know mathematics is difficult enough for most teachers. However, couple this challenge with that of implementing it with students who have been associated for so long with a mythology that has socially defined them as needing worksheets and computation, and the cognitive change for teachers becomes overwhelming. Consequently, we have a greater need for more concrete and explicit examples of reformed pedagogy being used with Latinos.

The purpose of this discussion is to offer an example of one teacher who teaches Latino students in ways that not only reflect current reformed mathematical practices but that ensure that *all* students learn. We give this teacher the pseudonym Mrs. Martinez.

BACKGROUND

We observed and videotaped Mrs. Martinez for more than two years as she taught mathematics to fifth graders. As we watched her interact with her students and watched with amazement the power of understanding within each student that was developing in front of our eyes, we came to recognize characteristics of her pedagogy that needed to be understood in a theoretical context beyond mere good practice. This context is influenced by such sociocultural theorists as Vygotsky (1978) and Bakhtin (1981).

One of the outcomes of current reforms in mathematics education is the recognition of mathematics as a socially constructed entity. As such, the subject has a cultural life of its own in that certain ways of thinking, knowing, and doing pertain to mathematics alone. It has its own symbols, syntax, and ways of speaking (Pimm 1987). The mastery of such cultural tools is interrelated with individual thought (Vygotsky 1978), which means that as one becomes proficient with the cultural tools and symbols, one comes to think in that cultural way. Consequently, learning mathematics substantially entails the acquisition of this mathematical culture through and with the mastery of its cultural tools. However, acquiring a culture and its mode of thinking is not accomplished by simply telling someone how things are done. Instead, it requires the immersing novice in the culture and actively making meaning of its tools through the use of those tools.

Mrs. Martinez engineered a mathematical cultural context that plunged students into the social norms, thinking, and practices associated with the subject. More important, and more critical to the process of immersion, were her own actions in helping students understand the strategies mathematicians use to convey meaning. As what Vygotsky (1978) refers to as the "enabling other," Mrs. Martinez guided, pushed, and modeled by her own spontaneous actions as a mathematician: trying to understand students' strategies, making her own estimates, speaking mathematically, using concrete models to comprehend the abstract, and learning (e.g., about her students' thinking) through a collective activity.

Vygotsky (1978, p. 89) noted that the "only 'good learning' is that which is in advance of development." By this he meant that children can do many learning activities with the guidance of an adult or in collaboration with others that are actually beyond their capability. But as they do them repeatedly in this active and interpersonal context, their understanding, or higher psychological functions, becomes internalized so that eventually they can do independently that which they had been able to do only in collaboration. The idea embodied by this entire process is what Vygotsky termed the "zone of proximal development" (Vygotsky 1978).

The implication here, beyond the obvious need for learning environments that actively engage children and that encourage collaboration, is that our focus should be on setting tasks that are slightly more advanced than what children can do easily and on allowing a longer span of time for seeing evidence of children's internalized development. As we shall see, the interactions between Mrs. Martinez and her students exemplify this state of "good learning."

THE PEDAGOGY OF CHANGE

Mrs. Martinez teaches in an old, crowded school whose students are nearly 100 percent Latino, primarily of Mexican descent. She is part of the bilingual education faculty. In this particular class, the students are proficient enough in English so that much of the instruction is in that language. However, Spanish is still spoken in the classroom; both the teacher and the students use it whenever they want or need to. Generally, Mrs. Martinez has about thirty students in her class and often has one of the highest enrollments in the school. The overall academic-achievement level for the district is one of the lowest in the country. Consequently, when students from Mrs. Martinez's fifth-grade class, many of whom entered one or two levels below grade, score at, or significantly above, level on standardized tests of achievement in mathematics at the end of the year, one must take notice.

During the first year of observation, visits were irregular but spaced approximately a month apart and field notes were gathered; in the second year, instruction was observed weekly for approximately two months using field notes and then twice a week for almost four months, using video taping along with field notes. From these observations, patterns emerged in Mrs. Martinez's instruction that were analyzed in greater detail using the videotapes. These patterns, or striking characteristics, are discussed in this section.

It is important to know some general characteristics of the mathematics lessons in order to have a fuller context for the discussion that follows. The daily mathematics lessons are long by typical school standards and range from forty-five minutes to an hour and a half, depending on the problems on which students are working. Most problems are centered on a theme such as circles, rectangles, or patterns. Some problems may be nonroutine in that they are more open ended and strategy oriented. In either situation, the problem is substantial and is contextualized with visuals and a story.

Mrs. Martinez does not use a textbook in class. Instead, she uses the textbook (along with professional journals) as a source of ideas for problems and a reference for both her and the students. Yet students do take textbooks or workbooks home in order to do problems there. During a lesson, textbooks are essentially never visible.

The lessons follow a routine in which a problem is given to the students on the chalkboard. Generally, students read the story problem individually and then in a group in order to comprehend what is being asked. Sometimes the students have a long discussion about the meaning of the problem before they actually start to work. In this way, a mathematics problem is used as the context for developing literacy skills. The students then work in pairs or individually, as they choose, to solve the problem. Each student has a calculator to use and, when appropriate, must record as part of a write-up the keystrokes that were used. As students work, Mrs. Martinez walks around the room observing them, asking probing questions as a way of guiding them, and assessing each student's capabilities. When all the students have solved the problem, a pair of volunteers is asked to present their solution at the chalkboard and explain it to the class.

At this point, the discussion is not about whether the solution is correct. Instead, the objective is to reinforce understanding and meanings, to talk mathematically, and to comprehend strategies. It is obvious that Mrs. Martinez is interested in more than simply solving the problem; she is interested in students' deeper thinking. Because students feel confident about their solutions, they are eager to present their work at the chalkboard and there is never a lack of volunteers.

From this well-established routine, some striking patterns emerge, two of which we wish to discuss here: (1) Mrs. Martinez's teaching for meaning and (2) her discourse.

Teaching for Meaning

No problem is too difficult and none is too easy because each problem is taken apart piece by piece for its meanings before students begin, after they find a solution, or both. The following excerpts of a dialogue from a class discussion exemply this process.

The students have been working in pairs on the problem given at the beginning of the dialogue. Even though most of the students solved the problem, Mrs. Martinez has observed that many of the students might not have fully understood it—and as she notes in the beginning, they need to be able to tell her about it.

> Maria planted one-third of the 12 trees, and Julie planted the rest. How many did Maria plant? How many did Julie plant?

1. *T:* Now we have a problem over here that a lot of you got a little help about, but you need to be able to tell me … Who would like to go and use a picture in a way to explain that problem? *(A girl [S_1] and a boy [S_2] are selected to go to the chalkboard and there is a short interchange about drawing the trees.)*

2. *T:* How many trees are you going to draw?

3. *S_1:* Twelve.

4. *T:* Why twelve?

   (One of the students starts to read the problem.)

5. *T:* But I still don't understand why you're making … you're drawing twelve trees.

6. S_1: One-third.

7.   *T:* I'm not even interested in the one-third yet. I want to know where you came up with twelve trees.

8. S_1: One-third of the twelve trees.

9.   *T:* So what is the total number of trees that we have?

10. S_1: Twelve.

11.   *T:* We have twelve trees altogether. All right, so now what? *(The student begins to use an algorithm.)* No, no, no, I just want it with a picture please. I don't want anything with numbers right now. I want to see it in a picture. How many trees do you have up there?

From this excerpt, we see Mrs. Martinez's emphasis on making sure students understand. She begins by saying she wants a "picture" of the problem (line 1) and not an algorithmic explanation as is typical. Furthermore, although the student obviously knows that the problem concerns a total of twelve trees, since she responds to a question with "twelve" (line 3) and she draws the right number of them (line 5), Mrs. Martinez is not satisfied because neither of these responses answers the important metacognitive question of how the student *knows* to draw twelve or what role this information plays in understanding the problem. In essence, Mrs. Martinez will not let the students assume anything.

14.   *T:* Twelve trees. Now if I read the problem a couple of times, there is something there that tells me what I should do with all my trees.

15. S_1: By four.

      (Members of the class shout "by three.")

16.   *T:* Wait a second, he has a good point, he says by four. Why is he saying by four? Evelyn *(who is not at the chalkboard),* why is he saying by four? Is he right? From the word problem—look at all the words there—is there any mention of a four in there?

17. S_3: No.

18.   *T:* I don't see any mention of the number four in there. So where would …? One-third. When you hear the word *one-third,* what do you see in your head?

19. S_1: Three.

20.   *T:* Roy, why don't you go write down, when you read the word, what did you see in your head immediately? One-third—that is all I want to concentrate on. Look at this word, one-third. What does that mean?

21. S_4: It means that….

22.   *T:* Write it down so I can see what you think it means.

      (Roy writes "12 divided by 3.")

23.   *T:* Nope, I don't agree with that. That doesn't make any sense to me. One-third, it says one-third, it doesn't say anything divided into twelve, it says nothing like that. I want to know what is one-third, what does it look like?

      (A student at the chalkboard draws a tree.)

24.   *T:* One-third does not look like a tree to me. Salvador, show me what one-third looks like.

      (Salvador comes to the board and draws a circle divided into three parts.)

25.   *T:* No, that looks like a circle to me, I don't know what…

      (Armando comes up and writes "1/3.")

26.   *T:* Look what Armando wrote: does that say one-third?

27.   *Chorus:* Yes.

28.   *T:* Are you sure?

The dialogue demonstrates the need to take time to make sure students understand important mathematical concepts. In this instance, Mrs. Martinez is checking everyone's understanding of one-third apart from the rest of the problem but still within its context. She does not discount what any student says, as demonstrated in line 16, but she wants all of them to understand, so she keeps asking for an explanation. She is not satisfied that Roy can demonstrate its application in the problem (line 23) or that Salvador can provide the typical representation of one-third: a circle divided into three parts (line 25). At the end of this excerpt, we see that even after the appropriate representation is offered, she is not going to let up (line 28).

42.   *T:* When I think one-third, I think a one, a division sign, and I see a three. Now, if I had twelve trees and I see one-third because I'm looking at that word problem and it says one-third, I still don't really understand the problem. What am I supposed to do here? Well, first of all maybe I should go ahead and use Salvador's picture. Salvador, could you show me one-third of your picture?

(Salvador returns to the chalkboard and shades in one-third of his original circle.)

43.   *T:* What does that one-third mean? Look at the word problem and look at what that means. Armando?

44. S_5: You have three pieces and just one is colored in.

45.   *T:* That means I took the whole group, the whole set. I had one circle and of that circle, I divided it into three equal parts. Right? Isn't that what the three in the bottom tells you? The three in the bottom, the denominator, tells you that there are three pieces.... And of those three pieces, how many are being used?

46. S_1: One.

47.   *T:* But I don't have a circle in the problem. It's talking to me about twelve trees and Maria planted one-third of them. So what can I do? Vanessa? *(Vanessa responds, and Mrs. Martinez repeats her response.)* I should divide my twelve trees into three groups? Why?

(There is a short exchange about drawing the groups of trees.)

48. S_6: Maria divides the group of trees.

49.   *T:* Stop right there. You divide the whole set of trees. This is one set of trees. You divide it into how many parts?

50. S_7: Four.

This exchange is very important even though there is very little student talk. It is here where Mrs. Martinez clearly assumes her role as the "more experienced other" and focuses her students' thinking on the dilemma that is present in the problem: One-third and twelve trees are not inherently related; they refer to different concepts. In order to solve the problem, the student has to consider which one to use or, if both are to be used, how to bring them together. She expertly engages the students in the thought processes of linking the trees with the fraction through her own self-talk and through the use of Salvador's drawing (lines 42 and 43). She stays with the idea of linking the two concepts and models it again in line 47 and seems to accomplish her goal when a student uses a complete sentence to describe what has to be done (line 48). Unfortunately, another student skips the crucial part of the process and goes directly to the solution again (line 50). The discussion continues for twice the length of this excerpt until the students in the class are able to demonstrate their understanding by easily answering her questions.

It is interesting that the climate in these types of discussions is extremely positive and students focus their attention on what is being said. This is not to say that no students find this discussion is a little boring, but they have a patience that seems to come from accepting that understanding is to their benefit and that even if they do understand a process, it does not hurt to review it. Mrs. Martinez creates this climate, in part because she does not ignore the students' responses but uses them to make meaning.

Mrs. Martinez's determination not to leave a problem until *all* students understand is atypical: teachers often advocate leaving some students behind in order to meet the need for others to move ahead. Although Mrs. Martinez is relentless in getting at students' thinking, she does it in a way that results in students' feeling confident in what they know.

In many classrooms, a problem such as the one presented here would have been discussed at the level of recognizing that 12 should be divided by 3. But in this example, each component of the problem was analyzed: (1) Why are we working with twelve? (2) What is the meaning of one-third in any context? and (3) What is the problem asking? (How many trees did each person plant?) (The portions of the dialogue that describe how the class arrived at the answer have been omitted in this paper.)

Characteristics of Discourse

Mrs. Martinez also is striking in her discourse. We shall discuss two patterns of her talk: her use of questions and her use of vocabulary.

Although a discourse style that is not "teacher telling" but that engages students in an instructional conversation (Goldenberg 1991) is advocated for effective instruction with Latino students, teachers seldom use such discourse with them (Ramirez and Merino 1990). Mrs. Martinez, however, is notable for the number of questions she poses to students to get them to express their thinking and to make meaning. In a typical mathematics lesson, an observer can be overwhelmed with counting the number of questions she poses to students. Mrs. Martinez uses her questions not merely to assess students' thinking but to develop it, and through some of her questions, she enculturates students into the practice of mathematicians. We can see this process in the following example.

The whole class is discussing the following problem after students have solved it themselves in pairs:

A red car, a blue car, and a green car are placed in a straight line. If the red car is put first in the line, in how many different ways can the other cars be put in line?

1. *T:* … So we know the cars are parked in a straight line. Then they give you a condition, telling you in this parking there is one thing you have to respect. Here's the condition: if the red car is put first, that means that I am going to have first a red car, right? What do they want to know, Miguel? They told me if the red car is put first in line. So I know my condition. To meet my condition, to meet my rule, I have to put the red car first. What do they want to know? They already told me something that I know and they know. The red car has to be first. Now, what do I need to do? What do I need to find out? Let Miguel [S_1] answer. Can anyone help Miguel there? You're letting him hang all by himself.

2. *S_2:* The combination?

3. *T:* I don't understand what you mean by combination.…

    (An exchange occurs between the teacher and some students who have simply answered with the word cars.*)*

4. *T:* Is that what it's asking you? Could you read the question for me? Not the conditional part of the question, but the question part of the question. The part that is asking you something, not the part that is telling you something. What is the part that is telling you something, Araceli? Read it for me.

5. *S_3:* If the car is put first in line. *(The student omits the word* red.*)*

6. *T:* OK, right, they're giving me some information, right? They're telling me something. They told me … they gave me information: if the red is put first in line. Now, what is the question? Read it please, Miguel.

7. S_1: If the red car is first.

8. *T*: No, that is not the question, sweetheart. Here they're giving me some information. They're making a condition. You can go on the field trip if you do your homework. OK. I'm giving you a condition. Did you do your homework? Yeah, so you're meeting the condition. The condition is if the car is put first in line, then what's the question?

9. S_1: How many different ways can the other two cars be put in line?

   (The teacher acknowledges this answer, and there is a short discussion of how to show the situation. The teacher returns to the question in the problem, and a student answers correctly.)

10. *T*: Two ways? How do you know there are two ways?

11. S_1: Because this is.... *(Miguel indicates with chalk how the cars line up.)*

12. *T*: That's right! Isn't it wonderful? Great job! I think he deserves an applause. Very good. Did you write it down on your paper, Miguel? You want to write it down real quick. If you do not have that explanation written down, put it down, please.

Again, keep in mind that Mrs. Martinez already knows that the students have solved this problem. She begins the discussion by asking two basic questions (line 1), which direct the students' thinking not toward a solution strategy but toward a broader metacognitive analysis of the general nature of a problem, that is, what is a condition and how do we know what is being asked? She asks students to explain themselves (line 3) and she continues to focus on the nature of a problem (line 6) by asking, "What is the question?" At last a student responds in the form of a complete sentence (line 9) and another gets the correct answer to the problem (line 10), but Mrs. Martinez still asks a final metacognitive question (line 10), "How do you know this is the correct answer?"

In this short excerpt, we can see that the questions are numerous and that they are not the kinds of questions ordinarily asked of "disadvantaged" Latino students (Ramirez and Merino 1990). The questions are clearly designed to have students think more substantially and in much greater depth. The students can make sense of this approach because they have solved the problem, and they are therefore dealing with the content of the questions in the context in which they implicitly occur.

The second aspect of Mrs. Martinez's discourse has to do with the way she infuses speaking mathematically (Pimm 1987) into her lessons. Throughout our observations, we were amazed at the students' mathematical vocabulary. We would be taken aback when students spoke about *mean, medians, modes,* and *data,* and even easily used such words as *quantitative, qualitative,* and *combination.* In listening to students' informal discussions, it was obvious that they knew what these words meant because they used them appropriately. Occasionally, one of us might offhandedly ask a student to explain a word just used as a way of testing her or his true comprehension. In such instances, the students never failed to demonstrate that they indeed understood the term.

How do the students develop this facility? Does Mrs. Martinez drill her students on vocabulary lists? If not, how do the students come to appropriate the kind of discourse that mathematicians take for granted? Mrs. Martinez does not provide vocabulary lists nor does she have her students memorize mathematical terms. Instead, she creates experiences in which these words are simply used to express meaning in mathematics. If we listen to her, we can readily see the origin of her students' discourse. She speaks using the words that her students can later be heard using. She does not water down her vocabulary, but as she speaks, she uses the context of mathematical problems to its fullest to immerse the students in the language of mathematics.

Consequently, the students acquire the language by hearing it used frequently in context in natural communication. Nevertheless, she deliberately supports the students' linguistic and cognitive acquisition by such practices as always writing words that might be problematic or new for her students (e.g., *data, radius, vertex*) as she speaks them or pointing to them if they are in a problem or in a drawing. The same technique has been used by other effective teachers of mathematics (Khisty 1995).

Also, she insists that students always draw a picture of the problem (as in the first example given) and copy the problem, drawing, and explanation into a daily writing log, which she checks each week. The students naturally use mathematical terms as they record their work and an explanation, and since the terms are on the chalkboard as part of the writing that went on during the problem solving, the students can easily refer to them for their logs. Keep in mind, however, that students are not merely acquiring new vocabulary. They are engaged in the process of developing mathematical thinking, and the words are an important factor in this development (Bakhtin 1981).

SOME CLOSING THOUGHTS

We have presented a glimpse of a classroom in which Latino students, including special education students, engage in mathematics in the way that we wish all students could but that is seldom used with Latinos. We have also attributed the students' progress squarely to the teacher's pedagogy, which in essence ignores all the common assumptions about what Latinos can or cannot do. We have identified key elements of Mrs. Martinez's practice that emerge to form a pattern of effective instruction.

However, we have not addressed the question of why Mrs. Martinez teaches this way. How does she know to ask the questions she asks and to support students' acquisition of mathematical concepts through discourse and context? And more important, why hasn't she accepted the common limiting assumptions about Latino students, as many of her colleagues have? Mrs. Martinez did not learn the most important aspects of her pedagogy through her preservice education or professional development, which raises the question, why not?

Specific answers to these questions are less important than what they signify, which is that when we challenge the conventional wisdom about Latino students and their capabilities, we can see radically different outcomes. The real question is, now that we know that instruction for Latinos can be different, how do we ensure that it is?

REFERENCES

Anyon, Jean. "Social Class and the Hidden Curriculum of Work." *Journal of Education* 162, no. 1 (1980): 67–92.

Bakhtin, Mikhail M. *The Dialogic Imagination.* Austin, Tex.: University of Texas Press, 1981.

Brophy, Jere, and Thomas Good. "Teacher Behavior and Student Achievement." In *Handbook of Research on Teaching,* 3rd ed., edited by Merlin C. Wittrock, pp. 328–75. New York: Macmillan Publishing Co., 1986.

Diaz, Stephen, Luis Moll, and Hugh Mehan. "Sociocultural Resources in Instruction: A Context-Specific Approach." In *Beyond Language: Social and Cultural Factors in Schooling Language Minority Children,* edited by California State Department of Education, pp. 187–230. Los Angeles: Evaluation, Dissemination and Assessment Center, California State University, 1986.

Goldenberg, Claude. *Instructional Conversations and Their Classroom Application.* Washington, D.C.: National Center for Research on Cultural Diversity and Second Language Learning, 1991.

Grubb, W. Norton. "The Old Problem of 'New Students': Purpose, Content, and Pedagogy." In *Changing Populations and Changing Schools,* Ninety-Fourth Yearbook of the National Society for the Study of Education, Part 2, edited by Erwin Flaxman and A. Harry Passow, pp. 4–29. Chicago: University of Chicago Press, 1995.

Gutierrez, Kris, and Brenda Meyer. "Creating Communities of Effective Practice: Building Literacy for Language Minority Students." In *Creating New Education Communities,* Ninety-Fourth Yearbook of the National Society for the Study of Education, Part 1, edited by Jeannie Oakes and Karen H. Quartz, pp. 32–52. Chicago: University of Chicago Press, 1994.

Khisty, Lena Licón. "Making Inequality: Issues of Language and Meanings in Mathematics Teaching with Hispanic Students." In *New Agendas for Equity in Mathematics Education,* edited by Walter Secada, Elizabeth Fennema, and Lisa B. Adijian, pp. 279–97. New York: Cambridge University Press, 1995.

Knapp, Michael, and Patrick Shields, eds. *Better Schooling for the Children of Poverty: Alternatives to Conventional Wisdom.* Berkeley, Calif.: McCutchen Publishing Corp., 1991.

Licón, Lena. *The Effect of Social Class and Ethnic Stereotypes on Preservice Teachers' Decision-Making.* Doctoral dissertation: Washington State University, 1979.

Moll, Luis. "Social and Instructional Issues in Literacy Instruction for 'Disadvantaged' Students." In *Better Schooling for the Children of Poverty: Alternatives to Conventional Wisdom,* edited by Michael Knapp and Patrick Shields, pp. 61–84. Berkeley, Calif.: McCutchen Publishing Corp., 1991.

Moll, Luis, and Stephen Diaz. "Change as the Goal of Educational Research." *Anthropology and Education Quarterly* 18 (1987): 300–11.

National Council of La Raza. *Literacy in the Hispanic Community.* Washington, D.C.: Policy Analysis Center, 1988.

Oakes, Jeannie. "Opportunities, Achievement, and Choice: Women and Minority Students in Science and Mathematics." In *Review of Research in Education* 16 (1990): 153–222.

Pimm, David. *Speaking Mathematically.* New York: Routledge & Kegan Paul, 1987.

Ramirez, J. David, and Barbara Merino. "Classroom Talk in English Immersion, Early-Exit and Late-Exit Transitional Bilingual Education Programs." In *Language Distribution Issues in Bilingual Schooling,* edited by Rudolfo Jacobson and Christian Faltis, pp. 61–103. Clevedon, England: Multilingual Matters, Ltd., 1990.

Vogt, Laurie, Catherine Jordan, and Roland Tharp. "Explaining School Failure, Producing School Success: Two Cases." *Anthropology and Education Quarterly* 18, no. 4 (1987): 276–86.

Vygotsky, Lev S. *Mind in Society: The Development of Higher Psychological Processes.* Cambridge, Mass.: Harvard University Press, 1978.

Teachers' and Students' Attitudes toward the Use of Manipulatives in Two Predominantly Latino School Districts

9

Maria L. Bustamante

Betty Travis

Many studies have reported on the effectiveness and benefits of using manipulatives in the classroom. Suydam and Higgins (1977) reviewed twenty-three research studies that addressed the effectiveness of incorporating manipulatives in instruction. They concluded that the use of manipulatives increased mathematics achievement more than instruction without manipulatives did. In a metanalysis of studies investigating the use of manipulatives, Sowell (1989) concluded not only that manipulatives had a significant positive effect on achievement but also that the use of manipulatives in instruction was effective in improving students' attitudes toward mathematics. According to Kober (1991, p. 5), "attitudes and beliefs are powerful forces that work beneath the surface to enhance or undermine students' mathematics performance."

Although many studies have researched the use of manipulatives and their impact on achievement, few studies have investigated teachers' and students' attitudes about the use of manipulatives in the classroom. Even fewer studies have investigated the question with minority students in minority school districts. The purpose of this study was to determine teachers' and students' attitudes toward the use of manipulatives in middle school classrooms in two minority school districts in San Antonio, Texas.

METHODOLOGY

Population

The sample consisted of 724 students and 34 mathematics teachers from two school districts with minority enrollments of approximately 98 percent and 92 percent. The student sample was predominately Latino (95.3 percent), which was representative of the total population in the two school districts. About 2.5 percent of the students were non-Latino white students, 1.7 percent were African Americans, and 0.5 percent were from other ethnic groups. The student sample consisted of 52.8 percent females and 47.2 percent males. Of the students, 52.6 percent were in the seventh grade, 46.3 percent were in the eighth grade, and the remaining 1.1 percent were sixth graders.

The teacher sample was 53 percent Latino, 44 percent non-Latino white, and 3 percent African American.

Instruments

Although many instruments were available to measure attitudes toward science and mathematics in general, no instruments measured students' and teachers' attitudes toward the use of manipulatives in particular. Consequently, the two investigators in this study developed questionnaires specifically for seventh- and eighth-grade students and teachers in the two school districts. The mathematics supervisors in the school districts assisted in the production of the questionnaires because the districts were interested in the study and needed evaluative data for other projects. The questionnaires were straightforward, uncomplicated, written in language appropriate for seventh- and eighth-grade students, and time efficient, so they could be completed in five to ten minutes. The questionnaires are shown in figures 9.1 and 9.2.

---

1. Before you started using manipulatives, did you feel comfortable working mathematics problems?
2. Now that you are using manipulatives, do you feel more comfortable working mathematics problems?
3. Do you feel manipulatives make mathematics more fun?
4. Do you feel using manipulatives help you understand the material better?
5. Would you like to continue using manipulatives in the classroom?
6. Would you like to use manipulatives in other classes like science?

Figure 9.1. Student questionnaire requiring a Yes (Y), No (N), or Undecided (U) response

---

1. Do you feel comfortable using manipulatives in your classroom?
2. Do you believe students benefit from using manipulatives in the classroom?
3. Do you feel manipulatives help lower-level students as well as higher-level students?
4. Do you believe manipulatives are suitable for all learning styles?
5. Do you feel sufficient training or in-service workshops are available?
6. Do you feel all necessary materials are available to you?
7. Do you believe you will use manipulatives in the future?
8. Do you feel administrators encourage you to use manipulatives in the classroom?

Figure 9.2. Teacher questionnaire requiring responses ranging from Strongly Agree to Strongly Disagree

Procedure

All the teachers participating in the study had opportunities to attend workshops or classes on the use of manipulatives. Of the students, 82 percent indicated that they had used manipulatives at one time or another. Table 9.1 shows a listing of some of the manipulatives and the percents of students who had used those manipulatives at various times in their schooling.

Table 9.1
Percent of Students Who Had Seen and Used Various Types of Manipulatives

Type of Manipulative	Percent
Algebra tiles	26.8
Fraction bar	51.9
Hands-On Equations®	41.4
Geometry models	46.5
Tiles	50.3
Base-ten models	41.3
Spinners	41.4
Geoboard	39.4
Lab gear	36.7
Pattern blocks	57.9

Student Survey

The data summarizing the responses of the students to the student questionnaire are shown in table 9.2.

Table 9.2
Summary of Responses to the Student Questionnaire: Yes (Y), No (N), Undecided (U)

Question	Percent of Females			Percent of Males		
No.	Y	N	U	Y	N	U
1	38.5	23.3	38.3	49.7	25.7	24.6
2	63.9	8.4	27.7	62.0	15.5	22.5
3	72.0	9.9	18.1	58.8	20.2	21.0
4	72.0	5.8	22.2	69.9	11.7	18.4
5	74.3	4.5	21.2	68.7	13.7	17.6
6	66.5	12.3	21.2	62.6	21.0	16.4

Since the investigators were interested in gender differences within the student population surveyed, a chi-square test was used to determine the correlation between the males' responses and the females' responses (table 9.2) to each question in the student questionnaire (fig. 9.1). The chi-square values for all the responses were significant at the .05 level, which indicates that the differences between the expected and observed frequencies exceed those expected by chance.

An interesting finding is the difference in female respondents' feelings of comfort in working mathematics problems before and after using manipulatives. Before they started using manipulatives, about 38 percent of the females and about 50 percent of the males felt comfortable working mathematics problems. After they had experience in using manipulatives, 64 percent of the females and 62 percent of the males felt more comfortable in working mathematics problems. Also, 72 percent of the female students stated that manipulatives make mathematics more fun, and 59 percent of the males had the same opinion. However, it is interesting that twice as many males (20%) as females (10%) thought that manipulatives do not make mathematics more fun.

Seventy-two percent (72%) of the females and 70 percent of the males agreed that manipulatives help them in understanding mathematics. Only 9 percent of the sample disagreed with this statement. Thus, it appears that approximately three-fourths of the students are being reached through the use of manipulatives. Considering that manipulatives make mathematics more fun for students and help them understand the material better, it might be expected that the students would want to continue using manipulatives in the future. Seventy-four percent (74%) of the females and 69 percent of the males responded positively to this question. Approximately 67 percent of the females and 63 percent of the males would like to use manipulatives in other classes.

Teacher Survey

The statistics summarizing the responses of teachers to the teacher questionnaire are shown in table 9.3.

If the Strongly Agree and Agree categories in table 9.3 are combined, it appears that almost 88 percent of the teachers felt comfortable using manipulatives. About 94 percent of the teachers thought that students benefit from using manipulatives, and 76 percent agreed that manipulatives are suitable for all learning styles. Only 50 percent of the teachers felt that sufficient training is available, and 62 percent felt that all necessary materials are available for their teaching.

Table 9.3
Summary of Responses to the Teacher Questionnaire

	Percent of Teachers				
Statements	**Strongly Agree**	**Agree**	**No Opinion**	**Disagree**	**Strongly Disagree**
A	47.1	41.2	6	3	3
B	55.9	38.2	3	3	0
C	52.9	29.4	9	6	3
D	38.2	38.2	0	20.6	3
E	26.5	23.5	9	35.3	6
F	23.5	38.2	3	26.5	9
G	41.2	35.3	3	6	0
H	35.3	44.1	20.6	0	0

DISCUSSION

The results of the study found that teachers and students believe manipulatives are useful in teaching and learning mathematics. Not only do students and teachers feel comfortable using manipulatives, but both groups also wish to continue using manipulatives as a teaching and learning tool. However, many teachers think that additional training should be given to teachers.

Several considerations limit the generalizability of this study. Since the study took place in a predominantly Latino environment, the results cannot be generalized to all classrooms. Since the school districts had requested such a study to investigate the teachers' and students' attitudes toward the use of manipulatives and the survey instruments were designed by the investigators with the assistance of the school district personnel, the results provide generalizable information only to those who are in similar situations.

CONCLUSIONS

Several conclusions can be drawn from an interpretation of the data: (1) Since the results indicate significant gender differences in the students' responses, it would appear that the use of manipulatives could be an equalizer in students' attitudes toward mathematics and in their comfort in doing mathematics; (2) It appears that approximately three-fourths of the students are being reached through the use of manipulatives.

Overall it seems that teachers have a positive attitude toward the use of manipulatives in teaching mathematics, although they have expressed some concerns about the additional training that is needed for the proper use of manipulatives in the classroom and the availability of appropriate materials. Their concerns are justified when the financial situation in the two school districts is considered. Although the two districts included in the study have a history of encouraging teachers to use manipulatives, funding for in-service training and classroom teaching materials has been limited and not every school has received the same level of administrative support in these areas. Studies such as this one can help in justifying the purchase of manipulatives and the teacher training that is necessary to incorporate manipulatives into the classroom.

REFERENCES

Bustamante, Maria. "Teachers' and Students' Attitudes Toward the Use of Manipulatives in Two Predominately Hispanic School Districts." Master's thesis, University of Texas at San Antonio, 1995.

Kober, Nancy. *What We Know about Mathematics Teaching and Learning.* Columbus, Ohio: ERIC Clearinghouse for Science, Mathematics, and Environmental Education, 1991. (ERIC Document Reproduction Service no. ED 343 793)

Sowell, Evelyn J. "Effects of Manipulative Materials in Mathematics Instruction." *Journal for Research in Mathematics Education* 20 (November 1989): 498–505.

Suydam, Marilyn N., and Jon L. Higgins. *Activity-Based Learning in Elementary School Mathematics: Recommendations from Research.* Columbus, Ohio: ERIC Clearinghouse for Science, Mathematics, and Environmental Education, 1977. (ERIC Document Reproduction Service no. ED 144 840)

Portafolio de Matemática
Using Mathematics Portfolios
with Latino Students

10

Leslie Garrison

Teachers, schools, or districts initiating a mathematics portfolio program first need to address basic questions of purpose and content: How will portfolios help meet the goals of the mathematics program? What materials will be included in the portfolio? How will that material be used? The answers to these questions vary from program to program; some portfolios are used primarily for student reflection and conferencing, whereas others assume a major role in determining students' learning and grades. Some portfolios follow students year to year and others reflect work over a shorter time. Portfolio programs in certain schools document students' development in problem solving, and others chronicle growth in mathematics procedures. The answer to basic questions of the design of a portfolio program should be guided by the goals of the mathematics program. But when portfolio programs are initiated among special populations, such as students who are linguistically diverse, other fundamental issues of language and concept development must also be addressed.

In areas with high Latino populations, special attention must be paid to ensure that mathematics portfolio programs are equitable and accessible to all students. Important issues to be addressed include the following: What language will be used in instruction? Will students use English or Spanish to write in their portfolios? Who will decide which language is used? This chapter describes how one elementary school with a large Latino population successfully implemented a mathematics-portfolio program to serve the needs of all its students.

In current educational practice, portfolios are most commonly used in language arts programs. Portfolios often contain a sampling of each student's best literary efforts and chronicle the development of writing skills. Although portfolios have been employed to document students' progress in language arts, using portfolios for the assessment of mathematics progress is a more recent phenomenon.

As portfolios are starting to be used in mathematics instruction, teachers raise questions about how they are to be used and what to put in them. In the area of mathematics, Jean Stenmark (1991, p. 35) suggests that

> A portfolio is a showcase for student work, a place where many types of assignments, projects, reports, and writings can be collected. Progress in, attitudes toward, and understanding of mathematics can be seen in a comprehensive way. The collection exemplifies the goals of the NCTM Evaluation Standards and shows much more than will a single test.

In this definition, Stenmark points out that the materials found in a portfolio can be from a variety of sources. Depending on the purpose of the portfolio, it can house selected daily assignments; the finished products from a unit of study; or personal writing and reflections on mathematical attitudes, accomplishments, and challenges. Regardless of the specific material it contains, a portfolio represents work collected over time, a characteristic that differentiates it from a single event such as a test or

The author would like to acknowledge the special contributions of the Mains Elementary School principal, Gloria Celaya; the resource teacher, Cecelia Wong; and Norma Chavez-Cruz, Sara Garcia, and Rosa Martinez, teachers at the school, for their professional excellence and invaluable assistance with this chapter.

even a unit. Students demonstrate progress and change in their skills, attitudes, and understanding of mathematics through the work collected in their portfolios.

The teachers and students at Mains Elementary School in Calexico, California, have taken the skills they initially developed in using language arts portfolios to formulate an exemplary mathematics-portfolio program.

THE MATHEMATICS PORTFOLIO PROGRAM AT MAINS ELEMENTARY SCHOOL

Mains Elementary School is part of the Calexico School District in southern California; it is located only a few blocks from the United States–Mexico border. All 550 students at Mains are of Latino descent, 88 percent are classified English-language learners, and 80 percent receive free or reduced lunches. The school, therefore, is a unique setting for mathematics-portfolio program that addresses the concerns of Latino students.

The mathematics-portfolio program at Mains School was developed incrementally starting in 1992. Initially, the staff and administration designed mathematics benchmarks to give direction to the mathematics program and ensure that students had mastered skills appropriate for their grade level. These original benchmarks were based on the skills required for the California Test of Basic Skills (CTBS). Dissatisfied with the narrow focus of the original benchmarks, the administration sought new instructional strategies and materials directed at developing and having students demonstrate a broader understanding of mathematics concepts. Writing was introduced into the mathematics program in an attempt to augment students' reasoning skills.

THE CONNECTION BETWEEN WRITING AND MATHEMATICS

The Mains Elementary School principal, Gloria Celaya, encouraged teachers to use writing in mathematics to help students improve their mathematics and communication skills. The value of combining mathematics and writing instruction is well documented in research: writing helps students show and practice skills and gives them an opportunity to create their own problems, analyze their work (Helton 1995), clarify their thinking, and relate personal experiences and attitudes (Elliot 1996). Writing also affords students the opportunity to reflect on and evaluate their work (Pokay and Tayeh 1996; Wolf 1989).

The use of mathematics journals was initiated at Mains School in 1993 to help students develop writing, thinking, and mathematical skills. In addition, the responses to open-ended problems supplied important instructional information as teachers became aware that many students had trouble explaining their mathematical reasoning in words. The teachers saw that even some of the best mathematics students were unable to explain coherently why $3 \times 4 = 4 \times 3$. The students were used to thinking of mathematics problems in terms of answers—not how they endeavored to solve them—and became perplexed when the correct answer was not considered sufficient. Therefore, Mains teachers developed lessons around the type of writing required in mathematics and over time saw improvement in their students' skills.

Following the success of the mathematics journals, the mathematics program at Mains School incorporated a more formal portfolio program in 1994. The purpose of the portfolio program was twofold: (1) to document that students' learning was in line with the National Council of Teachers of Mathematics (NCTM) Standards and school-developed goals and (2) to assess and evaluate the effectiveness of the school's mathematics program.

Before implementing the program, the teachers were trained by the principal and the resource specialist in instructional strategies that focused on developing problem-solving and mathematical thinking skills. The staff development focus was used to train teachers to successfully practice instructional methods that encourage students' understanding, to develop their skills in evaluating students' mathematical writing, and to familiarize students with this type of assessment.

THE CONTENT OF THE MAINS PORTFOLIO

School administrators held grade-levels meetings with teachers to develop the portfolio program. The NCTM *Curriculum and Evaluation Standards for School Mathematics* (1989) and the goals developed at the school provided the criteria for selecting the content of the portfolios. The content was specified by trimester and generally had the components listed in figure 10.1.

First-Trimester Content

- Mathematics benchmark pretest and posttest—examinations designed by the Mains faculty and administration that focus on the skills outlined in the NCTM *Standards*

- Journal entry—open responses to questions that ask students to express their feelings and thinking about some aspect of mathematics

- Open-ended questions—problem-solving exercises that have a variety of possible solutions. Students are asked to explain their solution strategy.

- Sample investigation—work from an extended unit in which students have explored a range of mathematics problems based on a central theme

---

Fig. 10.1. An example of portfolio content by trimester

Benchmark Tests

According to the NCTM *Curriculum and Evaluation Standards for School Mathematics* (1989, p. 44), students need to possess the ability to "model, explain, and develop reasonable proficiency with basic facts and algorithms." The Mains faculty determined that a knowledge of basic facts is the basis for number sense and estimation and is a necessary building block to higher mathematics. Thus, benchmark tests were created to document the students' knowledge of basic facts and their skill in performing algorithms.

These benchmark skills tests resembled standardized tests (e.g., the Iowa Test of Basic Skills and the California Test of Basic Skills) in both content and format: the students were expected to solve problems and choose the correct response from the four choices given (see fig. 10.2). The purpose of the benchmark tests was to prepare the students for annual standardized tests and ensure that they were learning the mathematics "basics" as defined by the Mains School grade-level benchmarks.

Many advocates of portfolios question the appropriateness of including multiple-choice tests in a portfolio, and their inclusion is somewhat unusual. However, the staff and administration at Mains School decided to include benchmark tests for the following reasons:

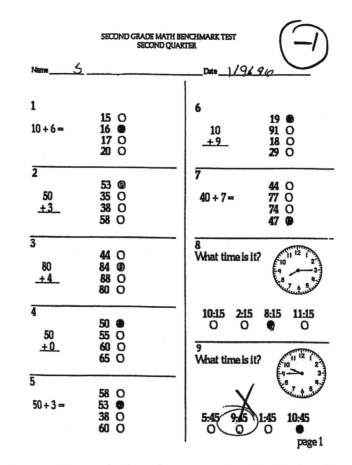

Fig. 10.2. An example of a student response sheet for a benchmark test

1. The skills measured were part of the school's mathematics goals.

2. The multiple-choice format gave students practice in the style of standardized tests which is very important because the placement of students in special programs is based in part on these test results.

3. Portfolios are used in parent conferences and should contain samples of all aspects of the mathematics program.

Journal Entries

The students were asked to write journal entries about a variety of mathematical topics to include in the portfolios. The students frequently used the "writing process" (Sebrnek, Meyer, and Kemper 1990, p. 11) to complete journal entries, so this section represents an integration of skills from different subject areas. The writing process, which is taught as part of the language arts curriculum at Mains and numerous other schools across the nation, involves brainstorming and organizing thoughts, writing a rough draft, editing the draft, and making a final copy. The use of this four-step process was evident because brainstorming, rough drafts, and final copies were included in the portfolios (see figs. 10.3 and 10.4). The integration of mathematics with other academic areas is recommended by the *Curriculum and Evaluation Standards for School Mathematics* (NCTM 1989) to help students make connections between mathematics and its real-world applications. Mains teachers also integrate mathematics and writing through the use of mathematics journals.

Journal writings collected over time document the growth of mathematical skills and reasoning skills and—with bilingual students—English-language development as well. Sandra, whose writing appears in figure 10.4, initially learned to read and write in Spanish. She began writing in English during the fourth grade, a change that is clearly documented in her mathematics portfolio. Her journal entries at the beginning of the fourth grade were in Spanish (see fig. 10.5) but by the end of that year she was writing journal entries in English (see fig. 10.6). A description of the work shown in figure 10.6 appears in the section headed Improving Instruction and Making Instructional Decisions.

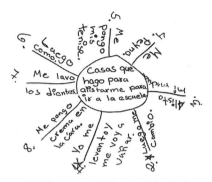

Write the steps you take to get ready for school.
Escribe paso por paso lo que haces antes de venir a escuela.

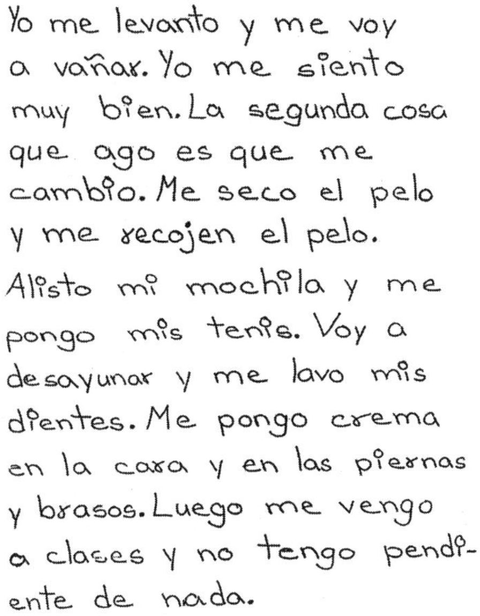

Yo me levanto y me voy a vañar. Yo me siento muy bien. La segunda cosa que ago es que me cambio. Me seco el pelo y me recojen el pelo. Alisto mi mochila y me pongo mis tenis. Voy a desayunar y me lavo mis dientes. Me pongo crema en la cara y en las piernas y brasos. Luego me vengo a clases y no tengo pendiente de nada.

I get up and take my shower. I feel very good. The second thing that I do is I change. I dry my hair, and they fix my hair. I get my backpack ready and put on my tennis shoes. I have breakfast, and then I brush my teeth. I apply lotion to my face, my legs, and arms. I then go to class and don't worry about anything.

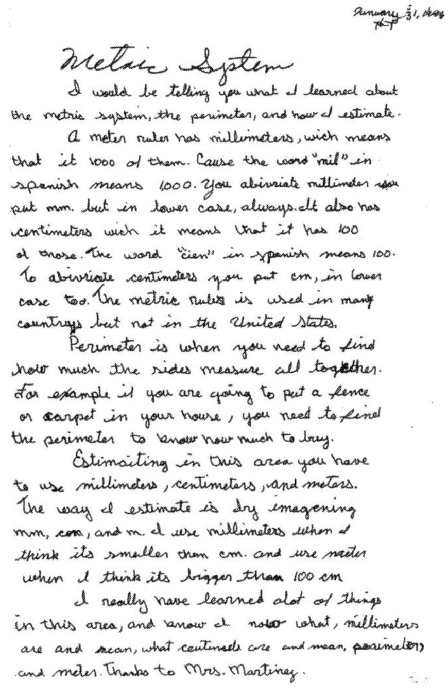

Fig. 10.3.

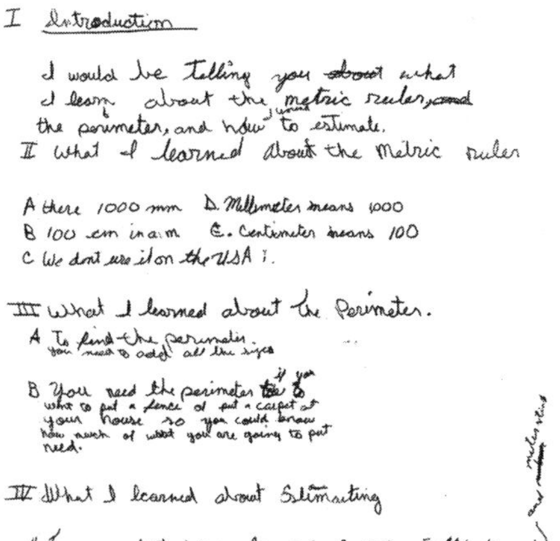

Fig. 10.4. Sandra's journal entry about the metric system

Students at Mains School begin reading and writing in English when they have demonstrated reading and writing competency in their primary language and demonstrated an oral command of English. As a result, most classrooms at Mains School have students with a wide range of proficiency in English, making the individualized nature of portfolios especially appropriate because students can respond in the more appropriate language.

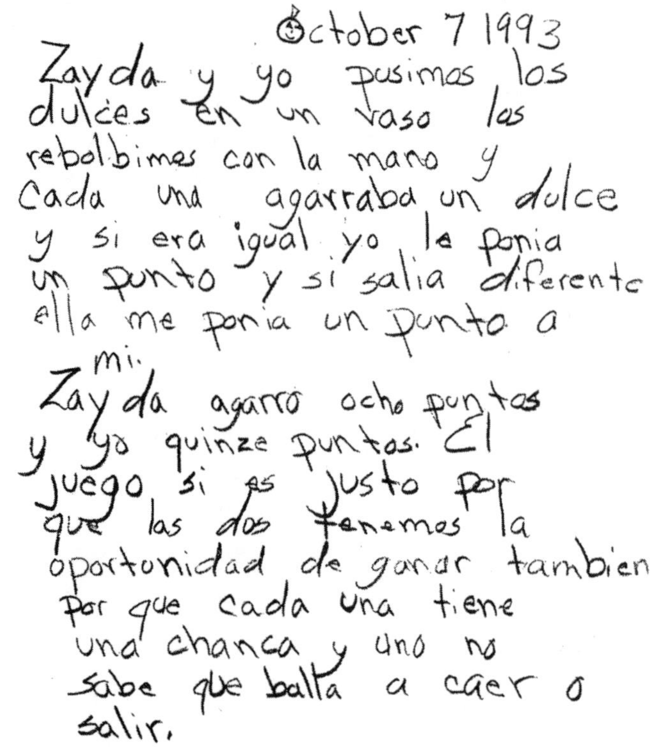

October 7 1993

Zayda y yo pusimos los dulces en un vaso las rebolbimes con la mano y cada una agarraba un dulce y si era igual yo le ponia un punto y si salia diferente ella me ponia un punto a mi.

Zayda agarro ocho puntos y yo quinze puntos. El juego si es justo por que las dos tenemos la oportunidad de ganar tambien por que cada una tiene una chanca y uno no sabe que balla a caer o salir.

Zayda and I put some candies in a jar and mixed them up with our hand. Each one of us would take a candy out and if they were the same, I would give her a point, and if they were different, she would give me a point. Zayda got eight points and I got fifteen points. The game was fair because we both had the same opportunity to win. Neither on knew what would fall or come out.

Fig. 10.5. At the beginning of the fourth grade, Sandra wrote her journal entries in Spanish.

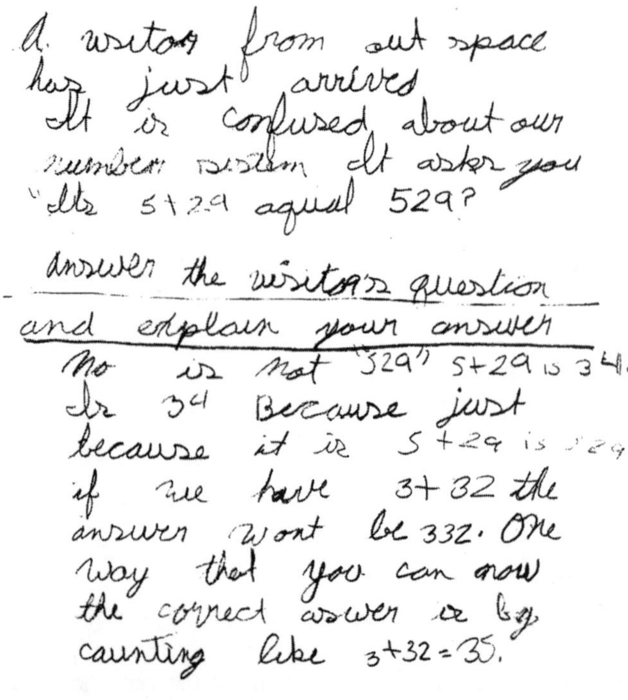

A visitor from out space has just arrived It is confused about our number system It asks you "Is 5+29 aqual 529?

answer the visitor's question and explain your answer No is not "529" 5+29 is 34. Is 34 Because just because it is 5+29 is 529 if we have 3+32 the answer wont be 332. One way that you can now the correct answer is by counting like 3+32=35.

Fig. 10.6. By the end of the fourth grade, Sandra was writing English in her journal entries.

Open-Ended Questions

The *Assessment Standards for School Mathematics* (1995, p. 89) gives the following definition of open-ended questions, based on Pandey (1991):

> Tasks that allow for various acceptable answers and for multiple approaches to an effective solution. Open-ended problems engage students in interesting situations and allow students at many levels of understanding to begin working on the problems, make their own assumptions, develop creative responses, and effectively communicate their solutions.

The samples discussed here were taken from portfolios in a newcomers' class, composed of fifth- and sixth-grade students who had recently immigrated to the United States. The curricular experiences provided through the Newcomers' Program assist students in understanding educational expectations and in developing language and academic skills to enable them to perform in a mainstream classroom. The Newcomers' Program introduces students to the educational methodology employed in the Calexico School District and elsewhere in the United States.

For example, students learn about the four-step process, the scientific method, literature studies, mathematics inquiry, and U.S. history and geography. English-language development, of course, is another curricular theme; students are gradually introduced to English through the Natural Language Approach, which mirrors the method used to learn the primary language. It introduces students to new words and phrases as the need arises within a context of day-to-day situations instead of using prescribed grammatical sequences. For example, color might be taught in conjunction with an art activity, not as isolated information presented in a predeteremined order.

At the beginning of the year, students in the newcomers' class are asked to respond to the following questions: What is mathematics? How is mathematics used? and How do I feel about mathematics? The responses range from Norma's relatively complete and philosophical answers (see fig. 10.7) to Hugo's short and incomplete replies (see fig. 10.8). Norma's response reveals her understanding of the scope and pervasive nature of mathematics, whereas Hugo's offers a narrow and limited view. Since Mains School keeps the language arts portfolios with the mathematics portfolios, Hugo's writing skills could be verified easily. A sample of a narrative revealed that Hugo generally communicates well in writing but has difficulty writing about mathematics.

The classroom teacher attributes the discrepancy in Hugo's performance to a difference in educational systems and expectations between U.S. schools and schools in Mexico. Hugo's two writing samples illustrate the difficulty some recent immigrant students have when encountering different educational expectations in mathematics. His mathematics training in Mexico had focused on problems that had only right or wrong answers, and since no one had ever explicitly told Hugo the answer to "What is mathematics?" he felt unprepared to respond. Even though Norma had had similar educational experiences in Mexico, she was better able than Hugo to transfer her writing and skills across disciplines.

Portfolios serve an important function for culturally and linguistically different students such as Hugo. The broad cross section of work they contain allows teachers to make instructional judgments on a range of students' work. In the hands of someone well versed in the cultural and linguistic background of the students, portfolios give enough information to make sense of ambiguous results in students' performance.

Sample Investigation

Mains teachers assign students at least two mathematics investigations each year. These investigations can come either from the district's newly adopted MathLand textbook series or from the list of state-endorsed "replacement units." These extended units, which build concepts contextually, give students ample opportunities to learn and understand the concepts presented.

Que son las matematicas
Para que se usan
Como me siento con las mate-
maticas

Las matematicas son
cosas formadas Por inumeros,
Problemas, Figuras geometricas y
otras cosas.

Las matematicas se usan
Para sacar la respuesta de
algo relacionado con numeros
y Problemas, en el mercado
Sacan la respuesta del dinero
que se tiene que pagar.
yo me siento bien
con las matematicas pero
son un poco dificiles pero
son parte de la educacion
del mundo.

What is mathematics?

What is it used for?

How do I feel about mathematics?

Mathematics is made up of numbers, problems, figures, geometrics, and other things.

Mathematics is used to figure out answers related to numbers and problems.

At the stores, they must figure out the total amount owed.

I feel good about mathematics. They are a little difficult, but they are part of education in the world.

Fig. 10.7. *Norma's responses to three questions*

¿Que son las matematica? 9/22

¿Para que se usan?

¿Como me siento con las matematica?

Las matematicas son tipos de
cuentas para saber problemas.

What is mathematics?

What is it used for?

How do I feel about mathematics?

Mathematics are types of accounts to solve problems.

Fig. 10.8. *Hugo's responses to the three questions*

A sample of Jorge's work from a second-grade unit (see fig. 10.9) represents one of the culminating activities from this unit. Students are asked to use new mathematical knowledge imaginatively to create an original mathematics word problem. Students also draw a picture that fully illustrates the problem. In this sample, Jorge has demonstrated his ability to create a mathematical problem, explain it fully in writing (in Spanish), and accurately represent it pictorially.

Había dos ratas que querían comer galletas en encontraron doce galletas en el parque. Las dos ratas fueron y agararon ciete galletas. Ellas se la comieron. ¿Ahora cuantas galletas quedar

There were two rats that wanted to eat some cookies. They found twelve cookies at the park. The two rats took seven cookies and ate them. How many cookies are left?

Fig. 10.9. Jorge created a mathematical problem, explained it in Spanish, and represented it pictorially.

ASSESSING WITH PORTFOLIOS

The National Council of Teachers of Mathematics (NCTM) published the *Assessment Standards for School Mathematics* in 1995 to assist teachers and administrators in developing assessment techniques in line with the NCTM *Curriculum and Evaluation Standards for School Mathematics* (1989).

The *Assessment Standards* outlines the following four purposes of assessment: to promote growth, to recognize accomplishment, to improve instruction, and to modify programs. Portfolios can play a major role in addressing these four purposes by providing progress and achievement information to teachers, parents, and external program evaluators (Asturias 1994). At Mains School, portfolios serve each of these assessment purposes.

Promoting Growth and Monitoring Students' Progress

The mathematics portfolios move with Mains students from kindergarten through sixth grade. During this time, students' work that demonstrates their mathematical skills, reasoning, and writing is compiled to clearly document their growth. At the end of sixth grade, the portfolios go home with their authors as a permanent record of their accomplishments.

Portfolios promote as well as monitor students' growth by helping teachers target instruction on the basis of past performance. Students' academic strengths and weaknesses are documented in a portfolio, allowing teachers to get a better sense of both the whole group's and individuals' areas that need attention.

Portfolios also document each student's learning for shorter periods of time. This individual monitoring is vital at Mains School, since many students transfer from schools both within and outside the United States. Migrant students make up more than 20 percent of the student population and attend Mains School for only part of each year. Repeated changes in the educational setting often produce gaps in migrant students' learning and is disruptive to their achievement. Teachers at Mains find it very challenging to differentiate between students who have knowledge gaps and those with learning difficulties.

Portfolios, because they collect a range of students' work over time, play an important role in identifying learning problems. Even when students have been at Mains School for a short time, portfolio work can demonstrate changes in their performance. Students who struggle academically are referred to the Student Study Team, a group of teachers and specialists who evaluate the learning of individual students and make recommendations about the type of instructional strategies and educational placements that might help the students improve their academic achievement. Teachers include portfolio work in every Student Study Team meeting, where students are considered for special services. On the one hand, portfolios help identify students whose low performance stems from lack of educational opportunity, which is evident when they demonstrate a strong gain in skills in relatively short periods. On the other hand, students whose portfolios fail to demonstrate gains over time are considered for special educational assistance.

Mathematics portfolios also serve as important communication tools for parent conferences. They contain a range of examples of work in mathematics, showing strengths and weaknesses in a more graphic manner than letter grades. The mathematics investigations contained in the portfolios also illustrate to parents the problem-solving and higher-level-thinking goals that have been incorporated into the Mains School mathematics program.

Recognizing Accomplishment and Evaluating Students' Achievement

Evaluations by teachers and peers and self-evaluations are included in Mains portfolios. Norma and Hugo completed self-evaluations of their work, which included both a numerical ranking (1–3) and an explanation of the score (see figs. 10.10 and 10.11). Norma's response was typical of students' early efforts to critique mathematical writing by focusing more on the writing than on the mathematical content. Hugo's self-evaluation shows that he was aware of the incompleteness of his response. Self-evaluations give teachers important feedback on whether students realize when they are having problems in mathematics and what they can articulate about those problems.

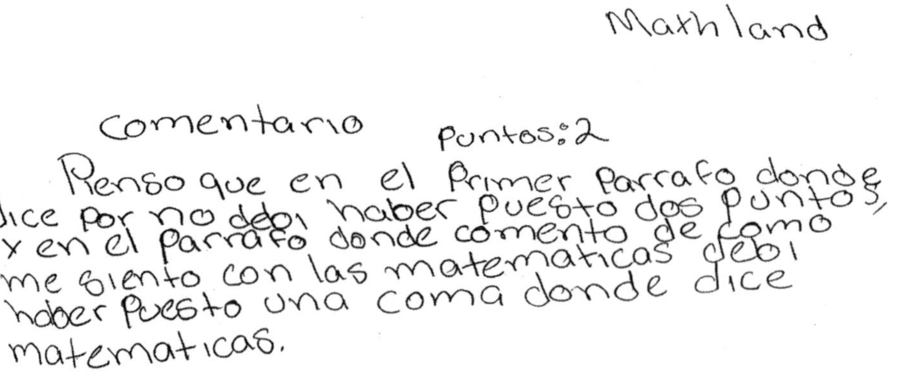

Math land

Comentario   Puntos: 2

Pienso que en el primer parrafo donde dice por no debi haber puesto dos puntos, y en el parrafo donde comento de como me siento con las matematicas debi haber puesto una coma donde dice matematicas.

Comments Points: 2

I believe that in the paragraph that says *por,* I shouldn't have placed a colon, and on the paragraph where I comment on how I feel about mathematics, I should have used a comma where it says *mathematics.*

Fig. 10.10. Norma's self-evaluation

Students develop peer-evaluation skills as part of the language arts program. They frequently review and evaluate the writing of their peers, and peer evaluations can be found in the writing portfolios of Mains students. For example, Rosa, a sixth-grade student and experienced peer evaluator, once gave a 2.5 rating to another student's mathematics writing after pointing out the need for more "mathematical language." Her comments demonstrate more sophistication than those made by students in the newcomers' class and attest to the evaluation skills developed through both the language arts and mathematics programs.

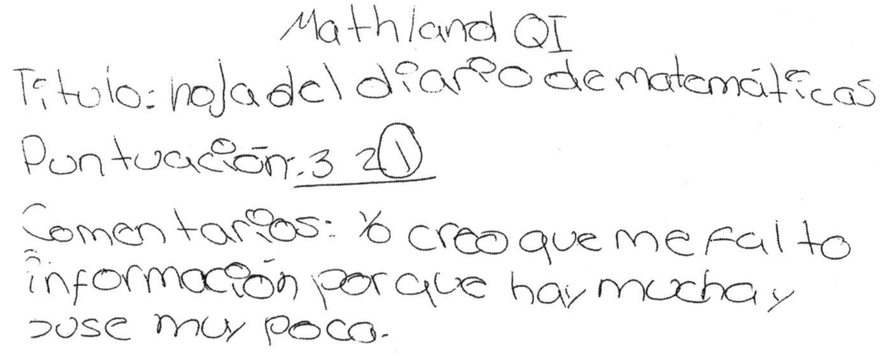
Mathland QI
Titulo: hoja del diario de matematicas
Puntuación: 3 2 1
Comentarios: yo creo que me falto información porque hay mucha y puse muy poco.

Title: page from the mathematics journal Points: 3 2 1

Comments: I believe that I was missing information because there was a lot and I put in very little.

Fig. 10.11. Hugo's self-evaluation

Teachers also evaluate the work found in the portfolios. The forms of evaluation include the number of errors on benchmark tests, written comments, and holistic scoring based on a rubric. These rubrics are usually five-point scales that evaluate both the conceptual and the procedural knowledge of mathematics.

The educational program at Mains School systematically teaches children the skills they need to perform successfully. Helping students develop the skills to make decisions and clearly explain their reasoning is important for all students but especially for students whose parents have low levels of educational attainment. Gloria Celaya, the Mains principal, underscores the need to develop students' reasoning skills carefully. She reminds the faculty that the parents of many Mains students have had limited educational opportunities. Parents who have not been exposed to reasoning patterns that are common in the schools cannot employ these strategies in the home.

The scientific method, for example, is unfamiliar to most Mains parents. The teaching staff at Mains, aware of this situation, explicitly teaches it as well as other reasoning strategies needed in school to ensure that all students have the tools for academic success. The success of the Mains School program stems from the faculty's knowledge of the needs of the students and their families and the teachers' ability to tailor the educational program to meet those needs.

Improving Instruction and Making Instructional Decisions

Working in grade-level groups, teachers determine the content of the portfolios. Their discussion and analysis of the mathematics program guides and articulates the portfolio program. The teachers at Mains assume greater ownership of the program when they help select the mathematics taught and the student work to be included in the portfolios.

Mains teachers reported receiving valuable instructional feedback from the mathematics and writing required in the portfolios. Students' explanations of mathematical concepts informed the teacher about the level of their students' understanding. On the basis of that information, teachers restructured lessons according to their students' needs.

Sandra's work (see fig. 10.7), for example, provides insights into her mathematical thinking. The problem requires Sandra to explain whether 5 + 29 is equal to 529. Her written response is in four parts: (1) the correct answer, (2) an attempt to explain the answer: "just because it is," (3) a similar example: 3 + 32 is not equal to 332, and

(4) a partial explanation of how to count to find the answer. An evaluation of her response shows that she knows the correct procedure to find the answer; however, she is not sophisticated enough to use place value to explain or justify the answer. She has given examples of the procedure, not an explanation of the underlying concepts.

Sandra's teacher should provide additional place-value activities, such as using base-ten blocks and a place-value chart, to reinforce the concept that in the number 529, the 5 represents 500, the 2 represents 20, and the 9 represents 9 units. The two numbers, 529 and 34, could then be compared. Addition activities using concrete objects help reinforce the concept of place value and explain the role it plays in addition.

Since portfolios are used schoolwide and materials are collected annually, the portfolio process holds both teachers and students accountable for their work. The teachers are conscientious about addressing the instructional areas to be covered in the portfolios, and the students want to complete and include their best efforts in this showcase.

Evaluating and Modifying the Program

The most powerful force behind the success of the Mains portfolio program is the school principal, whose vision, direction, and work made it possible. To keep herself informed about the progress of the portfolio program, Ms. Celaya checks selected portfolios from each class every trimester. The contents update her on both the classroom mathematics program and the students' progress. This information is the basis for her continued direction of the mathematics program. Program changes are usually introduced by the principal and then discussed, shaped, and agreed on by the faculty. This process takes time and requires teacher training, but both of these essential components have been built into the Mains portfolio program.

In spite of the regulation of the contents of the portfolios, I do not get the sense that either the mathematics program or the role of portfolios within that program has been predetermined. After talking with the principal, the resource teacher, and other teachers at Mains School, I realized that the students and teachers are developing and strengthening their skills every year. As each milestone, or benchmark, is reached in the program, the next step becomes evident and a new goal is selected. Currently, the groundwork is being laid for integrating the mathematics and the language arts portfolios to create on comprehensive portfolio of student work. Many of the mathematics essays in the portfolios (see figs. 10.3 and 10.4, for example) indicate that the language arts program has already had an effect on the students' writing in mathematics.

CONCLUSION

Portfolios are powerful tools for teachers of mathematics to showcase students' progress and assist in evaluation. With the twofold purpose of assessment and documentation in mind, the faculty at Mains Elementary School has developed a mathematics portfolio program that includes benchmark tests, journal entries, responses to open-ended questions, and work from extended units.

The Mains Mathematics Portfolio Program demonstrates the importance of—

1. having a committed administrative leader to train, monitor, and assist teachers in the development of the program;
2. developing a portfolio program collaboratively, over time, and with a commitment to teacher input and staff development.

Special attention needs to be paid to students' linguistic differences by allowing students to write in their primary language when appropriate. Furthermore, explicitly teaching the required skills enables students to develop and express their mathematical ideas effectively.

Educators looking for ways to make mathematics more meaningful to students would do well to investigate and pilot a mathematics portfolio program similar to the one used in Mains School.

REFERENCES

Asturias, Harold. "Using Students' Portfolios to Assess Mathematical Understanding." *Mathematics Teacher* 87 (December 1994): 698–701.

Elliot, Wanda Leigh. "Writing: A Necessary Tool for Learning." *Mathematics Teacher* 89 (February 1996): 92–94.

Helton, Sonia M. "I Thik the Citanre Will Hoder Lase: Journal Keeping in Mathematics Class." *Teaching Children Mathematics* 1 (February 1995): 336–40.

National Council of Teachers of Mathematics. *Assessment Standards for School Mathematics.* Reston, Va.: National Council of Teachers of Mathematics, 1995.

———. *Curriculum and Evaluation Standards for School Mathematics.* Reston, Va.: National Council of Teachers of Mathematics, 1989.

Pandey, Tej. *A Sampler of Mathematics Assessment.* California Assessment Program. Sacramento, Calif.: California Department of Education, 1991.

Pokay, Patricia, and Carla Tayeh. "Preservice Elementary Teachers: Building Portfolios around Students' Writings." *Teaching Children Mathematics* 2 (January 1996): 308–13.

Sebrnek, Patrick, Verne Meyer, and Dave Kemper. *Write Source 2000.* Burlington, Wis.: Write Source Publishing Co., 1990.

Stenmark, Jean Kerr. *Mathematics Assessment: Myths, Models, Good Questions, and Practical Suggestions.* Reston, Va.: National Council of Teachers of Mathematics, 1991.

Wolf, Dennie P. "Portfolio Assessment: Sampling Student Work." *Educational Leadership* 46 (April 1989): 35–39.

Taking On the Challenge of Mathematics for All

11

Richard G. Doty

Susan Mercer

Marjorie A. Henningsen

Beginning in 1989, the National Council of Teachers of Mathematics (NCTM) published a series of documents recommending drastic changes in mathematics curriculum, instruction, and assessment (NCTM 1989, 1991, 1995) in order to improve achievement for all students in mathematics. In concert with the national calls for reform, the state of California published a new framework for mathematics education in 1992 (California Department of Education 1992). All these documents emphasize the development of mathematical power for all students, which includes exploring mathematical ideas, making conjectures, problem solving and reasoning, communicating about mathematics, and making connections within mathematics and between mathematics and the real world.

At the same time, the Ford Foundation launched QUASAR (Quantitative Understanding Amplifying Student Achievement and Reasoning), a middle school mathematics education reform project designed to address some of the issues raised in the reform documents mentioned above. QUASAR was aimed at studying and improving the mathematics learning of students at six middle schools serving disadvantaged urban student populations around the country. The project was "based on the premise that the oft reported low levels of participation and performance in mathematics for poor urban students in the middle grades are not due primarily to a lack of student ability or potential but rather to a set of educational practices that fail to provide them with high quality mathematics learning opportunity" (Silver and Stein 1996, p. 476).

One of the six QUASAR sites, Spurgeon Intermediate School in Santa Ana, California, serves a large Spanish-speaking population in grades 6–8. Of the 1300 students, 75 percent are designated English-language learners (ELL), and 98 percent speak a language other than English at home. Latinos compose 88 percent of the student population at Spurgeon. Prior to QUASAR, the students at Spurgeon were homogeneously grouped for mathematics instruction on the basisi of ability. At the outset of QUASAR, however, tracking was eliminated, with the exception of a single section of algebra.

Also prior to QUASAR, instruction at Spurgeon was primarily textbook driven and characterized by an overemphasis on drill and practice in basic skills. Because the textbooks we were using were developed prior to the era of the NCTM Standards, there was much repetition in the content of the sixth-, seventh-, and eighth-grade regular-track classes. Manipulative materials and calculators and computers were used little

The authors gratefully acknowledge the support of the QUASAR staff directed by Edward A. Silver at the University of Pittsburgh, Learning Research and Development Center; the Spurgeon site administration; and most important, the teachers and bilingual instructional assistants of the Spurgeon Intermediate School Mathematics Department, Special Education Department, and Literacy Program, without whose commitment and enthusiasm no viable, positive change could take place. The preparation of this manuscript was partially supported by a grant from the Ford Foundation (no. 890-0572) for the QUASAR project. Any opinions expressed herein are those of the authors and do not necessarily represent the views of the Ford Foundation.

or not at all. Classroom lessons were primarily teacher directed, with the teacher doing most of the talking and students sitting quietly at their desks, participating only when called on to give brief one-word or one-number answers to the teacher's queries. The students did very little writing about mathematics.

Mathematics was viewed primarily as a static body of facts and procedures that students needed to memorize and be able to use in order to become proficient at mathematics. Problem solving was generally thought of as a special activity, such as a problem of the week, rather than an everyday part of students' classroom experience. In short, mathematics instruction at Spurgeon was similar to many typical traditional mathematics instructional programs in the United States (Stodolsky 1988).

IMPROVED STUDENT PERFORMANCE

Prior to QUASAR, Spurgeon also had a history of lower scores on standardized tests than other intermediate schools in the district. However, as QUASAR evolved (1991–95), a different picture of student performance emerged.

Comprehensive Test of Basic Skills (CTBS)

Over the course of the project, Spurgeon students improved their performance on the CTBS, which assesses students' basic computational skills and mathematics concepts and applications. Although basic-skills instruction was not completely abandoned during the project, it was no longer the primary focus of instruction at Spurgeon.

Fig. 11.1 compares the mean scaled score on the CTBS of students at Spurgeon with that of students in the district and at a comparable intermediate school over a three-year period (sixth graders in 1991–92, seventh graders in 1992–93, and eighth graders in 1993–94). As shown in figure 11.1, Spurgeon students started out in sixth grade performing below the average of both the district and the comparable school in computation, in concepts and applications, and overall. By the time they completed eighth grade, Spurgeon students were performing better than those at the comparable school on concepts and applications, and they were closing the gap in computation and overall performance.

We also looked at the performance of a cohort of 106 students (see figure 11.2) who were enrolled for three years in the QUASAR program at Spurgeon and took the CTBS in 1991–92, 1992–93, and 1993–94.

Figure 11.2 shows that the performance of the ad hoc "true" (i.e., three-year) cohort exceeded the performance of all Spurgeon students in computation, concepts and applications, and overall performance as they completed eighth grade. The performance of the true cohort demonstrates the progress that was made by the students who experienced the entire three-year QUASAR mathematics program at Spurgeon.

QUASAR Cognitive Assessment Instrument (QCAI)

Over the course of the project, the Spurgeon students also increased their proficiency in thinking and communication skills related to complex mathematical ideas. The QCAI is a program-level assessment developed specifically for use in the QUASAR project. It consists of a set of extended constructed-response tasks designed to assess students' knowledge of a broad range of mathematical content, their understanding of mathematical concepts and interrelationships, and their capacity to use high-level thinking and reasoning processes to solve complex mathematical tasks. For a more complete description of the QCAI, see Silver and Lane (1995).

Changes in performance on the QCAI at Spurgeon were examined for two two-year periods. Gains were based on increases in the percent of high-quality responses (three or four on a scale of 0–4 points) from one testing time to the next on eleven tasks. The tasks were common to the sixth- and seventh-grade and to the eighth-grade

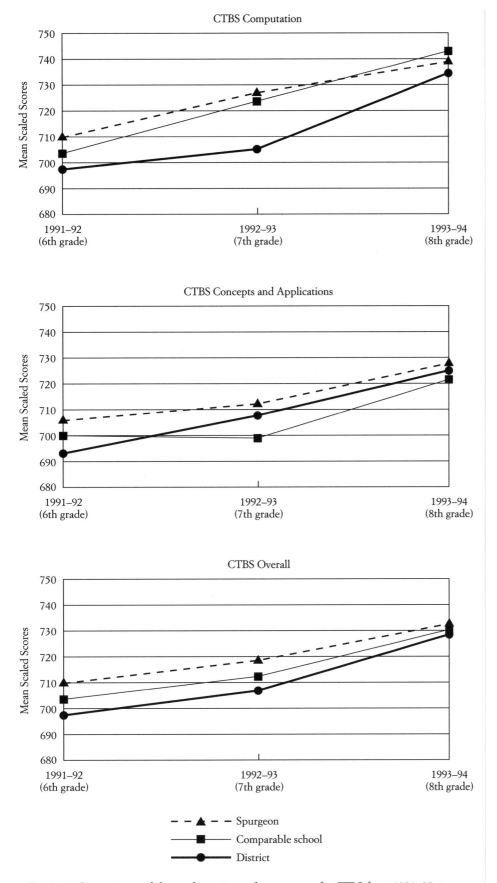

Fig. 11.1. Comparisons of the mathematics performance on the CTBS from 1991–92 to
1993–94 of students at Spurgeon Intermediate School, students at a comparable intermediate
school in the district, and students in the district as whole

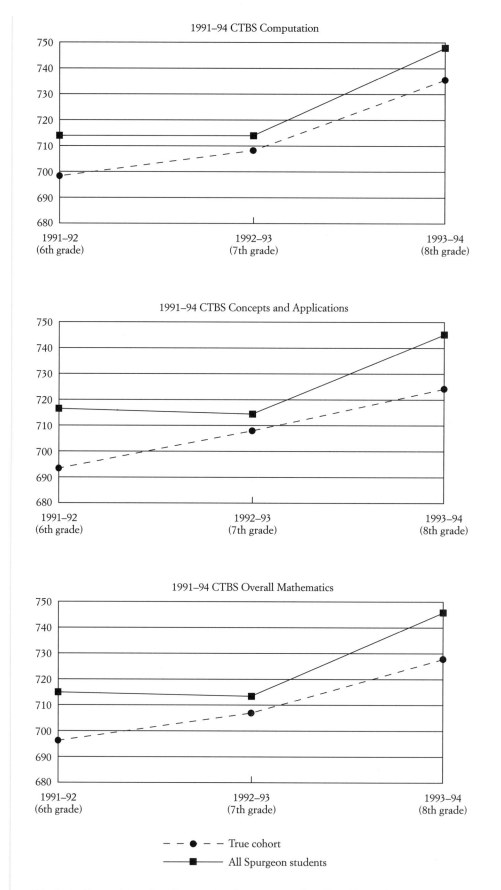

Fig. 11.2. *Comparison of mathematics performance on the CTBS from 1991–92 to 1993–94 of a true cohort of students at Spurgeon Intermediate School (106 students who were at Spurgeon all three years) and all students at Spurgeon.*

versions of the QCAI and were common across QCAI administrations. The average percent of responses attaining the two highest score levels increased 16 points from fall 1991 to spring 1993 and 25 points from fall 1992 to spring 1994.

What kinds of changes were going on at Spurgeon that might have contributed to the progress in mathematics being made by the students? Our experiences suggested that mounting a successful effort to improve mathematics instruction and student understanding at the school level was a huge challenge. Such an effort presents a number of unique problems for schools serving urban students who are primarily ELL, especially when the teaching faculty is primarily English speaking.

In the remainder of this paper, we describe how the Spurgeon mathematics faculty, as participants in QUASAR, took on these challenges for all their students. We begin by giving a general description of the QUASAR project at Spurgeon, of how the teachers organized themselves, and of the teachers' goals. Next we describe in detail the teachers' work involving language in the classroom.

LAYING THE FOUNDATION FOR TAKING ON THE CHALLENGE

Silver and Lane (1995, p. 51) point out the following:

> For too many students, conventional mathematics instruction, especially in middle grades, has consisted of students passively learning alone and in silence, solving exercises provided by a textbook or a worksheet, exercises for which a student's task is to produce a stylized response to a narrowly-prescribed question having a single correct answer which can only be validated by teacher approval and which is expected to be obtained without hesitation through application of the most recently taught procedure.

Prior to QUASAR, Spurgeon was no exception.

In an effort to help the Spurgeon teachers change their mathematics program, QUASAR supported a partnership between Spurgeon and a local university as well as other important resources in the district. The resource partners' role was to provide the teachers with intellectual guidance and staff development as we established goals for change and worked toward our goals. One of the important features was that the entire mathematics department, including a subset of interested special-programs teachers, participated in the project. The strategies and expertise of all the participants contributed to reaching all our students, regardless of their abilities and whether their needs involved academics, language skills, or behavioral problems.

In addition to QUASAR support, the mathematics department had the support of a progressive school administration and of district personnel as we experimented with our mathematics curriculum. The district's flexibility in allowing such experimentation was instrumental to our success. It was essential for the teachers to have the freedom to develop ownership of the ideas and activities that would affect their professional life and their students' learning of mathematics.

CHANGING THE APPROACH TO TEACHING MATHEMATICS

During the QUASAR project, the Spurgeon teachers developed a program that committed them to take on the challenges put forth by the California Mathematics Framework and the NCTM Standards documents. Changing the nature of the mathematics instruction included developing a new curriculum, changing teaching practices, and implementing different types of assessment. The changes in instructional practices included the use of manipulatives, multiple representations, calculators, and computers. We also emphasized cooperative work, student discussion, problem solving and reasoning, connecting algorithms with underlying concepts and meaning, and exploring concepts as a whole as opposed to isolated parts.

Along with the foregoing changes in instruction, the teachers developed a curriculum that they thought would provide a three-year mathematics experience that would be significantly different from what the students had experienced before QUASAR. At the outset of QUASAR, an appropriate commercially available curriculum did not exist, so we drew classroom activities and lessons from a variety of resources, including the Southern California Regional Algebra Project (SCRAP), the Middle Grades Mathematics Project, Math A (and the later version published by Glencoe), and units developed in the California Renaissance program. We increased the emphasis on several topics in our curriculum such as proportional reasoning, measurement, spatial visualization, probability and statistics, data organization, patterns and functions, and discrete mathematics. The project also needed to address the language needs of Spurgeon's Latino students.

A SUPPORT SYSTEM FOR CHANGE

The California framework states, "The critical factor in reform is support for teachers. Change takes time, and the typical faculty will need three to five years of sustained commitment and support to make the full transition to an empowering program" (California Department of Education 1992, p. x).

After struggling for the first year and a half of the project, we realized that trying to do everything simultaneously had become unwieldy. Therefore, we worked with the QUASAR staff and our resource partner to develop a small set of focal issues to guide our efforts. A focal issue is a small, manageable area of concern relating to reforming our instruction, curriculum, or assessment practices. It was important that the faculty work as a group to decide on each of the focal issues because if the effort was to be sustained, the faculty needed to feel ownership of the work they were planning. For each issue, we developed a descriptive statement and a plan with goals and specific activities.

Following the articulation of each focal-issue plan, we formed working groups, which we called focal issue committees. A focal issue committee consisted of mathematics and special-program teachers and bilingual instructional assistants who collaborated to facilitate the work and needs of the department regarding a specific focal issue. The committee held us accountable for working on the focal issues and for documenting our work.

Specific focal issues evolved over time and in accordance with our evaluation of our progress and needs. In 1993, we chose three focal issues to guide our efforts: (1) to generate strategies, methodologies, and practices that provide a safe environment where students are willing to participate actively; (2) to increase comprehensible input (instruction) and output (outcomes) for the large ELL population (discussed below); and (3) to develop a curriculum that prepares students to experience success through middle school and in high school.

One result of committee work on providing a safe environment was the development and administration of a student attitude survey at the beginning and end of each year. The committee facilitated the development of the survey, which was used by all the teachers, and then compiled the findings by class and shared them with the teachers to reveal the students' perceptions of their classroom experiences.

Another activity was observation of one another's classrooms. The goal was for teachers to observe successful examples of some of the specific strategies and techniques recommended by our colleagues and to give friendly individual feedback. A debriefing was held soon after the observation. The peer observation was perceived as nonthreatening and nonevaluative because the focus was determined by the teacher being observed. All teachers were observed at least once; some teachers conducted mutual observations on an ongoing basis.

The committee organized discussions about the curriculum, wrote curricular goals for our students, and defined the outcomes we hoped to see after students had had three years of mathematics instruction at Spurgeon.

The foregoing are just a few examples of the work facilitated by the focal issue committees. In the next section we describe our efforts to deal with the special needs of our Latino ELL students.

WORKING ON THE LANGUAGE ISSUES

Specific language issues were addressed primarily by a committee established to work on what we called "increasing comprehensible input and output in the classroom." What was initially viewed as a matter of translating from Spanish to English to help students understand instruction became a much more complex problem than we initially thought.

The first year of work on this focal issue emphasized vocabulary awareness and development and the implemention of Specially Designed Academic Instruction in English (SDAIE) methodologies, previously known as *Sheltered English*. The purpose of SDAIE is to provide in English comprehensible input to the core curriculum (Crawford 1994). Examples of these strategies include the use of manipulatives, the use of visuals, explaining vocabulary rather than just defining it, and allowing students to use their native language. These strategies are also recommended by NCTM as good instructional practices (NCTM 1991).

We decided that in order to have students actively participating, discussing, and communicating mathematical ideas and concepts, we needed to change the roles of the teacher, the bilingual assistants, and the students significantly. The traditionally accepted models of the teacher as giver of knowledge, the bilingual assistant as translator, and the student as passive receiver of information did not facilitate the type of mathematics learning our mathematics department wished to provide for our students.

To change the traditional roles, we decided to focus on (1) the relationships and interactions between the teachers and the bilingual assistants in the classroom and (2) the students' interactions and communication with the teacher, the bilingual assistants, and the other students in the classroom. As we struggled, not only with curricular issues but with improving teaching strategies and questioning techniques, we became increasingly aware of a largely untapped resource in our classrooms: the bilingual instructional assistant (BIA).

INTERACTIONS BETWEEN TEACHERS AND BILINGUAL INSTRUCTIONAL ASSISTANTS

The Role of the BIAs before QUASAR

At Spurgeon, the role of the BIA had traditionally been translator of teacher-presented lectures or of one-word student responses. Occasionally, the BIAs would share with the teacher an unexpected or lengthy student response made in Spanish.

A common occurrence was to have the BIA sit with a small group of selected ELL students (students with either the lowest English proficiency or the worst behavior) to translate verbatim the day's lessons without having a clear understanding of the lesson's direction. Many of the teachers hesitated to allow the ELL students to discuss a lesson among themselves in their native language or even with the BIA. Many teachers were afraid the BIAs might give the students the answers to problems.

What could be done to make this dismal interaction among teachers, BIAs, and students more effective and productive, less stressful, and more in tune with the department's goals? It seemed that one possibility was to make the BIAs a more integral and contributing part of the mathematics department.

Changing the Role of the BIAs

Team-building sessions were conducted to improve and broaden the link between the teachers and the BIAs. The teachers and BIAs needed to know one another better so that a trusting relationship could be built. We also encouraged the BIAs to take a more active role in instruction and encouraged the teachers to allow that to happen.

Efforts were made to include BIAs in all mathematics department meetings, focal issue committee meetings, and department retreats. The retreats were full-day meetings off campus, occurring about six times a year, in which the entire department, including the BIAs, participated in planning and in-service activities.

With support from the school administrators, the assignment of BIAs became more subject specific so that a consistent cadre of BIAs served predominantly in mathematics classes. Without this basic change in BIAs' assignments, it is doubtful that substantial progress could have occurred toward the goal of integrating the BIAs more fully into the department. The "math specific" BIAs (ranging in number at times from four to seven) were included in all department activities. Interested BIAs also participated with teachers in staff development programs that focused on mathematics content and pedagogy.

The BIAs' participation in the curriculum development process enabled them to gain a clearer understanding of the kind of instruction the teachers were trying to deliver and the kinds of student outcomes that were expected in the classroom. As dialogue between teachers and BIAs began to grow, the valuable input from the BIAs helped to shape all the activities of the Mathematics Department. In fact, the inclusion of the BIAs in the affairs of the department empowered them, as illustrated by one BIA's comment: "Now I feel I am listened to, whether I have a question to ask or a suggestion to make."

As time passed, more BIAs began to contribute their thoughts and perspectives in the meetings and retreats and also informally during the school day. Since this type of participation in an academic department was new for the BIAs at Spurgeon, it took some time for everyone to become comfortable with the situation. In fact, some BIAs and teachers never really achieved the level of comfort that the group had originally hoped for. Some BIAs and teachers, however, developed beyond our wildest expectations.

BIAs' Perspectives on the Changes

In group discussions with BIAs, they often related how their inclusion in the department's change process had brought with it a change of responsibility in the mathematics classroom and beyond. Instead of sitting with a small group, for example, they moved more freely around a class, making themselves available where needed.

Some BIAs could be observed previewing an upcoming lesson, helping a student at the overhead projector communicate with the class in Spanish or English, or walking around the room assessing whether the students were following the lesson or not. In some instances, BIAs began functioning more as another teacher in the room and as a resource for the entire class rather than for just a few specific ELL students. Some teachers and BIAs clearly developed mutually trusting relationships in the classroom and began working more as a team.

The BIAs demonstrated an increased sense of ownership of the mathematics program as their understanding and experience with the goals of the lessons broadened and as we grappled with specific lessons during full-day retreats. The BIAs noted a change in how they were perceived by the students and teachers. In an interview, one BIA commented, "I don't feel pushed aside anymore."

The BIAs also remarked that the students' respect had increased as they became facilitators rather than literal translators or answer givers. Their staff development experiences afforded them more confidence in responding to students' questions, and they responded more often on their own, without "checking with the teacher."

Some BIAs cited as positive their role in previewing and reviewing vocabulary or reviewing concepts. Many also noticed an increase in rapport and communication with the students since they had had more opportunities to guide the students in formulating their thoughts and ideas in Spanish.

Some BIAs also perceived that fewer teachers who spoke only English felt threatened by the use of Spanish in the classroom. They attributed this change to the rapport and trust that had developed between the teachers and the BIAs. Clearly, two conditions were essential for such trust to develop: (1) opportunities for teachers and BIAs to interact as professionals and (2) teachers' and BIAs' earnest engagement in such interactions.

OPPORTUNITIES FOR STUDENTS TO COMMUNICATE AND INTERACT

The California mathematics framework states, "Students learn mathematics best in their primary language; therefore, they must be given the opportunity to do mathematics and create their own meaning by speaking, writing and reading mathematics in their primary language" (California Department of Education 1992, p. 45). Elsewhere, Carrasquillo (1991) posited that "language is a very important component of Hispanic children's and youths' cognitive development and growth since it is a reflection of their underlying thought; it expresses and defines their ideal, concept and logic" (p. 58). Discussion among the teachers and assistants and the sharing of personal experiences enabled the teachers to slowly allow students to use more Spanish in the classroom.

The relationships and interactions of adults with students and students with students were addressed by the teachers and the BIAs in many ways. A focal issue committee conducted workshops on classroom practices and methods (e.g., modeling, preview and review techniques, questioning strategies, attention to vocabulary development, the use of students' primary language, the use of multiple representations, etc.). The department also encouraged more student-centered discourse and more varied opportunities for students to demonstrate their understandings.

For example, in spring 1995, classroom observations by the QUASAR staff revealed that in several lessons individual students (or groups of students) were encouraged to model solutions at the overhead projector or the chalkboard, explain their solutions, and in a few cases, entertain questions from their peers. This type of student activity had been much less prevalent in previous classroom observations.

By the end of the project, some teachers also gave the students some explicit criteria for good explanations. The students evaluated their peers' presentations according to a four-point rubric posted in the front of the room. The teacher also furnished guiding questions to help the students make their final evaluation.

For example, the students were instructed to consider the following points in addition to the rubric: (*a*) Did [the presenter] explain the solution fully? (*b*) Did [the presenter] use mathematical terms appropriately? and (*c*) Was [the presenter] able to give alternative explanations of the concepts or techniques? It appeared that the students used the criteria and guiding questions seriously.

Moreover, by making the criteria explicit to the students, the teacher gave the students a means of deciding what was important to include in their own presentations. Thus, the students had an opportunity to reflect on specific ways in which they might produce more-comprehensible and more-substantial mathematical explanations. The following example from an eighth-grade unit on solving equations will help illustrate further the kind of instruction and student participation we were aiming for.

Balancing Equations: A Classroom Example

In order to help students understand what they are doing when they solve an equation, we use the "balance model." Students use rectangular strips to represent unknown quantities and two-color tiles to represent integers. Starting with simple equations, they use the strips and tiles to represent equations and solve them by determining the value of the unknown while keeping both sides of the equation balanced. As they manipulate strips and tiles on "the balance," students write in mathematical terms what they did.

For example, if they take away six positive tiles from both sides of the balance, on paper they record that they subtracted six from both sides of the equation. In this way students can see the connection between manipulating the tiles and recording the manipulation symbolically. The students solve equations in groups and the BIA, also familiar with this model, walks around the classroom and helps the students in Spanish.

In one ELL class, at the end of the unit each group of students was given an equation to solve. The groups had to prepare a poster showing the balance at different stages, solve the equation, check their answer by substituting it in the original equation, and present their solution to the rest of the class. The students were required to script their presentation, and every student had to present a part. The following is an excerpt from the script of one group (fig. 11.3 shows the solution process as explained by the group):

> The problem that we had is $5x + -6 = -3x + 2$.
>
> This is the way we solved it. First we look at the problem and see if we could take some squares from each side, but we can't because we can't mix positive and negatives. In one side we have −6 and on the other side we have 2 so we add 6 positives to each side because it has to be balanced.
>
> Next, we saw that we had zeros on one side so we took them out because they don't count. After that we do the math and our new answer is $5x = -3x + 8$ because we add what was left.
>
> Next, we have to take away the x's so we add 3 positive x in each side. So, we do the math in the first side we add $3x$ and on the other side we also add $3x$ so we had $8x = 8$.
>
> Now, that we have done all the balance work, we work hard on the math. We look at the answer and divide what we have left, that means that we divide 8 into 8 and the answer is $x = 1$.
>
> Now we do the checking and it works like this: we always represent (replace) our answer in all the x's that are in the equation, that means: $5(1) + -6 = -3(1) + 2$. We have to get the same answer, $5(1)$ is 5 and then we add −6, so the answer is −1. The other side has to be the same. We times −3(1) is −3 and we add 2 the answer is −1. −1 equals −1. It checks.

In this example the students worked together on a complex problem, using manipulatives that helped them understand what they were doing mathematically. Because of the way the assignment was set up, the students had the opportunity to demonstrate what they knew about the problem beyond just giving a final answer. This was beneficial not only to the students but also to the teacher, who learned much more about how the students were thinking than if they had been required to say only that "*x* equals 1."

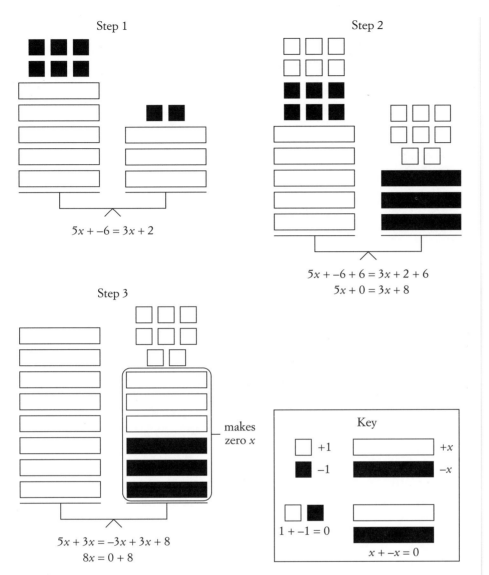

Fig. 11.3. An ELL group's diagram illustrating their solution to 5x + –6 = –3x + 2

By the end of the project, most teachers were trying to engage students in activities and projects like the one described above. Students were encouraged to work together to solve and share their results. At the close of the unit of study, these students might also have been asked to reflect on their own learning by providing written mathematical explanations and examples of what they had learned, as well as a self-assessment of what grade they deserved and justifications for their choice.

Students' Perceptions

A focal issue committee developed a six-question, open-ended survey in which the students were asked to reflect on three areas: (1) what helped them understand mathematics better, (2) how they felt when working individually or in groups, and (3) what type of activities they liked in their mathematics class. The teachers were then asked to put in writing their reflections on their students' perceptions and describe how the students' perceptions might influence and alter their teaching practices.

The students responded that the following helped them understand mathematics better:

- "When teachers explain what to do"
- "Shows us why we do it"
- "Use the overhead"

- "Explains slowly"
- "When the teacher uses words I understand"

Another student remarked, "[the teacher] tells me how to do it without telling me the answer."

A different student stated, "[the teacher] shows us how to solve a certain problem in different ways. This helps us because we can choose the technique that is easier to apply to that problem. This also helps us to not get stuck on a problem because we know different ways of solving it."

Several ELL students wrote that they understand when things are explained in Spanish, either by the teacher or the BIA. One student wrote in Spanish, "Algunas veces que no entiendo inglés y la maestra lo explica en español y entoncies entiendo más mejor" ("When I do not understand the explanations in English and the teacher explains it in Spanish, I then understand it much better").

In response to the question about group work, a large majority of Latino students stated that they learned when allowed to work in groups, even when working on individual assignments, because the group was there to help. Several students stated, "Four heads are better than one." One average-achieving student wrote about group work, "Love it ... all of us have different ideas then when you put different ideas together we get a GREAT idea, its fun."

Another student wrote, "Ayudo a mi grupo para resolver el problema y entiendo más el trabajo que tenemos que hacer y ... me siento mejor, más segura de lo que estoy haciendo" ("I help my group to solve the problem and I understand what we have to do ... I feel better, more confident of what I am doing"). In addition, working in groups allowed students to help one another when communicating answers in English, since each group has students with different levels of English proficiency but most are proficient in Spanish.

When asked about the activities they liked, a majority preferred tasks that allowed them to be actively involved in the class, for instance, doing projects, using calculators and computers, using manipulatives (dice, spinners, tiles, linking cubes, fractions pieces, base ten blocks, etc.), cutting, pasting, and coloring. One student liked "when we do our own projects and can be creative."

Most teachers took the students' responses seriously and used them as a learning tool in reviewing their teaching practices. For example, one teacher wrote, "The majority of my students mentioned that they don't understand when the teacher talks fast. I realize that I have a tendency to speak fast and now I am conscious of it. I am now making it a goal to speak slower." Another teacher reflected, "Almost all of the students liked to work in groups, with calculators, blocks, computers and be an active participant. I realize that I need to incorporate those activities more often in my lessons." And another teacher said, "I was glad I administered this survey despite the amount of time it took to read through the responses and reflect upon what my students had to say. I felt like most of them were being very honest and not just telling me what I wanted to hear. I felt fortunate that they felt comfortable enough to speak honestly and openly. All in all, this survey gave me a lot to think about."

The survey revealed a positive change in the students' attitudes toward their mathematics classes. Even though we expect students to use higher-level thinking skills, solve problems, and explain the process and steps to an answer, they do not mind the challenges when we work hard to help them understand and when they are allowed to work in groups, to be active, and to use their native language when needed.

CONCLUSIONS

Since the inception of QUASAR, we have made mathematics significantly more accessible to all students at Spurgeon. We have attempted to combine the resources of a diverse community of educators, each contributing a specific expertise to address the needs of our English-language learners. Drawing on content knowledge from the mathematics teachers, methodologies and modifications from special education teachers, SDAIE strategies from the Literacy teacher and from the BIAs, we improved the link between teachers and students.

Spurgeon has moved a long way from the lecture-based, textbook-driven, teacher-as-giver–student-as-receiver instructional model so prevalent at our site prior to the project. The following are common practices that could be seen at Spurgeon:

- All students, including ELL, special education, and literacy students, have access to a rich and broad curriculum.
- Students work in groups, using their native language and solving complex problems and doing projects.
- Students have access to manipulatives to better understand abstract mathematics concepts and calculators to solve multistep problems.
- Students are required to explain orally or in writing, in English or their native language, their problem-solving processes.
- Bilingual instructional assistants interact throughout the classroom.
- Teachers are more reflective about what is happening in their classroom.
- Teachers are open in seeking collaboration with, and the support of, their peers and the BIAs when needed.

As we took on the challenge of improving our students' mathematical understanding, we knew the curriculum and instructional practices had to change. But we did not initially realize how much the roles of teachers, instructional assistants, and students would be affected. When we envisioned students taking risks, we never knew how much the teachers needed to risk as well. Teachers had to be willing to try new practices and then reflect on their work in order to change, modify, and improve it. Taking on the challenge also meant that teachers had to be willing to share concerns and frustrations with one another in order to improve.

Taking on this challenge was not just about changing the curriculum or methodologies; it has also been a continual process of reflecting on what is working and what is not. We have learned that there is always more to be accomplished. The success of our approach continues to influence and affect student outcomes positively both in large-scale testing and within the classroom. In the QUASAR project we refer to these efforts as "the revolution of the possible."

REFERENCES

California Department of Education. *Mathematics Framework for California Public Schools.* Sacramento, Calif.: California Department of Education, 1992.

Carrasquillo, Angela L. *Hispanic Children and Youth in the United States: A Resource Guide.* New York: Garland Publishing, 1991.

Crawford, Alan N. "Communicative Approaches to Second Language Acquisition: From Oral Language Development into the Core Curriculum and L2 Literacy." In *Schooling and Language Minority Students: A Theoretical Framework,* edited by Charles F. Leyba, pp. 79–131. Los Angeles: Evaluation, Dissemination, and Assessment Center, 1994.

National Council of Teachers of Mathematics. *Assessment Standards for School Mathematics.* Reston, Va.: National Council of Teachers of Mathematics, 1995.

———. *Curriculum and Evaluation Standards for School Mathematics.* Reston, Va.: National Council of Teachers of Mathematics, 1989.

———. *Professional Standards for Teaching Mathematics.* Reston, Va.: National Council of Teachers of Mathematics, 1991.

Silver, Edward A., and Suzanne Lane. "Can Instructional Reform in Urban Middle Schools Help Students Narrow the Mathematics Performance Gap? Some Evidence from the QUASAR Project." *Research in Middle Level Education* 18, no. 2 (1995): 49–70.

Silver, Edward A., and Mary Kay Stein. "The QUASAR Project: The 'Revolution of the Possible' in Mathematics Instructional Reform in Urban Middle Schools." *Urban Education* 30, no. 4 (1996): 476–521.

Stodolsky, Susan. The Subject Matters: Classroom Activity in Mathematics and Social Studies. Chicago: University of Chicago Press, 1988.

Staff Development to Foster Latino Students' Success in Mathematics
Insights from Constructivism

Gary Ivory

Dolores R. Chaparro

Stanley Ball

12

For two years, the first two authors of this chapter worked on a project to help students in the Ysleta Independent School District (ISD) in El Paso cope with the mathematics portion of the Texas Assessment of Academic Skills (TAAS), a standardized test consisting entirely of word problems. From 1990 to 1995, the first six years that TAAS was administered, the gaps in passing rates between white students not of Latino origin and Latino students had been about 30 points. In 1995, the statewide passing rates for the two groups at the tenth-grade level of the TAAS mathematics test were 74 percent and 43 percent, respectively. Since passing the TAAS is a graduation requirement and since the Ysleta ISD is 84 percent Latino, we were greatly concerned about helping students improve their performance. Although we did not see test scores as the be-all and the end-all of mathematics instruction, we did believe that such gaps in test scores revealed problems that we had to address.

We attempted in 1994–95 to implement an instructional innovation to improve students' technical-language proficiency and ultimately their performance on the TAAS mathematics test. Our efforts involved six tenth-grade geometry teachers who had volunteered to participate. At the end of the year, we were chagrined to realize that our efforts seemed to have had little impact on the teachers' practices. We regrouped and planned another attempt for 1995–96, this time with eighteen seventh- and eighth-grade mathematics teachers.

For 1995–96, the third author joined the project, bringing with him a fervent commitment to the philosophy of constructivism. Together we came to believe in three ways that constructivism could guide efforts to improve the mathematics learning of Latino students.

1. Constructivism argues for improving mathematics performance by addressing students' language capabilities.

2. Constructivism has implications for staff development to which we were largely inattentive in our 1994–95 effort.

3. Constructivism challenges educators to go beyond traditional views of how evaluations should be conceived and conducted.

We shall discuss each of these insights in light of our differing efforts and experiences in the two school years.

This study was funded by the Ysleta Independent School District. We are grateful to the teachers and students who participated and to Lucille Armendariz-Housen, Naomi Assadian, Linda Calk, Irma Bañuelos Ivory, Judy Miller, Rachel Ortiz, April Padilla, and Nick Pike for their assistance in preparing this article.

113

LANGUAGE DEVELOPMENT IN MATHEMATICS

Language Difficulties in Mathematics in the 1994–95 Project

Our striving to pinpoint the difficulties Latino students had with the TAAS mathematics test and to help them overcome those difficulties led us to research on technical-language proficiency (Mestre 1988; Spanos et al. 1988). The researchers had hypothesized that the levels of language proficiency needed for mathematics problem solving were higher than those needed for basic interpersonal communication and cognitive academic language proficiency. They called attention to four features of mathematics word problems that make them difficult: (1) semantic features—the specialized vocabulary of mathematics; (2) syntactic features—the grammatical idiosyncrasies of mathematics word problems, such as more-frequent use of the passive voice and the use of prepositions and logical connectors that the reader must understand precisely; (3) pragmatic features—references to contexts with which the reader is assumed to have some familiarity; and (4) mathematical symbols.

Mestre (1988) and Spanos et al. (1988) documented Latino students' difficulties with these features by tape-recording students' small-group discussions of how to solve mathematics word problems and then analyzing the tapes and categorizing the difficulties they noted. Two implications of their findings are that mathematics teachers have to become more alert to the possibility that students' difficulties are related to language and that teachers have to work to help students gain facility with that language. The researchers in the study reported by Spanos et al. then produced a workbook of exercises and prescriptions for group activities to help students become more conversant with the language of algebra (Crandall et al. 1987).

We planned to collect similar data in fall 1994, taping tenth-grade students in small groups discussing how to solve TAAS-like problems and developing similar workbooklike instructional materials for teachers to use in spring 1995. Whereas the Mestre (1988) and Spanos et al. (1988) studies had depended on audiotape recorders, we videotaped the students. We invited the students' mathematics teachers to facilitate the discussions if they wished to, but often they did not. The teachers who chose to facilitate the discussions will be referred to hereinafter as *facilitators*.

Although we gave all the facilitators a handout to read explaining the role of facilitator, we did not offer them training or practice before we began filming. In fact, the facilitators had difficulty giving up their teaching roles, frequently wanting to guide students' problem-solving efforts when we would have preferred them to take a less directive role.

As we had expected, the analysis of the videotapes revealed that students had major difficulties with the language of the TAAS problems. We were surprised to discover that they had almost as much difficulty with some rudimentary mathematics knowledge and skills. Finally, they had a significant lack of problem-solving skills (Ivory et al. 1995). The simple workbook of language activities we had envisioned at the beginning of the project no longer seemed adequate.

Constructivist Insights into Language Development

Constructivism encompasses views of learning comprehensive enough to explain all three of our findings. We shall support that claim first by contrasting constructivism with empirical realism and then by showing how constructivism's emphasis on the social nature of learning implies that language is developed simultaneously with knowledge.

Gergen (cited in Schwandt [1994, p. 125]) distinguished constructivism from empirical realism by highlighting realism's commitment "to the view that the facts of the world are essentially *there* for study. They exist independently of us as observers, and if we are rational we will come to know the facts as they are." Schwandt went on to explain, "Constructivists are deeply committed to the contrary view that what we take to be objective knowledge and truth is the result of perspective. Knowledge and truth are created, not discovered by mind."

As Schifter (1996, pp. 494–95) pointed out, these different perspectives on knowledge result in different approaches to instruction:

> The drill-and-practice approach to math instruction has an affinity for a static and timeless conception of mathematical truth ("all the mathematics there is has always already been out there"). The constructivists, on the other hand, argue that mathematics is a human invention.... In this view, then, to "do" mathematics is to conjecture—to invent and extend ideas about mathematical objects—and to test, debate, and revise or replace those ideas."

Rohrkemper (1989, p. 143) wrote that we learn in a *social/instructional environment:* "By social/instructional environment I refer to parents, teachers, tasks, and peers that students influence and are influenced by as they engage in learning, be it about themselves, their community, or two-digit division." Thus, students' use of language becomes central to the whole learning process.

According to constructivism, then, we learn as we process information received from the senses or created by reflection and make sense of it by agreeing on symbols to represent common experiences. The social-linguistic exchange creates a language for sharing and simultaneously aids each individual's actual concept formation. Language acquisition and content acquisition occur simultaneously and are facilitated by meaningful social interaction. One way to promote such interaction in the classroom is with small groups. As students use words, they decide whether communication is taking place by sensing the actions of the receivers. In small groups, students are more likely to take risks with new words as symbols of new learning. As their language risk taking pays off they are empowered with increased communication and problem-solving ability.

We conclude from these constructivist tenets that if learners do not have opportunities to use language—oral or written—about a given topic, the learning process may be hindered. We believe that the learning of students from minority cultural or linguistic backgrounds or from lower socioeconomic backgrounds is hindered because such students do less verbalizing about academic content (Heath 1983; Westby 1987). De Avila (1988) documented that teachers simplified their language and used extremely simple logic when speaking with English-language learners.

We fear that similar behavior (either less verbalizing by the students or oversimplifying of language or logic by teachers) occurs with many language-minority students. As former classroom teachers and as observers of teachers, we have experienced how difficult it can be sometimes to engage students in a discussion of curriculum topics. The temptation has at times been overwhelming to lecture or to show a film and hope the richness of the medium helps the students "get it." The affinity of traditional mathematics teaching for drill and practice may be due to more than its connection to empirical realism. It may also be due to teachers' feeling that when they fail to get students to discuss mathematics, drill and practice at least makes them look as if they're learning.

The writings of De Avila (1988), Heath (1983), and Westby (1987) and our own experiences suggest, then, that Latino students have probably had fewer opportunities to use language in studying mathematics. In this light, what we saw on our videotapes is not surprising. Constructivism suggests that students who have fewer opportunities to develop the language of mathematics will not only be less proficient with the specialized language but they will also have a weaker grasp of mathematical concepts and be less competent at the unstructured tasks confronting them in word problems—all difficulties we observed on the videotapes. To put it simply, we now believe that if Latino students have inordinate difficulty with mathematics tests, it is often because they have had insufficient experience in talking and writing about mathematics.

Videotaping in the 1995–96 Project

In the second year of our project, we had the seventh- and eighth-grade mathematics teachers facilitate nearly all the discussions. We had given each teacher a handout on how to facilitate, plus an hour and a half of training and practice in the role of facilitator. These teachers struggled much less with this role than their counterparts from the previous year had. They seemed more able than the previous year's teachers to sit quietly and allow students to discuss and to make mistakes as they worked toward the solution of a problem.

During both years, two teachers noted that after the students were filmed in discussions, some became more assertive and confident problem solvers in the classroom. This development seemed surprising at first, since the discussions were for diagnosing problems, not for improving performance. But it is entirely consistent with constructivism that if students are asked to discuss, are listened to, and are required to explain or defend their thinking, they will actually begin to discuss, explain, defend, and think better.

STAFF DEVELOPMENT

Staff Development in the 1994–95 Project

For our 1994–95 project, we had begun with the assumption that we could handle the time-consuming tasks of making and analyzing the videotapes and then simply present teachers with a digested version of our findings. Furthermore, we provided only six hours of staff development to the six tenth-grade teachers in the study. During those six hours, we had them discuss their perceptions of the difficulties in TAAS mathematics problems, showed them selections of videotape, and listened to their assessments of students' efforts to solve the problems. Then we presented them with copies of Chamot and O'Malley's (1994) *The CALLA Handbook: Implementing the Cognitive Academic Language Learning Approach.*

Chamot and O'Malley developed CALLA (the Cognitive Academic Language Learning Approach) to facilitate the learning of three kinds of students: (1) English-as-a-second-language (ESL) students who have social-communication skills but insufficient academic-language skills for their grade level, (2) students who have academic-language skills in their first language and some beginning-level skills in English but who need help transferring concepts and skills learned in their first language to English, and (3) bilingual English-dominant students who have not yet developed academic language skills in either language (Chamot and O'Malley 1994, pp. 9–10). We believed that although many Latino students in the Ysleta district were not limited in English proficiency and never had been, they still met the third criterion.

To help such students succeed with academic content, Chamot and O'Malley (1994) made three recommendations: (1) that ESL classes assist students in learning the language of academic content, (2) that each content teacher consciously assist students with the language of his or her content area, and (3) that teachers deliberately teach students learning strategies, that is, tactics to help them learn new material. During the staff development session and subsequent feedback sessions, we reminded the six geometry teachers to help the students with the technical language of TAAS mathematics, emphasized to them the importance of teaching learning strategies, and underscored the benefits of having students work in small groups.

Constructivist Insights into Staff Development

Paris and Byrnes (1989, p. 174) emphasize the difficulty of getting students to learn new content if that content is at variance with schemata they have already constructed, arguing, "It would be maladaptive for a child to abandon completely and immediately a theoretical perspective … on the basis of new evidence that seems to contradict current theories."

Staff development specialists, although they work with adults, ignore this principle at their peril. Furthermore, their ignoring it is particularly ironic because they may be urging teachers to give students more time and opportunities to construct new schemata in response to new information while simultaneously denying the teachers those very same means of learning. As Darling-Hammond and McLaughlin (1995, p. 598) remind us, "Teachers learn by doing, reading, and reflecting (just as students do); by collaborating with other teachers; by looking closely at students and their work; and by sharing what they see." In our 1994–95 study we paid insufficient attention to teachers' needs to learn in the ways alluded to by Darling-Hammond and McLaughlin.

Staff Development in 1995–96

For 1995–96, we planned a much more thorough approach, requiring the middle school teachers to commit to thirty hours of staff development instead of the six we had carried out the previous year. Although doing so meant a substantial increase in time, effort, and financial support, we believed that the results would be worth the effort.

After the teachers facilitated the students' discussions for videotaping, we spent an hour and a half with them in small groups, guiding them in viewing and analyzing the videotapes, and then paid them to spend more time viewing their tapes individually. This time was only a prelude to the thirty hours to which they had already committed. To begin the thirty hours, we brought all of them together for a two-hour meeting in which individual teachers presented segments of videotape and initiated discussions of what the tapes revealed about students' difficulty with TAAS mathematics problems. We had instructed the teachers during the videotaping sessions to listen to the students, to question them, and to avoid directly helping them unless they seemed completely stalemated in their efforts. This videotaping experience and the two-hour discussion led to teachers' becoming more aware of the verbal interaction in the classroom. By listening to students' comments on tape and in class the teachers achieved a heightened realization that students' perspectives on problems are quite different from what teachers might assume.

We followed this staff development session with others on the principles of constructivism, the tenets of second-language acquisition (Collier 1995), and learning strategies. We eschewed lecture for group problem solving as much as possible in these sessions. It was extremely important that we model the instructional behaviors we wanted the teachers to emulate.

In fact, we issued the teachers their copies of *The CALLA Handbook* (Chamot and O'Malley 1994) only after the several hours of videotaping and viewing tapes and the first ten hours of staff development meetings. Then we constantly strove to promote their involvement with, and ownership of, the recommendations in *The CALLA Handbook*. For example, we introduced the CALLA learning strategies by having the teachers try to solve mathematics word problems in French and Spanish (simulating the experience of language-minority students) and describe the strategies they used. We listed the strategies they reported using, then showed them the list of CALLA strategies and asked how many of the strategies they had used corresponded to those in the CALLA list. We wanted the teachers to develop and express their own beliefs about, and experiences with, language and mathematics learning and problem solving before we confronted them with prescriptions, just as we hoped they would promote similar experiences with their students.

We presenters followed each staff development session with a debriefing period among ourselves in which we discussed the teachers' learning, what we hoped to accomplish next, and how we would model the principles of constructivism in accomplishing it. Some of these debriefing sessions raised our anxiety levels considerably when we neared the deadlines for having the next staff development session prepared but could not agree on the best way to foster the teachers' constructions of new ways of viewing their students and mathematics teaching. Our stressful planning sessions began to seem worthwhile when we heard the teachers make comments such as the following.

- "This has been a good sharing with each other."
- "Why didn't I learn this five years ago?"
- "For the first time in a long time, we're getting something we can use in the classroom."
- "Middle school teachers used to have a sense of unity, and we haven't had that the last couple years. We're getting the unity here again."

EVALUATION

We believe that staff development projects are most effective when they proceed through a cycle of three components: (1) examining evidence of students' learning, (2) implementing staff development on the basis of the student needs identified through the first component, and (3) analyzing systematically collected outcome data. This third component fulfills two needs: (1) it provides feedback on how effective the staff development effort has been, and (2) it starts the cycle over again, providing new data to guide the planning of future staff development.

Evaluation of the 1994–95 Project

In 1994–95, we instructed the tenth-grade teachers to spend six weeks implementing CALLA in a randomly selected treatment class and not to implement CALLA in a control class for purposes of comparison. We monitored their compliance by observing their teaching when it was possible and by having them turn in weekly checklists.

Although the teachers' reports and comments in the feedback sessions had suggested to us that they were being effective in implementing CALLA, our observations revealed the inadequacies of our six hours of training in fostering their understanding and implementation of CALLA methods. We realized that pressured to "cover" a great deal of mathematical content, most teachers only mentioned or defined particular learning strategies for their students and devoted insufficient time to helping the students internalize and gain facility with any strategies. Their weekly checklists suggested that they had done almost nothing to help the students with specific aspects of technical-language proficiency. Furthermore, although they did group the students, we saw little indication that they were able to take advantage of small-group activities to enhance the students' language development in mathematics.

Constructivist Views of Evaluation

We have argued that constructivism can provide important insights into students' achievement and that it can help guide staff development for teachers. We believe further that it can make findings from evaluations more relevant to users.

Guba and Lincoln (1989) argue that evaluation findings are not final, unimpeachable descriptions of reality. Rather, they are at best jumping-off points to spark discussion, debate, and new, more sophisticated constructions of reality among stakeholders—"persons or groups that are put at some risk by the evaluation" (p. 40). Since various stakeholders can have constructed various realities, "one of the major tasks of the evaluator is to conduct the evaluation in such a way that each group must confront and deal with the constructions of all the others" (p. 41). They further argue that the value of evaluation findings is not in their generalizability to other populations and situations but in the way they enable new constructions of meaning by stakeholders. Therefore, the usefulness of evaluation data from a staff development project becomes apparent only when one shares those data with the participants in the evaluated project and in future projects.

Evaluation in 1995–96

Teacher Logs and Classroom Observations

In 1995–96, we grappled with ways to assess the impact of the program that would be consistent with constructivist views of knowledge. We had spent much time emphasizing to the teachers a constructivist view of communication. On occasion, the teachers would relate an exchange they had had with a student about a mathematics lesson and note, "The student interpreted the situation in such and such a way, but that was not what I said." We would point out that when a teacher states that she or he has told a student some piece of information and then asked the student to respond, a constructivist will assume that the student will respond according to what he or she heard. Whatever words the teacher used in an attempt to communicate to the student must be judged against the student's ensuing response. As these teachers listened to one another, they gained an appreciation of the idea that "telling students" does not necessarily mean that students have "learned" and that they must be more aware of what students "hear" as well as what they themselves "say."

Having established these ground rules for thinking about communication, we could not just give the teachers another set of weekly checklists to fill out as a way of documenting their implementation of CALLA. Completed checklists would not have given us the kind of detail that would enable us to judge the extent to which the teachers' views of what they were doing matched our views of what we thought they should be doing.

Our Interpretations of Teachers' Logs and Classroom Observations

We opted instead for weekly two-page log entries in which the teachers were to write descriptions of activities in their classes that exemplified their attempts to implement facets of CALLA. The teachers were to describe the activities and tell why they served as valid examples. We reminded the teachers that we were looking for their true reports and reflections. We emphasized that honest comments, questions, and specific details would be helpful and that glowing but untrue reports and wildly enthusiastic but unsupported testimonials would not be. We explained that even though we were to write an "evaluation," we would use it not to judge but to furnish food for thought. In fact, we used information from log entries, as we went along, to plan staff development sessions. Of the fifteen teachers who completed the program, thirteen turned in logs. During the eleven-week implementation period, we received about 100 single-spaced pages.

In addition to the logs, we completed twenty-three classroom observations, covering fourteen teachers in the process. This small number of observations was hardly enough to give a reliable sense of what the teachers were doing. But the observers used a standardized form that we had developed, and their reports offered another view of the workings of this project.

We used the log entries and the classroom observers' reports to answer three questions:

1. How effectively did teachers learn to foster technical language development in students?

2. How effective were the teachers in leading students to conduct intelligent discussions of mathematical content and problem solving?

3. How effectively did the teachers learn to teach the students to use learning strategies?

This third question is particularly interesting in light of O'Malley and Chamot's (1990, pp. 154–55) statement that

> Very little attention has been given to training in which teachers are familiarized with techniques for learning strategy instruction. Virtually all learning strategy training in both first and second language contexts has been conducted by researchers.... no mention is made of how teachers have been or can be trained to teach learning strategies to their students.

Preliminary answers to these questions follow:

1. Helping students with the technical language of mathematics was not an instructional tactic that the teacher used thoroughly. In log entries, only six of thirteen teachers (46%) reported even minimal attempts to call students' attention to vocabulary. The observers' reports confirmed the impressions from the log entries. This perception was also similar to that from the 1994–95 project.

2. The teachers seemed more effective in leading students to participate in intelligent discussions of mathematical content and problem solving. The log entries of twelve teachers (92%) provided evidence that the teachers fostered students' conversations about mathematics. Our classroom observations confirmed that in general the teachers made attempts to do so. We noted, however, that in some instances the attempts were unsuccessful, either because the teacher was not effective in following up on the initial prompt or because the students resisted the effort to have them converse on the topic in question.

3. Finally, we examined the extent to which the teachers taught the students to use CALLA learning strategies. The logs showed that all thirteen teachers had taught the students to use learning strategies during the eleven-week implementation period. The teachers taught thoroughly an average of 2.7 strategies and superficially covered an average of 2.3 additional strategies. In our observations we witnessed nine teachers (64%) giving thorough instruction on one or more CALLA learning strategies. We observed the other five (36%) alluding to the strategies or encouraging the students to use them, although we did not see those five teachers give thorough instruction on the strategies. Since the strategies involve complex skills, we considered that the evidence from the logs and observations pointed to an impressive accomplishment.

Later we concluded that the teachers had implemented these three components in roughly the same proportions as we had emphasized them in our staff development sessions. In retrospect we saw that we had done almost nothing to help the teachers develop their students' technical-language proficiency and that only toward the end of our work together had we held a well-planned session on promoting discussions of mathematics among students. We had, however, worked with them intensively on teaching learning strategies.

DISCUSSION

Constructivist Views of Evaluation

With Guba and Lincoln's (1989) advice in mind, we are still striving to develop our understanding of constructivist ways to assess project outcomes. After the 1995–96 project ended, all three of us were pulled away from it by the demands of new professional roles and responsibilities. But our experience with this project has left us with new insights into the place of evaluation data in constructivist-oriented projects. We will call on these insights if another opportunity arises to work on a similar project.

Teacher Logs and Classroom Observations

A teacher's log is a construction of reality that the teacher believes will interest the reader. The reader's cataloguing of themes or variables from log entries is yet another construction. For classroom observation, developing a standardized form and then filling it out in a number of classrooms resulted in constructions. Generalizing from the completed items on the form to make broad statements about what occurred in the classrooms added yet another construction of meaning.

If we get other opportunities to work with teachers on similar projects, we will use the data gathered from the logs and observations to foster dialogue with the teachers about these issues: How can we help teachers help students with the technical language of mathematics? How can we help teachers enhance their use of questioning strategies so that they are more effective in promoting students' discussion of mathematical content and problem solving? How can we overcome students' resistance to being more thoughtful about mathematics and the use of learning strategies? What questions do teachers think can be answered from their log entries and from observations of their teaching?

Constructivist Approaches to Planning Future Staff Development

We found evidence of both positive outcomes and needed improvements in our staff development projects. We were pleased with the teachers' efforts to teach learning strategies; we would like to see more attention given to the technical language of mathematics and more success in conducting small-group discussions. We believe that the teachers could benefit from further learning in all three areas that would grow from deeper insights into constructivism and more study and practice with CALLA activities.

Had we had the time and resources to continue intensive work with these teachers, we would have planned future staff development on the basis of our evaluation data. But following Guba and Lincoln's (1989) advice, we would have presented our evaluation data to the teachers, led them to share their various constructions of those data, used the questions from the preceding section to spark discussion, and worked toward consensus on what kinds of staff development the group felt would be most helpful.

From our construction of the evaluation data, we suspect that the teachers could benefit from learning more specifics to promote the acquisition of technical-language proficiency and more specifics about how to direct small-group discussions. The content and the priorities would have to emerge, however, from constructions developed with the teachers of their needs and wants.

CONCLUSIONS

We began the 1995–96 project in the belief that Latino students' difficulties with mathematics were exacerbated by traditional mathematics-teaching behaviors. Among such behaviors, we included an overemphasis on lecture; the hurried presentation of a great amount of mathematical information at the expense of making sure that students internalize some basic understandings; and the practice of simplifying material to promote students' success by, for instance, having students give short answers as the teacher leads them step-by-step through problem-solving processes that make sense to the teacher, with little or no consideration of whether they make sense to the student.

Our study of CALLA and our introduction to constructivist views of learning have increased our skepticism about the effectiveness of some of those traditional behaviors. We are confident that students' understanding and self-reliance as problem solvers will be fostered by new behaviors such as attention to the technical language of mathematics; group problem solving; experimentation with various approaches to solving problems; student explanation, discussion, and debate; and deliberately teaching students strategies they can use to regulate their own learning. Thus, we see ourselves in the process of constructing new views of mathematics teaching. But in addition, we find ourselves linking these views to constructivist models for staff development and evaluation.

We end with the declaration of three hopes: first, that giving students more opportunities to construct and explicate mathematical meanings will make them better mathematicians; second, that designing staff development to help teachers construct new views of teaching and learning will make them better mathematics teachers; and third, that giving teachers (and students as well) a greater voice in interpreting the findings of program evaluations will make us better evaluators and designers of effective programs in the future.

REFERENCES

Chamot, Anna U., and J. Michael O'Malley. *The CALLA Handbook: Implementing the Cognitive Academic Language Learning Approach.* Reading, Mass.: Addison-Wesley Publishing Co., 1994.

Collier, Virginia P. *Promoting Academic Success for ESL Students: Understanding Second Language Acquisition for School.* Elizabeth, N.J.: New Jersey Teachers of English to Speakers of Other Languages–Bilingual Educators, 1995.

Crandall, JoAnn, Theresa Corasiniti Dale, Nancy C. Rhodes, and George Spanos. *English Skills for Algebra.* Englewood Cliffs, N.J.: Prentice Hall Regents, 1987.

Darling-Hammond, Linda, and Milbrey W. McLaughlin. "Policies That Support Professional Development in an Era of Reform." *Phi Delta Kappan* 76 (1995): 597–604.

De Avila, Edward A. "Bilingualism, Cognitive Function, and Language Minority Group Membership." In *Linguistic and Cultural Influences on Learning Mathematics,* edited by Rodney R. Cocking and José P. Mestre, pp. 101–21. Hillsdale, N.J.: Lawrence Erlbaum Associates, 1988.

Guba, Egon G., and Yvonna S. Lincoln. *Fourth Generation Evaluation.* Newbury Park, Calif.: Sage Publications, 1989.

Heath, Shirley Brice. *Ways with Words: Language, Life, and Work in Communities and Classrooms.* New York: Cambridge University Press, 1983.

Ivory, Gary, Linda Calk, Lucille Armendariz-Housen, and Dolores Chaparro. "Analyzing Videotape of Hispanic Students' Discussions of Standardized Mathematics Test Items." Ysleta Independent School District, 1995. (Duplicated)

Mestre, José P. "The Role of Language Comprehension in Mathematics and Problem Solving." In *Linguistic and Cultural Influences on Learning Mathematics,* edited by Rodney R. Cocking and José P. Mestre, pp. 201–20. Hillsdale, N.J.: Lawrence Erlbaum Associates, 1988.

O'Malley, J. Michael, and Anna U. Chamot. *Learning Strategies in Second Language Acquisition.* New York: Cambridge University Press, 1990.

Paris, Scott G., and James P. Byrnes. "The Constructivist Approach to Self-Regulation and Learning in the Classroom." In *Self-Regulated Learning and Academic Achievement: Theory, Research, and Practice,* edited Barry J. Zimmerman and Dale H. Schunk, pp. 169–200. New York: Springer-Verlag, 1989.

Rohrkemper, Mary M. "Self-Regulated Learning and Academic Achievement: A Vygotskian View." In *Self-Regulated Learning and Academic Achievement: Theory, Research, and Practice,* edited Barry J. Zimmerman and Dale H. Schunk, pp. 143–67. New York: Springer-Verlag, 1989.

Schifter, Deborah. "A Constructivist Perspective on Teaching and Learning Mathematics." *Phi Delta Kappan* 77 (1996): 492–99.

Schwandt, Thomas A. "Constructivist, Interpretivist Approaches to Human Inquiry." In *Handbook of Qualitative Research,* edited by Norma K. Denzin and Yvonna S. Lincoln, pp. 118–37. Thousand Oaks, Calif.: Sage Publications, 1994.

Spanos, George, Nancy C. Rhodes, Theresa Corasaniti Dale, and JoAnn Crandall. "Linguistic Features of Mathematical Problem Solving: Insights and Applications." In *Linguistic and Cultural Influences on Learning Mathematics,* edited Rodney R. Cocking and José P. Mestre, pp. 221–40. Hillsdale, N.J.: Lawrence Erlbaum Associates, 1988.

Westby, Carol. "Learning to Talk—Talking to Learn: Oral-Literate Language Differences." In *Communication Skills and Classroom Success: Therapy Methodologies for Language-Learning Disabled Students,* edited by Charlann Simon, pp. 189–213. San Diego: College Hill Press, 1987.

TexPREP and Proyecto Access
Making Mathematics Work for Minorities

13

Julio C. Guillén
Manuel P. Berriozábal

International comparisons of the performance in mathematics and science of students from the United States and those from other countries show that the achievement level of American students in these areas is below that of students in other industrialized nations, such as Japan and Germany. Medrich and Griffith (1992) summarized past studies in mathematics and science by country and reported that the United States ranked in the middle for thirteen-year-olds and near the bottom for students in the final year of secondary school mathematics. The rankings for the sciences were higher for ten-year-olds' core tests but lower for the core tests of students in the last year of secondary school.

At the national level, in a follow-up study to the report *A Nation at Risk* (U.S. Department of Education, National Commission on Excellence in Education 1983), Blank and Engler (1992) examined data from several surveys assessing the progress of grades K–12 students in science and mathematics in the United States. They observed that scores on the National Assessment of Educational Progress had increased since 1982 but that the level of students' proficiency was still low. They further observed that students scored below the level of proficiency that is expected of them for their age and grade level. The authors recommended that mathematics educators should give more emphasis to mathematical reasoning, higher-level problem solving, and applications in their teaching because few students performed at acceptable levels in these areas.

O'Neil (1991) concurs with Medrich and Griffith and with Blank and Engler when he says that far too few students receive instruction in advanced topics in mathematics and science in grades K–12. He further argues that cultural values, attitudes, the media, and other factors contribute to a belief that for many students, high achievement in mathematics and science is either not worth striving for or is unattainable. One of the solutions he proposes is that all students should be required to take college preparatory mathematics before they enter college.

Some people view socioeconomic status (SES), race or ethnicity, and gender as factors that may influence the low achievement of U.S. students in mathematics and science. Hoffer, Rasinski, and Moore (1995) examined the relationships between gender, SES, the number of courses taken and completed in mathematics and science by high school students, and their scores on standardized tests. Their findings indicated that (1) gender was not a factor in the number of mathematics and science courses completed, (2) students from higher-SES families completed more courses in these subjects than students from families in lower SES levels, (3) African American and Latino students completed fewer courses in these subjects than students in other groups, and (4) within groups of comparable socioeconomic status, the number of courses completed was similar across races.

They also reported that in general, increases in test scores from the end of the eighth grade to the end of the twelfth grade were strongly related to the number of mathematics and science courses that students completed in high school, regardless

123

of gender, race or ethnicity, or SES, and that students who completed more courses in these subjects showed greater gains in their test scores.

Peng and Hill (1995) observed that at an early age all students have equally positive attitudes toward mathematics and science learning in school and have similar aspirations for mathematics- and science-related careers. However, as children get older, more minority students become unprepared to enter these fields as they fall behind in mathematics and science learning. Peng and Hill also say that a larger percent of minority students come from poor families and lack educational resources such as books and computers and that they are more likely to attend disadvantaged schools. Moreover, Peng and Hill affirm that minority parents are more likely than other parents to have a low educational level and to be unemployed and that they are less likely to provide academic support or serve as role models in mathematics and science learning to their children.

On the topic of mathematics-related intervention programs, Ortiz-Franco (1982) makes a distinction between two types of variables—affective and external—that should be taken into consideration in such programs for minorities. Affective variables such as enjoyment of mathematics might be affected by parental support, the existence of accelerated mathematics programs for young students, and the perceived usefulness of mathematics to future career plans or rewards. External variables such as counselors; teachers; curriculum; the identification and education of gifted minority students; peer interaction; and participation and support from the schools, the local community, and industry should also be features of an intervention program for minorities. This model, he explains, is based on intervention programs involving white women.

Another concern for education researchers and government education organizations that is related to intervention programs is the great number of engineers and others in mathematics-based professions that will be required in the twenty-first century. Matthews (1990) notes that a shortage of more than four hundred thousand science and engineering personnel is expected by the year 2000. On the basis of those prospects some investigators have stressed the need for a minority population that is better educated in mathematics and science to fill the jobs in mathematics-based careers.

Anderson (1992) urges all students to become involved in mathematics if the United States is to respond successfully to the projected employment needs in technical careers. He emphasizes the importance of a mathematics education for minority students in particular to meet that challenge. Wiley (1989) points out that the chronic underrepresentation of minorities and women in mathematics, science, and engineering education will have serious ramifications for America's technological future. A workforce made up increasingly of minorities, women, and the economically disadvantaged will be inadequately prepared unless more of these groups increase their participation in science and technology.

A report by the National Science Foundation (NSF) (1996) also stresses the need for making full use of all the human resources in the United States—including women, minorities, and persons with disabilities—to achieve success in international competition, to assert world leadership in science and engineering in an increasingly global economy, and to create an improved quality of life. The report presents data showing the underrepresentation of these groups in science and engineering.

For example, in 1993, minorities, women, and persons with disabilities who held Ph.D. degrees in science and engineering constituted only 7.8 percent of the entire pool of doctorates in these subjects. The other groups mentioned in the report are Asian, 9.8 percent, and white, 83.8 percent. This disparity has obvious repercussions in the job market. The NSF report also shows that 84.6 percent of the science and engineering labor force is white, 12.3 percent consists of minorities, women, and persons with disabilities; and 9.8 percent is Asian. Along the same lines, Davis (1996) presents data showing that women and underrepresented minorities have lower levels of employment in private business and industry. Scientists and engineers from these groups who hold doctoral degrees are likely to be employed in universities or four-year colleges. Women and underrepresented minorities with bachelor's degrees in science and engineering are most likely to be employed in government but less likely than other groups to be employed by private, for-profit companies.

The various reports and studies discussed above concur that in order to meet the demands of an increasingly technical society, the number of persons knowledgeable in mathematics, sciences, and technology—particularly women, minorities, and persons with disabilities—should be significantly increased. They also suggest that early intervention programs could be an important part of the effort to increase the number of minority scientists.

These intervention programs would stress the study of mathematics, science, and engineering beginning at the middle school level; they would be coupled with career awareness and exposure to the college environment. To face this challenge, states, local communities, schools, funding agencies, and professional organizations are developing programs to encourage students, particularly women and those in under-represented groups, to enter the fields of mathematics and science. Some examples are presented in the subsequent section.

SOME SOLUTIONS

As reported by Clarke (1994), the National Governors' Association has been working with states to develop policies and programs to assist the states in increasing the number of students choosing careers in science and engineering. That report discusses statewide programs from California, Connecticut, Georgia, Michigan, Montana, North Carolina, and Vermont. Most of the activities in the programs are aimed at preparing students to take college preparatory courses in mathematics and the sciences and at increasing the participation of women, Native Americans, and other minority groups in those fields. Examples of other, local programs are presented in several reports such as Archer (1993), Hayden and Gray (1990), Fitzgerald (1990), Orzech and Borden (1990), and the Mathematical Association of America (MAA) (1997).

In particular, Archer (1993) describes the efforts of three urban districts participating in the Urban Schools Science and Mathematics Program to enhance mathematics and science education in the middle grades and to prepare more African American, Latino, and female students for careers in technology and the sciences. Career awareness, science fairs, a school banking program, efforts to build self-esteem, and professional development for teachers are features of those programs. Hayden and Gray (1990) describe a "Saturday Academy" with three basic components (electrical engineering, computer science, and mathematics) that is designed to provide enrichment experiences for academically talented minority youth without cost to them.

A summary of more-recent and current programs is presented in the Strengthening Underrepresented Minority Mathematics Achievement directory (MAA 1997), which cites 119 programs supported by foundations, agencies, industries, universities, organizations, and individuals. Sixteen entries in that summary are related to a program started in 1979 in San Antonio, Texas: the Texas Prefreshman Engineering Program (TexPREP). The following section describes this intervention program.

THE TEXAS PREFRESHMAN ENGINEERING PROGRAM

Since summer 1979, a partnership consisting of various Texas colleges and universities has conducted the Prefreshman Engineering Program (PREP). Initially limited to San Antonio, the PREP educational model has been adopted by twenty community and senior colleges in eleven cities in Texas. This state-wide program is called the Texas Prefreshman Engineering Program, or TexPREP (Berriozábal 1997). In 1997, the TexPREP model was replicated in seven states across the country under the name Proyecto Access.

The purpose of TexPREP is to identify achieving middle school and high school students with the potential to be engineers or scientists and to give them needed academic reinforcement so that they can successfully pursue engineering and science studies in college if they choose to do so. To accomplish its purpose, TexPREP has developed an academic model with college mathematics as the focus of its curriculum.

In addition to the academic component, participating students also receive information about professional opportunities in mathematics-based careers. Guest speakers' personal experiences expose the participants to a multitude of careers in engineering, mathematics, and science. Women and minority students are special targets of TexPREP.

Program Curriculum

TexPREP is an academically intense, eight-week summer program that stresses the use of technology and the development and application of abstract reasoning skills, problem-solving skills, and test-taking skills. The program guides the identified promising students in acquiring the knowledge and skills required for success in mathematics-based professions. TexPREP runs in June and July.

The middle school participants begin with PREP 1 in their first summer in the program and move on to PREP 2 and PREP 3 in subsequent years. All three programs include abstract reasoning, problem solving, guest speakers, field trips, and test taking practice.

A typical day at TexPREP for first-year students starts at 10:00 a.m. with a guest speaker, usually a scientist or engineer. At 11:00 a.m., the students study logic; at 12:00 noon, they have lunch; at 1:00 p.m., they pursue problem solving; at 2:00 p.m., they investigate engineering or computer science; and at 3:00 p.m., they study or do research. The schedules for the second and third years are essentially the same, but the mathematics and problem-solving components differ from year to year, as shown in figure 13.1.

PREP 1
Problem Solving 1: Prealgebra, algebra, or geometry
Logic
Computer science
Engineering

PREP 2
Problem Solving 2: Prealgebra, algebra, or geometry
Physics
Algebraic structures

PREP 3
Problem Solving 3: Data analysis
Probability and statistics
Technical writing

Fig. 13.1. The TexPREP curriculum

In all three years, the students are issued written course notes, and they attend daily classes in the form of lectures, demonstrations, or presentations. In addition, group projects and teamwork encourage the students to create a cooperative learning environment. The students are held accountable for their own learning and that of their peers. In addition, the students are given class and daily homework assignments and laboratory projects. Tests and final examinations are administered to assess their progress and achievement level in each course.

On the first day of the program, the participants at each site are usually divided into small seminar groups of twenty students. Placement in a group is determined by a combination of a student's performance on a placement examination and academic grade level. Rarely, for example, would a seventh-grade student be placed in a group of predominantly ninth-grade students.

At all TexPREP sites, the instructors include college faculty members, middle school and high school teachers, air force and navy officers, and civilian engineers and scientists. The faculty members normally teach three classes each day and are available to work individually with participants before and after each class day.

Also, undergraduates studying engineering and science serve as "program assistant mentors." Each mentor accompanies his or her group to each class, grades homework, reviews difficult material with the participants, assists them in their projects and homework, and prepares them to take examinations.

With a grant from the National Science Foundation in 1991, a writing team consisting of twenty-eight San Antonio PREP instructors and eleven high school students who were San Antonio PREP graduates compiled a TexPREP start-up kit. This kit consists of an operations manual and a complete set of curricular materials covering the aforementioned subjects. Since 1992, these materials have been in use at all TexPREP sites.

TexPREP students are expected to maintain at least a 75 percent average in their academic performance throughout the eight weeks of the summer program. However, participants receive a certificate for successful completion if their final average is 70 percent or better. This practice accommodates low performance in the final examinations.

The retention rate from the beginning to the end of the program each summer is between 80 and 85 percent. Students drop out mainly because of academic underperformance. Statewide figures for 1996 indicate that 2534 participants successfully completed the summer program out of the 3055 who started it. In San Antonio, 1155 completed the summer program out of the 1360 who started it.

In addition to the reinforcement provided by the interaction with teachers outside the classroom, all-day access to a mentor, cooperative assignments, counseling services, free lunches, and stipends for poverty-level students, the Texas Education Agency has authorized local school districts to grant one unit of elective credit applicable to high school graduation for each year of successful completion of the TexPREP curriculum. Middle school students can bank earned credits until they enter high school.

Program Recruitment

The recruitment of summer participants begins in early winter. The offices of the various TexPREP sites send program brochures and applications to mathematics and science teachers, counselors, and principals at all local middle schools and high schools, as well as to local minority advocacy groups like the League of United Latin American Citizens, the National Association for the Advancement of Colored People, associations of housing-project residents, and local chapters of the Texas Alliance for Minorities in Engineering. Brochures and applications are also sent directly to students who were first- and second-year participants in the previous summer. Those students are invited to apply for the subsequent summer.

The staff members at each TexPREP site also accept invitations from local schools and PTA groups to make presentations about TexPREP. They make a special effort to visit predominantly minority schools.

A majority of the participants each summer come from inner-city school districts. At the time of application, they must be middle school or high school students and must ordinarily have a B or better grade-point average. They are selected on the basis of grades, recommendations from teachers or counselors, and demonstrated interest in science or engineering.

Program Assessment

In 1979, when PREP was started at the University of Texas at San Antonio, some education professionals advised that the program was doomed to failure because middle school and high school students would never want to spend their summer studying mathematics and its applications. Furthermore, some people in academia made negative comments to the effect that minority students would not succeed in a structured and disciplined environment. The popular media echoed that negativism: "The Mexican-American community is not where engineers come from anyway," read a line in *SA: The Magazine of San Antonio* (Walker 1979). However, periodic evaluations of the program have proved that TexPREP has been successful.

In its nineteen years of operation, more than 14 000 students have successfully pursued at least one summer of TexPREP. Of those students, 80 percent have been members of minority groups and 54 percent have been women. At least 50 percent have come from low socioeconomic and educationally at-risk environments.

Each year, all TexPREP sites conduct a follow-up survey of former participants. In 1996, 3182 of the 5503 former participants responded to the survey. Data from that survey show the following record of achievements:

1. The high school graduation rate of TexPREP scholars is 99.9 percent.
2. Of the TexPREP scholars, 92 percent have entered college; 71 percent of those college entrants are Latino.
3. Of the college entrants, 88 percent graduate from college.
4. Of the college graduates, 75 percent are members of minority groups and 70 percent are Latino.
5. Of those TexPREP scholars who graduate from college, 56 percent do so as science or engineering majors.
6. Of the engineering and science graduates, 70 percent are members of minority groups and 63 percent are Latino.

Table 13.1 shows more details by ethnicity and gender for the seventeen-year period 1979–95 and summarizes the college participation rates of former TexPREP scholars. Because of their effectiveness, which is evident in those statistics, the original San Antonio PREP and the current TexPREP programs have been cited as successful model intervention programs by public and private agencies such as the National Research Council, Mathematical Sciences Education Board; the U. S. Department of Energy; the U. S. Congress; the Texas State Senate; the Ford Motor Company; and many other organizations. In 1997, San Antonio PREP received a Presidential Award for Excellence in Science, Mathematics, and Engineering Mentoring.

Funding for TexPREP

Since a significant number of minority students come from low-income families, TexPREP does not charge any tuition or fees to them. Thus, the economic status of the student is not a barrier for participating in the program. Consequently, operating a statewide program such as TexPREP is an enormous economic challenge. For example, the cost of conducting the program in 1996 alone was $3.2 million. Financial and in-kind support for the program over the years has been provided by various public and private agencies (the number of sponsors or benefactors ranges annually between 200 and 250). For instance, the National Aeronautics and Space Administration (NASA), the U.S. Department of Energy, and the U.S. Department of Agriculture—Texas Department of Human Resources are public agencies that have provided funding for TexPREP.

Examples of in-kind support include the following: local school districts contribute the full-time services of middle school and high school teachers; the air force and navy contribute the full-time services of officers trained in engineering who serve as instructors; local industries hire undergraduate engineering and science majors for

Table 13.1
Summary Data of College Participation Rates and College Majors of TexPREP Graduates for the Seventeen-Year Period 1979–95, by Ethnicity and Gender

Major Field of Study	Native American			White			African American			Latino			Asian and Other			Total		
	Gender			Gender			Gender			Gender			Gender			Gender		
	F	M	Total	F	M	Total	F	M	Total	F	M	Total	F	M	Total	F	M	Total
Engineering	2	1	3	42	76	118	28	31	59	218	333	551	18	35	53	308	476	784
Science	4	1	5	69	74	143	52	35	87	307	292	599	39	36	75	471	438	909
Other	4	1	5	66	69	135	45	22	67	487	367	854	27	17	44	629	476	1105
Undecided	0	0	0	10	4	14	11	6	17	58	48	106	6	4	10	85	62	147
Subtotal	10	3	13	187	223	410	136	94	230	1070	1040	2110	90	92	182	1493	1452	2945
No college	0	2	2	9	8	17	10	16	26	73	112	185	3	4	7	95	142	237
Total	10	5	15	196	231	427	146	110	256	1143	1152	2295	93	96	189	1588	1594	3182

the summer and contribute their services as mentors; and in some TexPREP sites, local colleges of education identify graduate students in counseling who serve as counselors at no cost to the program.

One of the latest contributions to TexPREP is a $1 million grant from NASA to the Hispanic Association of Colleges and Universities to replicate the TexPREP program in seven states. This program, called Proyecto Access, is described in the following section.

PROYECTO ACCESS

Proyecto Access was developed in 1996 by the Hispanic Association of Colleges and Universities (HACU) in collaboration with the University of Texas at San Antonio (UTSA), and with financial support from the NASA. This project was designed as a replica of TexPREP to serve Latino students in grades K–12 in communities near seven colleges and universities outside Texas whose student enrollment is at least 25 percent Latino. These colleges are Jersey City State College, Jersey City, New Jersey; Hostos Community College, Bronx, New York; Richard J. Daley College, Chicago, Illinois; Florida International University, Miami, Florida; Los Angeles City College, Los Angeles, California; New Mexico State University, Las Cruces, New Mexico; and Pima Community College, Tucson, Arizona.

Each of the seven institutions was expected to recruit 50 middle school students for PREP 1 in summer 1997. The summer program of Proyecto Access runs from June to August depending on the academic calendar of the school districts involved. However, because of the successful history of TexPREP, a greater number of applications were received, and the sites accepted an average of 60 students to launch their programs. A total of 539 students applied, 426 were accepted, and 349 successfully completed the eight weeks of the program. See table 13.2 for summary statistics by grade, ethnicity, and gender. The graduation and retention rates from all these sites are similar to those of the TexPREP program. The long-term results from all seven Proyecto Access sites will not be available until the PREP 1 students enroll in college in the year 2001 and graduate four to five years thereafter.

The staffing at each Proyecto Access site followed that of TexPREP: a director, a secretary, a database manager, instructors (college professors and middle school or high school teachers), mentors, and counselors.

Table 13.2
Data for Proyecto Access for Summer 1997, by Grade Level, Ethnicity, and Gender

Applied

Ethnicity	5			6			7			8			9			10			Total		
	F	M	Total	F	M	Total	F	M	Total	F	M	Total	F	M	Total	F	M	Total	F	M	Total
Native American	0	0	0	0	2	2	0	0	0	1	0	1	0	0	0	0	0	0	1	2	3
White	0	0	0	5	1	6	11	13	24	7	15	22	1	1	2	0	0	0	24	30	54
African American	0	0	0	11	4	15	13	11	24	10	0	10	0	0	0	1	0	1	35	15	50
Latino	0	1	1	39	40	79	78	83	161	37	25	62	29	16	45	2	3	5	185	168	353
Asian and Other	0	0	0	2	1	3	38	30	68	1	7	8	0	0	0	0	0	0	41	38	79
Total	0	1	1	57	48	105	140	137	277	56	47	103	30	17	47	3	3	6	286	253	539

Started

Ethnicity	5			6			7			8			9			10			Total		
	F	M	Total	F	M	Total	F	M	Total	F	M	Total	F	M	Total	F	M	Total	F	M	Total
Native American	0	0	0	0	2	2	0	0	0	1	0	1	0	0	0	0	0	0	1	2	3
White	2	2	4	7	2	9	9	11	20	6	14	20	2	1	3	0	0	0	26	30	56
African American	0	2	2	10	11	21	9	12	21	2	0	2	2	0	2	1	0	1	24	25	49
Latino	2	2	4	25	44	69	52	59	111	31	25	56	15	12	27	2	3	5	127	145	272
Asian and Other	0	1	1	5	4	9	17	11	28	1	6	7	1	0	1	0	0	0	24	22	46
Total	4	7	11	47	63	110	87	93	180	41	45	86	20	13	33	3	3	6	202	224	426

Completed

Ethnicity	5			6			7			8			9			10			Total		
	F	M	Total	F	M	Total	F	M	Total	F	M	Total	F	M	Total	F	M	Total	F	M	Total
Native American	0	0	0	0	1	1	1	0	1	0	0	0	0	0	0	0	0	0	1	1	2
White	1	0	1	7	1	8	8	9	17	4	11	15	2	1	3	0	0	0	22	22	44
African American	0	0	0	9	6	15	8	9	17	2	11	13	2	0	2	1	0	1	22	26	48
Latino	2	1	3	20	38	58	44	43	87	25	19	44	13	10	23	1	3	4	105	114	219
Asian and Other	0	0	0	2	3	5	14	10	24	1	5	6	1	0	1	0	0	0	18	18	36
Total	3	1	4	38	49	87	75	71	146	32	46	78	18	11	29	2	3	5	168	181	349

Each site added unique features to the basic model to fit their local conditions. For instance, at Jersey City State College, a chess club, Web-page development, Saturday follow-up, and graphing calculators were incorporated into the program (Guillén and Riggs 1997). For coordination purposes, the directors of the seven sites attended meetings and workshops in San Antonio, Texas, and Miami, Florida, and the executive director of the national program, the database coordinator, and HACU representatives visited all sites twice—before and during the summer program.

In summary, for the first summer, Proyecto Access proved to be as successful in all seven states as TexPREP has been in Texas. The good results from the same model might be attributed to the highly structured curriculum, the recruiting procedures, and all the support for the academic component. In part because of this success, NASA has awarded another $1 million for HACU to continue Proyecto Access in 1998 and to open a new site in Denver, Colorado. In summer 1998, all eight sites will run PREP 1 with new students, and the seven original sites will also operate PREP 2 for their 1997 PREP 1 graduates.

SUMMARY AND CONCLUSIONS

In this article we discuss two successful early intervention programs—TexPREP and Proyecto Access—in mathematics, science, and engineering that are designed to serve women and minorities. For more details on these projects, please consult Berriozábal (1997) and Guillen and Riggs (1997).

The success of these programs can be attributed to the structure of the program, to the student selection process, and—most important—to the active participation of the community, from parents to government agencies. Guillen and Riggs (1997) describe in detail the involvement of families, local school officials, local mass-media organizations, and other members of the community at large in Proyecto Access at Jersey City State College in summer 1997. They also discuss how both the students and the community benefited from the program.

TexPREP and Proyecto Access programs, with their emphasis on serving minority students, particularly Latinos, are successful also because they communicate to the participants that they highly value education and stress the importance of education and the fact that hard work has its rewards. The experiences of TexPREP and Proyecto Access have disproved the myth that women and minorities cannot learn mathematics, science, and engineering in a structured academic environment.

If similar programs were initiated throughout the United States with the same degree of success, it is possible that twelve years after full implementation, proportional parity could be achieved in the representation of minorities in the science and engineering disciplines. We estimate that full implementation would require at least 400 000 middle school and high school minority participants each summer at a cost of approximately $1 billion each year in today's dollars. Certainly, when our society spends billions of dollars annually on, say, prisons, we can afford to invest such a comparatively small amount in the development of our human resources for our future well being in the world economic and technological market. TexPREP and Proyecto Access are effectively responding to the challenge of preparing minority students to be part of the scientific and technical workforce of the twenty-first century.

On the basis of the success of TexPREP and Proyecto Access, we make the following recommendations:

1. Any intervention program in mathematics, science, and engineering must espouse an educational philosophy that stresses personal excellence and wholesome intellectual development.

2. Academic intervention programs must emphasize the acquisition of self-esteem through hard work, commitment, and achievement on the part of the student.

3. College scholarships must be created for low-income high school students who excel in the college-preparatory, mathematics-based intervention program.

4. Two-year, state-of-the-art, postsecondary, high-technology vocational programs must be established as an alternative for successful graduates of mathematics intervention programs who decide not to pursue mathematics-based studies in a four-year college or university.

Programs such as TexPREP and Proyecto Access contribute to the development of a diverse workforce capable of responding to the demands of the technological world of the twenty-first century. Our overall objective is to educate women and minorities to become masters, not servants, of technology.

131

REFERENCES

Anderson, Beverly J. "Equity and Excellence in the Mathematical Sciences: A Challenge to America." Paper presented as the keynote address of the American Philosophical Society at the William Penn Foundation Symposium on Mathematics, Science, and Engineering, Philadelphia, 9 October 1992.

Archer, Elayne. *New Equations: The Urban Schools Science and Mathematics Program.* New York: Academy for Educational Development, 1993.

Berriozábal, Manuel P. "The Texas Prefreshman Engineering Program: Filling the Pipeline for Workforce Diversity." In *Proceedings of the 1995 National Symposium and Career Fair of the Society of Mexican American Engineers and Scientists,* edited by Gilberto Flores, José Garibaldo, and Fabian Rivera, pp. B-1–B-14. Long Beach, Calif.: Society of Mexican American Engineers and Scientists, 1997.

Blank, Rolf K., and Pamela Engler. *Has Science and Mathematics Education Improved since "A Nation at Risk"? Trends in Course Enrollments, Qualified Teachers, and Student Achievement.* Science and Mathematics Indicators Report. Washington, D.C.: Council of Chief State School Officers, Science and Education Assessment Center, Science and Mathematics Indicators Project, 1992.

Clarke, Marianne. *Achieving Equity in Mathematics, Science, and Engineering Education.* Washington, D.C.: National Governors' Association, 1994.

Davis, Abiola C. *Women and Underrepresented Minority Scientists and Engineers Have Lower Levels of Employment in Business and Industry.* SRS Data Brief, vol. 1996, no. 14. Arlington, Va.: National Science Foundation, Division of Science Resource Studies, 1996.

Fitzgerald, Sallyanne H. "Responding to National Concerns: A University/Secondary School/Business Partnership in Mathematics and Science Education." *School Science and Mathematics* 90, no. 7 (1990): 629–37.

Guillén, Julio C., and Richard Riggs. "Proyecto Access: Jersey City State College, NASA, and Hudson County Community." In *Jersey City State College Academic Forum* 6 (fall 1997): 5–6.

Hayden, Linda B., and Mary W. Gray. "A Successful Intervention Program for High Ability Minority Students." *School and Mathematics* 90, no. 4 (1990): 323–33.

Hoffer, Thomas B., Kennith A. Rasinski, and Whitney Moore. *Social Background Differences in High School Mathematics and Science Coursetaking and Achievement.* NCES 95-206. Washington, D.C.: U.S. Department of Education, National Center for Education Statistics, 1995.

Mathematical Association of America. *Directory of Mathematics-Based Intervention Projects: Strengthening Underrepresented Minority Mathematics Achievement (SUMMA).* Washington, D.C.: Mathematical Association of America, 1997.

Matthews, Christine M. *Underrepresented Minorities and Women in Science, Mathematics, and Engineering: Problems and Issues for the 1990s.* CRS Report for Congress. Washington, D.C.: Library of Congress, Congressional Research Service, 1990.

Medrich, Elliott A., and Jeanne E. Griffith. *International Mathematics and Science Assessments: What Have We Learned?* Research and Development Report 92-011. Washington, D.C.: U.S. Department of Education, National Center for Education Statistics, 1992.

National Science Foundation. *Women, Minorities, and Persons with Disabilities in Science and Engineering.* Washington, D.C.: National Science Foundation, 1996.

O'Neil, John. *Raising Our Sights: Improving U.S. Achievement in Mathematics and Science.* Alexandria, Va.: Association for Supervision and Curriculum Development, 1991.

Ortiz-Franco, Luis. "Suggestions for Increasing the Participation of Minorities in Scientific Research." In *Aspects of American Hispanic and Indian Involvement in Biomedical Research,* edited by J. V. Martinez and Diana I. Marinez, pp. 29–39. Bethesda, Md.: Society for the Advancement of Chicanos and Native Americans in Science, 1982.

Orzech, Miriam W., and Sue Borden. *SMILE: Science and Mathematics Investigative Learning Experiences.* Corvallis, Oreg.: Oregon State University, 1990.

Peng, Samuel S., and Susan Hill. *Understanding Racial-Ethnic Differences in Secondary School Science and Mathematics Achievement.* Research and Development Report 95-710. Washington, D.C.: U.S. Department of Education, National Center for Education Statistics, 1995.

U.S. Department of Education, National Commission on Excellence in Education. *A Nation at Risk: The Imperative for Educational Reform.* Washington, D.C.: U.S. Department of Education, National Commission on Excellence in Education, 1983.

Walker, Tom. "The Rise and Fall of UTSA." *SA: The Magazine of San Antonio,* November 1979, p. 63.

Wiley, Ed III. "Minorities Key to Maintaining Nation's Cooperative Edge, Analyst Says." *Black Issues in Higher Education* 5, no. 23 (1989): 13.

The Minority Mathematics and Science Education Cooperative (MMSEC) Success Story

14

Olga M. Ramirez

John E. Bernard

The purpose of this article is to share with the mathematics and science education community the experiences of the Minority Mathematics and Science Education Cooperative (MMSEC) in southern Texas. We begin with a general description of the MMSEC, follow with a discussion of some aspects of the implementation of the project, and conclude with a general statement of some of the lessons learned through the MMSEC. We hope that other educators can benefit from our failures and successes so that eventually our collective efforts can improve the representation of Latinos in mathematics-based careers.

MMSEC DEFINED

The Minority Mathematics and Science Education Cooperative is a comprehensive, long-range intervention model that assists schools in educating minority children more effectively in mathematics and science. MMSEC targets schools with a preponderance of culturally or socioeconomically diverse students from traditionally disadvantaged populations. MMSEC's strategy is to improve grades K–5 students' attitudes and academic achievement by developing their teachers' knowledge of, skills in, and attitudes toward mathematics and science. To do so, teachers receive (1) extensive developmental, multi-level, and spiraling content and pedagogical training; (2) opportunities to question, discuss, and learn with peers and selected university faculty and to observe, practice, and model active, hands-on teaching; (3) occasions to share their experiences and needs with, and request help from, peers, university faculty, and school administrators; and (4) released time for staff development and peer visitations, recognition for their efforts, and up-to-date equipment and instructional materials for their schools. These MMSEC provisions help teachers change from "where they are" to "what they can be" as teachers.

This success story summarizes the effort at the University of Texas—Pan American (UT—PA)/Edinburg Consolidated Independent School District (C.I.S.D.) MMSEC site in southern Texas during the first of two state-level MMSEC school cycles (1989–93 and 1993–96). Monthly from September through May and in a three-week course in June, this site-based experience expanded teachers' knowledge of mathematics and science through content courses and expanded their pedagogical knowledge and skills through training in approaches that motive students to learn by active involvement in meaningful activities. In addition, a three-day Training Institute was held each summer in Austin, Texas.

The MMSEC project was made possible through Texas Higher Education Coordinating Board Eisenhower Mathematics and Science Higher Education Grants and National Science Foundation Grants. The authors acknowledge and thank the principals and teachers of the UT—PA/Edinburg C.I.S.D. MMSEC Team for their contributions.

MMSEC enhances the skills and proficiency of the teachers who actually teach mathematics and science to minority children. Too often, these are the very teachers who shy away from staff development in mathematics and science or who are systematically overlooked by conventional staff development programs that have not appreciated their potential to become exemplary teachers. MMSEC brings excellence in learning and excitement into mathematics and science classrooms; moreover, it opens doors to opportunities in careers requiring strong foundations in mathematics and science.

MMSEC also includes three affective components that individually and collectively bolster teachers' perceptions of students' ability to succeed: (1) higher expectations for students' achievement, (2) awareness and respect for the diversity of students' cultures, and (3) efforts to include the parents of minority children in the education process. This agenda promotes changes in school environments that lead to greater achievement.

MMSEC COMMITMENT

At the UT—PA/Edinburg C.I.S.D. site, the MMSEC participants developed the "Declaration of Professional Conscience for Teachers" (Goodman 1980) whereby they adopted the belief that schools can be no better than the people working in them. Thus, this site's MMSEC team of university faculty, school administrators, and teachers publicly expressed their professional commitment to make MMSEC schools warm, friendly, supportive places where administrators and teachers work together to make children and parents welcome. Moreover, they committed themselves to improve the overall conditions of mathematics and science education.

With the adopted declaration came much responsibility. Directly trained MMSEC teachers (i.e., those who received direct training from university teacher educators) share their new skills and content and pedagogical knowledge with their peers and model higher expectations of their students and sensitivity to their students' cultures and to the parents' role in the children's education.

The principal's support and leadership is vital, since directly trained teachers require time to reflect on what they have learned, to plan on how to implement new knowledge in their classrooms, and to share formally and informally with their peers. Principals who understand and value this process implement creative ways to give their teachers the time to move toward their goals so that the responsibility does not become a burden. In short, MMSEC principals encourage and invest in MMSEC teachers, whom they cultivate and nurture to become model teachers.

THE SELECTION OF SITES

The UT—PA/Edinburg C.I.S.D. site was one of eight MMSEC sites selected by the Texas Higher Education Coordinating Board in 1989 to participate in the state cooperative. The foremost selection criteria were that the institution serve a significant number of minority and disadvantaged elementary school students and that it show a strong commitment to improve students' mathematics and science learning and achievement levels. A deciding factor in the selection of the UT—PA/Edinburg C.I.S.D. site was the collaborative relationship the education partners had established in previously funded Dwight D. Eisenhower Mathematics and Science projects.

Lamar and San Carlos Elementary Schools, selected from a pool of fourteen in Edinburg, Texas, were identified for having "bottom" achievement levels in reading and mathematics; no science scores were available, but they were thought to be low. The teachers and principals of these schools overwhelmingly supported their selection.

These schools' enrollments were about 99.9 percent Mexican-American; 94.5 percent of the children were from low-income families, 50 percent were from migrant-farm-worker families, and 90 percent were either in Chapter 1 Migrant or Chapter 1 Regular programs providing free or reduced lunches.

THE MMSEC PLAYERS

The significant players at the UT—PA/Edinburg C.I.S.D. site included the site coordinator (the MMSEC grant director), who was a university faculty member; one or two university teacher educators in mathematics or science; the participating district's assistant superintendent of curriculum and instruction; the director of special funded programs; the parental involvement coordinator; and three principals, two from the MMSEC intervention schools and one from a control (i.e., non-MMSEC) school. During the fourth year, the district's curriculum director and migrant director were appointed district MMSEC codirectors and worked closely with the site coordinator. Each site also had its local site evaluator, who was responsible for evaluating the data collected by the MMSEC state-level evaluator.

Ultimately, twenty-two teachers of grades K–5 from the two MMSEC schools served either as lead teachers or "key teachers." Each year approximately three hundred students of directly trained teachers and eight hundred students of indirectly trained teachers (i.e., teachers trained solely by directly trained MMSEC teachers through peer coaching) acquired new knowledge and teaching methods that they implemented in their mathematics and science classrooms with hands-on materials that had been commercially purchased or made in make-it-and-take-it workshops supported by the grant and provided by the school district.

In addition, the Dwight D. Eisenhower Mathematics and Science Higher Education Grants Program Director and the MMSEC State Coordinator represented the Texas Higher Education Coordinating Board. Their visionary direction and relentless dedication inspired confidence and hope that the MMSEC efforts would result in a school where successful mathematics and science curricula were in place and were highly valued.

BASELINE MATHEMATICS AND SCIENCE CONDITIONS AT THE MMSEC SCHOOLS

At the outset, the conditions for teaching mathematics and science were lamentable at the UT—PA/Edinburg C.I.S.D site. "Each teacher," the MMSEC teacher participants stated, "was on their own. We were very conservative, unorganized, would not share ideas or materials, and we would teach only mathematics and science information we felt a bit more comfortable with regardless of what was actually expected."

They further claim that their approaches to teaching mathematics and science were very "dry" and oriented toward lecture, with a heavy, page-by-page use of textbook lessons void of meaning and excitement. They admit that important mathematics and science concepts were taught sporadically with minimal attention to their real-world importance and little or no attention to developing the concepts over time. In addition, most of the teachers say that they either did not know how to use hands-on materials or lacked adequate materials.

These teachers felt frustrated because major portions of classes were spent reviewing for the Texas Assessment of Academic Skills with drill and practice of sample test items. To put it bluntly, mathematics and science were for the most part taught with a "halfhearted" and "back burner" attitude.

In fact, at the beginning of their involvement in the project, the MMSEC teachers stated that they felt very tense about teaching mathematics and science because of their lack of knowledge and inadequate preparation. Mathematics was taught for about one hour each day, and science was taught one hour a week. "The students," the teachers said, "were not learning mathematics and science."

"Students," the teachers continued, "displayed signs of boredom and found mathematics and science dull as they were forced to sit and listen to lecture presentations followed by ditto sheet work."

"No one at their schools nor the district level," the teachers thought, "provided dependable leadership for bettering mathematics and science teaching."

The teachers were afraid to ask for help out of fear of reprisal or loss of respect should their lack of teaching ability be revealed. Although the district made an effort to provide some staff development in mathematics (but none in science), usually only three teachers out of sixty from any given school were sent for training, and no provision was made to reach the others. "This," the teachers declared, "was not enough!"

Moreover, although the teachers were thought to be sensitive to the children's cultures, values, and family issues prior to MMSEC, in retrospect, even the teachers of the same ethnic and cultural background as their students now admit their naïveté about these affective areas. In fact, they stated, "We thought we didn't practice prejudiced behaviors in the classroom, and we found that we were doing it unconsciously and unintentionally."

Additionally, although teachers from these schools were already making attempts to include parents in their children's schooling, after becoming involved in the MMSEC evening sessions for parents (see the section on the parental-involvement component on page 140 for more details), they affirmed the importance of parental involvement.

DEVELOPING LOCAL MMSEC PLANS AND SELECTING KEY PERSONNEL

MMSEC project plans at the UT—PA/Edinburg C.I.S.D. site were initially agreed to primarily by the site coordinator, administrators, and principals. However, it was the teachers at the two schools who convinced the principals that the project would be worth participating in. As the project proceeded, the MMSEC teachers assumed greater responsibilities and were invited and encouraged to partake in greater decision making, complementing site-based management practices that had just been instituted in the school district. Throughout the duration of the project, the site coordinator (the university MMSEC grant director) was the person who had the primary responsibility of maintaining the integrity of MMSEC. At this particular site, the MMSEC site coordinator was known and respected by the principals and teachers. For this reason, an atmosphere of trust and collegiality and a sense of purpose permeated the relationship between the project coordinator and the site staff from the inception of the project.

After the Lamar and San Carlos Elementary Schools were selected as the MMSEC schools, the principals assisted in the selection of teacher-participants for the program. They determined that the curriculum assistants at each school would assume the role of MMSEC lead teachers and that the MMSEC key grade-level teachers would be experienced teacher-volunteers or teachers recommended by their peers to assume that role.

WORKING RELATIONSHIPS AMONG THE PRINCIPAL ENTITIES

Working relationships between the principal entities of MMSEC were not without difficulties. However, despite the various levels of hierarchical decision making and authority and the physical distances between the headquarters of the participating entities, communication breakdowns never occurred. All participants agreed on the goal of improved conditions for teaching mathematics and science, but the means of reaching our goal were not always clear or accurate. However, when logistical problems occurred, the ultimate goal (i.e., improving mathematics and science conditions) was never blocked or overshadowed by the difficulties or uncertainties.

The dedicated local MMSEC team, by trial and error and with a problem-solving attitude, adjusted appropriately. When problems arose, they were viewed as part of the change process.

The MMSEC team were convinced that serious educational reform was occurring that was worthy of their investment. More important, they could be proud that the change was due to their involvement and sacrifices.

MMSEC CONTENT TRAINING

During summer 1989, the local MMSEC site team attended the first MMSEC Summer Institute. At that institute, the MMSEC model consisting of three content components (mathematics, physical science, and life science) and three affective components (enhancing students' expectations, cultural awareness, and parental involvement) was explained in detail. The specific sequence of content training was decided by the site participants, but the sequence of training in affective areas was designated by the state-level director and coordinator to provide appropriate training and direction annually at state-level summer institutes.

The UT—PA/Edinburg C.I.S.D. site conducted the first mathematics in-service training course during the initial nine months of the project, and the first three-week mathematics summer content course was held in June 1990. The first-year content included mathematical concepts and generalizations and processes of mathematical constructs, and it incorporated manipulatives and other appropriate instructional materials. The pedagogical training included small-group, hands-on, experiential, technology-supported simulations and emphasized a discovery approach. The second year's nine-month in-service-training period combined mathematics, which was covered in the first four months, and physical science, which was covered in the last five months. The second summer course was devoted to physical science. The mathematics training was conducted by two mathematics or mathematics education university teachers, and the physical science training was conducted by two university physical scientists.

A similar nine-month in-service course in the life sciences took place in the third year and in the summer of that program year. The life science training was conducted primarily by a university biologist and two consultant-specialists in fish and spiders.

Chemistry training occurred during the fourth and final year of the project. It was conducted primarily by a university chemist and a university science educator.

The university faculty members were invited to participate as MMSEC trainers because of their interest in, and experiences with, elementary school teachers or students and their ability to communicate effectively the objective of adopting higher expectations for academic achievement. They were also expected to be willing to change their traditional teaching practices. Thus, various approaches such as field trips, laboratory experiments, videos, models, role playing problem-solving situations, and make-it-and-take-it workshops were integrated into the training these educators provided. More-conventional lectures and textbook studies were also included, but they were the exception rather than the rule. These methods were congruent with the philosophy of MMSEC to effect change in the teaching of mathematics and science in the schools and in higher education.

MMSEC AFFECT TRAINING

The GESA Component

Toward the end of the first year of the MMSEC, the Gender/Ethnic Expectations and Student Achievement (GESA) training modules were presented at the two sites with varying degrees of success. At one school, the GESA models were a great success, but the results were more modest at the other site. MMSEC schools valued GESA because it is based on the very belief they eventually embraced; that is, that in order to ensure equitable quality and excellence, schools need to confront directly the issue of gender, racial, and ethnic bias in teachers' interactions with students (Grayson and Martin 1988).

All the teachers from the MMSEC schools were invited to participate in the GESA training. Approximately 75 percent of them received the training, and approximately 50 percent of those originally trained implemented GESA behaviors (wait time, positive reinforcement, feedback, higher-order questions, grouping and organization, physical closeness, classroom management and discipline, enhancing students' self-concept) in their classrooms with adequate consistency. During the fourth year of MMSEC, teachers who had not received the initial GESA training were given in-service GESA training. Between the second and fourth years, indirectly trained teachers learned about GESA either by observing directly trained MMSEC teachers as they implemented GESA behaviors or by being observed by directly trained teachers. In a nonthreatening manner, the observers later shared with the observed teacher what they had seen.

The teachers admitted, " We were [initially] hesitant about having the GESA training. We were very insecure about having other teachers coming to observe us. We were afraid of criticism."

Today, those same teachers comment, "We have no idea how we could have ever taught effectively without practicing GESA behaviors. We're so glad GESA training was provided."

After one of the training sessions one teacher commented, "Where was GESA when I attended the university! I never realized what I was doing when I didn't call on the child without his hand up. I never wanted to put him in an embarrassing spot. Instead, I was sending the message to that child that I had no expectations of him."

The MMSEC teachers at the two sites proclaim that GESA is suited for every school because such training has ramifications for equitable teaching behaviors that are far more encompassing than one can imagine. As noted by MMSEC teachers, "a better, fairer future is more readily available for everyone when children are respected and appreciated for their uniqueness."

Modifications in teaching behaviors that resulted from the GESA training include greater teacher mobility about the classroom, more direct contact with each child, more encouragement of children to interact, and greater opportunities for students to respond to questions or to express opinions. The self-analyses made by the teachers as a result of their GESA experiences indicated that such training had had a powerful, positive influence on most of them.

An important aspect that sold the GESA component to the MMSEC teachers was the specific, positive attention given to GESA by the site coordinator and the university trainer by modeling and discussing GESA behaviors in the in-service sessions during the first year of mathematics training. Moreover, GESA was embraced by the site team as an important, integral component of the project rather than seen as an imposition.

The Cultural-and-Contextual-Awareness Component

During the initial part of the second year of the project, the cultural-and-contextual-awareness component required MMSEC teachers to become involved in activities that promoted awareness of their students' cultures. The UT—PA/Edinburg C.I.S.D. site team chose first to do an awareness assignment; hence, they surveyed their students to find how many of them were from migrant families, single-parent homes, rural areas, farm worker families, and the like. The demographic data enabled the teachers to know better the socioeconomic conditions of their students and gave them a basis for discussing issues affecting their disadvantaged students.

An awareness of students' racial background and heritage is essential to knowing, understanding, respecting, and positively dealing with their diverse cultures. But the MMSEC teachers realized that a deep understanding of children's diverse cultures requires more than a knowledge of their race, gender, heritage, language, age, values, habits, foods, nationality, holidays, feasts, heroes, or the like. As important as these cultural and contextual factors are, to know, understand, respect, and positively deal with the diverse cultures of schoolchildren requires a much deeper level of consciousness.

The MMSEC teachers at the UT—PA/Edinburg C.I.S.D. site made a conscious effort to reflect more deeply and to adjust appropriately when dealing with their students' life circumstances. The sample remarks in figure 14.1 were shared by the directly trained MMSEC teachers, who explained that respecting each child's circumstances was a way of respecting the cultural and contextual situations of his or her life.

Situation 1

Negative Remark Made by a Indirectly Trained MMSEC Teacher: "I don't care if the mom had to go take the baby to the doctor. My student should not have to stay home to watch the three-year-old. This is why students like this fall behind in school."

Culturally Sensitive Response Made by a Directly Trained MMSEC Teacher: "That's true, but we need to present other options to the mother. Maybe during a home visit, you can talk to her about Head Start or to ask a neighbor to help out during a dilemma. We need to stress the importance of the child coming to school, yet the mother probably needs to become aware of other options to evaluate problematic situations that will interfere with this happening."

Situation 2

Negative Remark Made by a Indirectly Trained MMSEC Teacher: "Why should I spend time having the migrant students catch up in class? They enroll late and leave early, so why should I kill myself teaching them?"

Culturally Sensitive Response Made by a Directly Trained MMSEC Teacher: "We have to insure a student's success so that they will be able to be better prepared for a more prosperous future. If this was your child, would you want him or her to be ignored by teachers?"

Situation 3

Negative Remark Made by a Indirectly Trained MMSEC Teacher: "Why should I work with this child who has already been retained? He already had his chance to learn. I need to focus on the other children."

Culturally Sensitive Response Made by a Directly Trained MMSEC Teacher: If you keep on neglecting that retained child, then for sure he will be a dropout. Instead keep building on what he knows. Show him that you expect more; help him try. He will produce more and he will succeed if you practice caring for him."

Fig. 14.1

The Parental-Involvement Component

The third MMSEC Summer Institute, held in July 1991, focused on the rationale for involving parents in their children's education. It was suggested that parents be considered critical collaborating contributors because they are the "glue" that holds all services together for the child. For the MMSEC teachers at the UT—PA/Edinburg C.I.S.D. site, this concept was not difficult to accept, since the district was already developing a parental-involvement component. Thus, with assistance from the district parental-involvement coordinator, a plan of action for parental involvement focusing on MMSEC activities was easily developed and followed.

The plan for parental involvement included five evening sessions in the 1991–92 school year that covered issues of parental involvement in mathematics and science and four similar activities in the 1992–93 academic year. At these sessions, MMSEC teachers presented parents with various mathematics or science activities being taught to their children and similar to those disseminated in *Family Math* (Stenmark, Thompson, and Cossey 1986). The parents attending the evening sessions at Lamar or San Carlos Elementary Schools were enthusiastic and highly motivated to learn the material. It was very stimulating to hear the parents, whose own formal education had been minimal and substandard and who in some instances were recent immigrants, commenting at the conclusion of those evening sessions that they wished they had more to offer to their children. Their enthusiasm for learning mathematics and science, often for the very first time, was inspirational.

As parents and teachers related in positive ways, a special bond was forged between the families of the children and the MMSEC schools. Those experiences affirmed that teachers and parents working side by side toward a common goal can complement and support each other in educating children. Asked why they were there, several parents responded, "We were asked more than three times to come, so we felt we were really wanted." Others mentioned, "We realize that we have a lot to learn about what takes place in school."

Indeed, the MMSEC parental-involvement component touched both parents and teachers and strengthened MMSEC teachers' and principals' perception that positive relations between schools and parents are extremely valuable and worth fostering for the sake of the children.

Peer-Coaching Component

By the middle of the second MMSEC year, the teachers receiving direct content training were frequently asked to begin sharing their newly acquired knowledge with other teachers. To accomplish this, a peer-coaching structure (Chapman and Laurel 1990) whereby principals and teachers scheduled MMSEC demonstration lessons once a month was developed by the site coordinator in collaboration with the district parental-involvement coordinator. An orientation meeting to discuss peer coaching was held for the teachers.

Although questions and concerns were raised at the orientation meeting, it was agreed that peer coaching would be tried. Within a month of the orientation meeting, the directly trained teachers gave demonstration lessons to their students or other teachers' students while other students observed. All teachers in the MMSEC schools participated by observing one another's classrooms by grade level.

One teacher commented, "It was the best thing that happened to our campus. The students really enjoyed having other teachers present lessons. Structured peer coaching such as this should be done more frequently. It was very tiring, but well worth it."

An indirectly trained MMSEC teacher related, "I loved the science experiments presented by my peers. I observed a variety of teaching styles and classroom-management techniques that I feel I would like to use in my classroom."

Indeed, this component proved to be exceptionally successful in promoting the dissemination of academic content to indirectly trained MMSEC teachers as well as in convincing them that they had a lot to learn from one another about teaching mathematics and science. The students were particularly fascinated with having other teachers present lessons, as the following comments indicate:

"Thank you for coming."

"What are you going to do next time?"

"I like it when you come to our room."

"I am going to show my brother what I learned today."

"Tell my teacher where she can get the materials you have."

In fact, it was the peer-coaching element that excited every teacher about MMSEC and that proved to be the catalyst for bonding them because it was through peer coaching that every teacher at the schools became more directly involved with MMSEC.

During spring 1990, the MMSEC teachers were asked to talk about cultural and contextual issues once a month with other grade-level teachers who were not receiving direct training. These discussions included questions brought up during the cultural-and-contextual-awareness training at the statewide second MMSEC Summer Institute held in August 1990.

By the end of the second year, the GESA and cultural-awareness training, coupled with the peer-coaching element, had calmed the MMSEC teachers' apprehensions about sharing new learnings, observing one another teach mathematics and science, reflecting about their students' cultural circumstances, accepting their weaknesses in teaching mathematics and science, and embracing the commitment to grow.

MMSEC FUNDING SOURCES

Each year's funding for MMSEC came from three grants: one for the nine-month school-based project, one for the summer course, and one for the three-day summer institute. The MMSEC schools received funding primarily from the Dwight D. Eisenhower Mathematics and Science Higher Education Grants Program administered by the Texas Higher Education Coordinating Board. Twice, during the 1991 and 1992 summer courses, the grants were funded by the National Science Foundation (NSF).

EXAMINING CHANGES IN TEACHING BEHAVIORS

In examining the changes in teaching behaviors, we made distinctions between directly trained MMSEC teachers, indirectly trained MMSEC teachers, and teachers from the control (non-MMSEC) school (Borich and Montgomery 1991; Montgomery 1992, 1993). Montgomery's (1993) report observes that when the participating sample of teachers was restricted to include only those trained at least once under the three components of MMSEC, in comparison to teachers in the control school (and controlling for Year 1 scores), a greater number of differences favoring the participating MMSEC teachers emerged.

Participating MMSEC teachers reported (1) a stronger belief than non-MMSEC teachers that they enjoy teaching mathematics, life science, and physical science; (2) that they know how to use mathematics, life science, and physical science teaching materials more effectively than non-MMSEC teachers to develop their students' mathematical and scientific knowledge and thinking; (3) that their students enjoy life science; and (4) that their schools are pleasant places in which to work.

At the UT—PA/Edinburg C.I.S.D MMSEC site the total number of years a student was taught mathematics by a teacher directly trained in mathematics was positively correlated with three (mathematical computation, mathematical problem solving, and total mathematical achievement) of the four student achievement variables as well as with all five attitude variables (school, class, reading, mathematics, and science).

Also self-reported by the teachers, validated by the school principals, and confirmed by the MMSEC state-level evaluation report (Montgomery 1993) was that as a result of the project the MMSEC directly trained teachers are less restrictive in their selection of mathematics and science activities than their indirectly trained counterparts. Project evaluation data also confirm that directly trained MMSEC teachers moved away dramatically from using dittos and from maintaining rigid, structured classrooms into modeling such teaching behaviors as establishing activity centers and creating a more flexible classroom structure. Cooperative-group work (Davidson 1990) is the standard rather than the exception in those classrooms. Teachers more frequently incorporate hands-on manipulatives to teach mathematics and science.

Furthermore, the documentation of classroom visitations made by the site evaluator, the site coordinator, and the accompanying university educators confirmed that the directly trained MMSEC teachers show more self-confidence and exhibit more flexible decision making and more positive assertiveness and risk-taking behaviors than non-MMSEC teachers. Directly trained teachers admit that they are more relaxed and are having fun when teaching mathematics and science, that they are more sensitive and responsive to their students' needs, and that they seem to "think on their feet" when conducting mathematics and science lessons.

In fact, these teachers state that *teaching for understanding* has become more important for them than teaching to the test, as they were once accustomed to doing. In their newly defined teaching roles, directly trained MMSEC teachers are leaders in modeling good teaching behaviors and in serving as teacher-mentors to their peers.

Consequently, the directly trained MMSEC key teachers at the UT—PA/Edinburg C.I.S.D. site have had a significant number of professional accomplishments. Out of the fourteen directly trained teachers, one was promoted to curriculum assistant and one to a counseling position; three became GESA certified instructors and served in that capacity in at least three other projects; and ten served as mathematics-curriculum writers, as mathematics peer-coaching mentors, or as experts in make-it-and-take-it mathematics-activity demonstrations in districtwide school projects.

The students of directly trained MMSEC teachers are known to be on-task, focused, and goal-directed and to enjoy the freedom to move around in their classrooms while being monitored and carefully guided through learning activities by their teachers. They are actively involved and interested in their learning. These students take the initiative to ask more questions and participate more readily in learning activities.

In comparison, the indirectly trained MMSEC teachers who have worked closely with the key teachers are exemplifying some of the behaviors mentioned above. However, some indirectly trained teachers who have had minimal commitment to MMSEC are, as expected, still hesitant about change and tend to depend on dittos for teaching and for assessment. They do not make as much use of student-activity centers, cooperative-group work, and hands-on teaching. Instead, their teaching styles still embrace lecture types of lessons, with children in more passive roles.

As a result, the students of the indirectly trained teachers are not as motivated to learn as the students of the directly trained teachers. Consequently, the indirectly trained teachers seem more stressed about not being able to reach their students effectively.

Moreover, the indirectly trained teachers are less likely to ask for help and are unable to envision outcomes. These weaknesses can perhaps be attributed to their lack of direct training or to their reluctance to accept and assimilate new teaching ideas. It has been noted by school principals and program evaluators that the indirectly trained teachers occasionally expressed feelings of being left out, even though they were sometimes reluctant to learn from their peers and were not enthusiastic at the outset about being considered to be MMSEC key teachers.

IMPORTANT LESSONS LEARNED

MMSEC is successful when personnel are willing to make a very strong, sustained commitment to improving learning conditions for minority students and their teachers. A project such as this will work if affective areas are given as much attention as cognitive areas—or more. The affective areas of training (students' expectations, cultural awareness, parental involvement) and the peer-coaching component were crucial to enhancing the educators' perceptions of the need to understand and work with the human circumstances of minority students and their teachers and principals.

A strong working relationship among the granting agency, the university, and the school district is essential for the success of a project such as MMSEC. This type of relationship can develop over time through smaller-scale projects in which the cooperating parties expand their commitment to improving mathematics and science education. Success can still occur, however, if at the outset the parties are prepared to take on a project of such magnitude.

For the MMSEC team at the UT—PA/Edinburg C.I.S.D. site, such preparedness involved cultivating a team-building approach to goal setting, apportioning responsibility, and maintaining growth. The school principals are essential to the team-building process. The principal holds the MMSEC team together and sustains participation by his or her leadership. With the endorsement of the school principals, most MMSEC teachers follow through with the project objectives with more explicit attention and awareness and give the project its due importance.

The university site coordinator is also important in keeping the project functioning, since he or she is responsible for managing the budget and coordinating activities so that the project's goals are attained. The site coordinator is also responsibile for keeping the lines of communication open between the funding agencies and the schools. With strong and consistent leadership and effective management, the site coordinator acts as a filter and mediator between individuals and the various constituencies connected to the project. He or she ensures that participants understand and work toward the goals set by the MMSEC. The university site coordinator acts as an authority figure who empowers constituents and promotes adherence to professional standards in mathematics and science education at all times.

Other important lessons learned from the MMSEC project include the following: Training elementary school teachers in mathematics and science content and methods requires sensitive and patient teacher educators. Teacher educators should, if possible, have experience working with elementary school teachers and should adjust to meet the cognitive and affective goals of the project. In particular, they should pay close attention to the teachers' and principals' understanding and receptivity of the content and methods. It is imperative that criteria for teacher educators include the following:

1. Experience working with elementary school teachers
2. A knowledge of grades K–12 (not just K–5) mathematics or science curricula and evaluation standards such as those in NCTM (1989), content knowledge (e.g., see Billstein, Libeskind, and Lott [1990]; Musser and Burger [1988]), pedagogical expertise (consult Burns [1992]; Post [1988]; and Fuys, Geddes, and Tischler [1988]), and a knowledge of psychological perspectives appropriate to mathematics and science learning (see Skemp [1971]; Davis, Maher, and Noddings [1990]; Dienes [1960]; Gagné [1971]; and Bruner [1971])
3. Sensitivity to the culture and conditions of minority students
4. An enthusiastic, nonthreatening, and flexible demeanor

5. A willingness to modify their own teaching behavior so that their modeling influences those whose standards they are trying to elevate

6. Reflection on the selection of mathematics and science activities to make sure that they are relevant and appropriate for elementary school teachers and their students without compromising content and rigor

7. A sensitivity to the need for selecting science and mathematics activities that are easily adaptable to the conditions of the local schools

Teacher educators are encouraged to present content objectives with laboratory and hands-on manipulative activities that are easily adapted. Repetition of content and methods is necessary to elementary school teachers' feeling comfortable and able to implement the content and teaching methods within a reasonable time. Universities are encouraged to collaborate with public schools to identify and reward faculty whose expertise lies in these areas.

Moreover, principals should be encouraged to formulate peer-coaching programs that match the GESA and cultural and contextual training. Peer coaching should be implemented as soon as possible in order to ensure that directly trained teachers can visit one another's classrooms to support one another. Also, the directly trained teachers should be allowed to share their knowledge with the indirectly trained teachers as soon as possible after they complete their training.

In addition, all instructional materials should be purchased in large quantities and in time for teachers to use them immediately after having been introduced to them. It is strongly recommended that a centrally located place, such as a learning-resource center or library, be identified where materials can be kept, cataloged, and made accessible to all teachers. The logistics, including timing and coordination, of accessibility to the materials should be addressed and clearly worked out as early as possible.

Most important, since a project such as MMSEC entails intensive effort and time, the cooperating school district administrators can ensure its success if they become involved with the project on a contining basis. The district should be willing to contribute released time for participating teachers to attend the training sessions, to prepare their classroom demonstrations, and to share lessons with other teachers. Further, financial support such as matching funds to purchase additional materials or to fund make-it-and-take-it workshops as needed should be considered strongly. Without voluntary local support of projects like MMSEC, reform in mathematics education will falter (National Research Council, Mathematical Sciences Education Board 1989). At the UT—PA/Edinburg C.I.S.D. site, MMSEC is recognized as a success story because a conscious effort toward reform was being institutionalized without compulsion.

Even though the teachers' commitment to MMSEC ideals took time to solidify, they eventually came to believe that mathematics and science can be learned by them and their minority and disadvantaged students. They came to accept wholeheartedly that mathematics and science are important areas of study; that means are available to teach these content areas effectively, that is, with understanding; and—most important—that disadvantaged students can learn mathematics and science when given an equitable opportunity full of enjoyable, meaningful activities that contribute to a well-balanced mathematics and science curriculum.

By offering culturally or socioeconomically diverse elementary school students from traditionally disadvantaged populations model intervention programs such as MMSEC, schools with a preponderance of Latino students are certain to encourage active engagement with mathematical and scientific ideas and thus to break some of the barriers that have kept Latino students from being prepared to pursue careers in mathematics and the sciences (U.S. Department of Education 1991; National Research Council, Mathematical Sciences Education Board 1989, 1990; Hyde 1989; Sparks 1983; Taylor 1986). In short, this MMSEC success story has been a lesson in "creating a better world" and encourages teachers of Latino and other elementary school students from traditionally disadvantaged populations to believe that they can be success stories, too (cf. Tobias, 1990).

REFERENCES

Billstein, Rick, Shlomo Libeskind, and Johnny W. Lott. *Mathematics for Elementary School Teachers: A Problem Solving Approach,* 4th ed. New York: Benjamin-Cummings Publishing Co., 1990.

Borich, Gary D., and Ellen Montgomery. *The Ten Best Things about MMSEC: First Interim Evaluation Report on the Minority Mathematics and Science Education Cooperative.* Paper submitted to the Eisenhower Mathematics and Science Education Grants Office of the Texas Higher Education Coordinating Board, March 1991.

Bruner, Jerome S. "Bruner on the Learning of Mathematics—a 'Process' Orientation." In *Readings in Secondary School Mathematics,* edited by Douglas B. Aichele and Robert E. Reys, pp. 166–77. Boston: Prindle, Weber, and Schmidt, 1971.

Burns, Marilyn. *About Teaching Mathematics: A K–8 Resource.* Sausalito, Calif.: Math Solutions Publications, 1992.

Chapman, Jim, and Elva G. Laurel. "Powerful Collaborations between Universities and School Sites." *Kappa Delta Pi Record* 26, no. 3 (1990): 77–79.

Davidson, Neil, ed. *Cooperative Learning in Mathematics: A Handbook for Teachers.* Menlo Park, Calif.: Addison-Wesley Publishing Co., 1990.

Davis, Robert B., Carolyn A. Maher, and Nel Noddings. *Constructivist Views on the Teaching and Learning of Mathematics. Journal for Research in Mathematics Education* Monograph No. 4. Reston, Va.: National Council of Teachers of Mathematics, 1990.

Dienes, Zoltan P. *Building Up Mathematics.* London: Hutchinson Educational, 1960.

Fuys, David, Dorothy Geddes, and Rosamond Tischler. *The van Hiele Model of Thinking in Geometry among Adolescents. Journal for Research in Mathematics Education* Monograph No. 3. Reston, Va.: National Council of Teachers of Mathematics, 1988.

Gagné, Robert. "Gagné on the Learning of Mathematics—a 'Product' Orientation." In *Readings in Secondary School Mathematics,* edited by Douglas B. Aichele and Robert E. Reys, pp. 157–65. Boston: Prindle, Weber, and Schmidt, 1971.

Goodman, Kenneth. "A Declaration of Professional Conscience for Teachers." Unpublished paper. Tucson, Ariz.: University of Arizona, 1980.

Grayson, Dolores A., and Mary Dahlbert Martin. *GESA (Gender/Ethnic Expectations and Student Achievement): Teacher Handbook.* Earlham, Iowa: Graymill, 1988.

Hyde, Arthur A. "Staff Development: Directions and Realities." In *New Directions for Elementary School Mathematics,* 1989 Yearbook of the National Council of Teachers of Mathematics, edited by Paul R. Trafton, pp. 223–33. Reston, Va.: National Council of Teachers of Mathematics, 1989.

Montgomery, Ellen. *Minority Mathematics and Science Education Cooperative, July 1991 through August 1992: Third Interim Evaluation Report.* Paper submitted to the Eisenhower Mathematics and Science Education Grants Office of the Texas Higher Education Coordinating Board, March 1993.

———. *Minority Mathematics and Science Education Cooperative, September 1990 through May 1991: Second Interim Evaluation Report.* Paper submitted to the Eisenhower Mathematics and Science Education Grants Office of the Texas Higher Education Coordinating Board, March 1992.

Musser, Gary L., and William F. Burger. *Mathematics for Elementary Teachers: A Contemporary Approach.* New York: Macmillan Publishing Co., 1988.

National Council of Teachers of Mathematics. *Curriculum and Evaluation Standards for School Mathematics.* Reston, Va.: National Council of Teachers of Mathematics, 1989.

National Research Council, Mathematical Sciences Education Board. *Everybody Counts: A Report to the Nation on the Future of Mathematics Education.* Washington, D.C.: National Academy Press, 1989.

———. *Reshaping School Mathematics: A Philosophy and Framework for Curriculum.* Washington, D.C.: National Academy Press, 1990.

Post, Thomas R., ed. *Teaching Mathematics in Grades K–8: Research Based Methods.* Newton, Mass.: Allyn & Bacon, 1988.

Skemp, Richard R. *The Psychology of Learning Mathematics.* New York: Penguin Books, 1971.

Sparks, Georgea Mohlman. "Synthesis of Research on Staff Development for Effective Teaching." *Educational Leadership* 41 (November 1983): 65–72.

Stenmark, Jean K., Virginia Thompson, and Ruth Cossey. *Family Math.* Berkeley, Calif.: Lawrence Hall of Science, University of California at Berkeley, 1986.

Taylor, Ross, ed. *Professional Development for Teachers of Mathematics: A Handbook.* Reston, Va.: National Council of Teachers of Mathematics and National Council of Supervisors of Mathematics, 1986.

Tobias, Sheila. *They're Not Dumb, They're Different: Stalking the Second Tier.* Tucson, Ariz.: Research Corporation, 1990.

U.S. Department of Education. *America 2000.* Washington, D.C.: U.S. Department of Education, 1991.

A Model of Tutoring That Helps Students Gain Access to Mathematical Competence

15

Yolanda De La Cruz

A knowledge of mathematics and science is essential for all members of our society. Our technological society increasingly expects our students to be able to understand and apply mathematical and scientific ideas. Achievement levels in these areas among students are cause for concern. An ever growing body of research documents that the American educational system is differently effective for students depending on their social class, race, ethnicity, language background, gender, and other demographic characteristics (D'Ambrosio 1990; Ogbu and Matute-Bianchi 1986; Erickson 1987; Mullis, Owen, and Phillips 1990; Oakes 1990). This differential effectiveness has been more pronounced for Latino students in mathematics than for their non-Latino white counterparts (De La Cruz 1991; Secada 1992; De La Cruz 1995a, 1995b, 1995c; Secada and De La Cruz 1996).

In my view, school reform programs have been developed without sufficient attention given to attaining the academic goals required for success among high-risk populations, and consequently implementation has been difficult. The reality of inequality in the daily lives of children must be taken into account in order to understand how to begin working with the constraints that interfere with gaining access to usable knowledge. The focus must be not only on high-quality instruction but also on how to provide effective support to students so that they can develop a positive image of themselves as successful learners. When children are included as partners in the learning process, they become active participants in that enterprise (De La Cruz 1996b).

Their participation in the learning process enables them to initiate creative, productive strategies. Moreover, when children are included as partners in learning, they feel that they belong in that process. Belonging and inclusion become the means by which children deal critically and creatively with their reality and discover how to participate in the transformation of their world.

This paper reports on the experiences gained from working for three years in an after-school tutoring project designed to improve mathematics teaching and learning environments for urban children in grades 1–3. We worked intensively in urban classrooms where teaching was done by project teachers collaborating with classroom teachers, by classroom teachers alone, and in an after-school tutoring program. Curriculum materials were written and continually adapted as needed, and individual children were tutored by research teachers, peers, parents, older students, and teacher's aides.

The after-school tutoring program was one effort to create more mathematics teaching and learning opportunities for teachers and students. From that work, theories of developmental levels in children's conceptual structures and models for some aspects of mathematics teaching and learning were developed (Fuson et al. forthcoming; Fuson, Smith, and Lo Cicero 1997; Fuson and De La Cruz unpublished).

The research reported in this paper was supported by the National Science Foundation (NSF) under grant no. RED 935373 and by the Spencer Foundation. The opinions expressed are those of the author and do not necessarily reflect the views of the NSF or of the Spencer Foundation.

This report focuses on the tutoring model, the Growth through Learning Model, developed from the After-School Mathematics Tutoring Program (ASMT). The tutoring model, shown in figure 15.1, illustrates how students can overcome constraints that have prevented them from gaining access to mathematical concepts. The Growth through Learning Model describes a holistic approach to teaching and learning through mentoring.

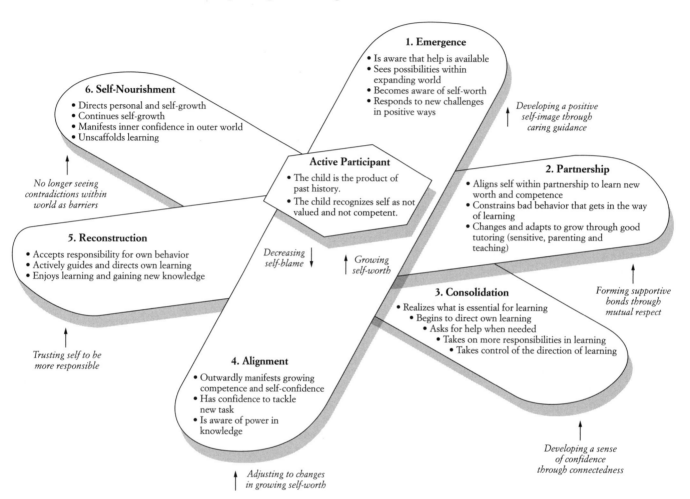

Fig. 15.1. The Growth through Learning Model

THE ASMT PROGRAM

The ASMT Program involved older students (in grades 4–8) in tutoring younger Latino students (in grades 1–3). Latino and non-Latino students were involved both as tutors and tutees. The experiences of the program illustrate the importance of teaching to the whole child and the importance of children's developing a positive self-image while gaining access to mathematical knowledge. Furthermore, the success of the ASMT Program shows the importance of operating on the affective domain of the learner and the positive impact of that intervention on her or his cognitive domain.

A major goal of the ASMT Program was to create an environment through which the younger students built on their basic mathematics knowledge to progress to further understanding. This environment was conducive to developing self-respect and self-worth to prevent the kind of academic retrogression that often contributes to dropping out of school.

Self-worth and self-blame have significant but opposite effects on learning. Mandler's (1984) analysis of mathematics classrooms suggests that negative beliefs about self can decrease effective mathematics learning. Students need supportive environments that increase self-worth and decrease self-blame. The Growth through Learning Model recognizes the significant but opposite influences that self-worth and self-blame have on learning and acknowledges the equally important effect of successful learning on self-worth.

The goal of the ASMT Program was set as part of an ongoing effort to seek ways to help young students develop mathematical understandings while the staff of the project identified constraints that prevent successful learning. The teachers in the large, urban, Midwestern school that housed the project have large classes and little time to help individual students. The families attempt to help their children when they can, but they are busy working and have little time to assist their children with academic work. When the parents come home, they often do not have the energy— and quite often they do not have either the required knowledge or pedagogic techniques—to help their children with schoolwork.

The ASMT Program also offered older students worthwhile after-school activities. For example, instead of suspending older students as punishment for infractions of school rules, the principal encouraged them to volunteer for the ASMT Program. If older students were found staying around the school with nothing to do, they were invited to attend the training sessions to prepare them to mentor and tutor younger children in mathematics.

The older students were required to sign a written commitment for the semester and attend the ASMT Program three days a week for an hour and fifteen minutes each session. Training sessions were held when students were able to meet with staff before, during, or after school as needed. The parents and teachers were eager to encourage these students.

The Students

The program began with ten pairs of students, with one younger and one older student in each pair, and grew to fifteen pairs over a period of eight weeks. The younger students, the tutees, were chosen by their teachers because they were unsuccessful in mathematics and were developing behavior problems. The older students, the tutors, were chosen for reasons mentioned earlier. The younger students were identified as *Los Novatos* (the novices), and the older ones were called *Los Expertos* (the experts).

The experts and the novices had commonly shared sociocultural histories or similar life experiences. *Shared histories* in this instance mean common experiences of poverty and difficulty in learning mathematics. Shared histories were important in the growth of the participants in this program because the inexperienced tutors were not afraid to help the younger students in an area in which they both were relatively weak. The older students became experts in the eyes of the novices even though they did not have that status outside the tutoring program. The members of some of the pairs were of different socioethnic backgrounds, for example, Latino and African American.

Although the experiences in the tutoring program provided insight into the growth of the experts as a result of their having "expert" status and experiences, this chapter focuses mainly on the novices and their growth in mathematics. However, our discussion also reports on some aspects of the program that affected the experts.

The tutoring challenges were accepted by the younger children because they were helped, and therefore affirmed, to be capable learners. These experiences inspired them to want to learn more mathematics. The novices were able to achieve success in the ASMT Program because they had caring tutors who took their responsibility seriously and made great efforts to help their tutees change.

The Program Director

The program director created an environment similar to that of a large family in which tutoring was conducted in a nurturing and nonthreatening way. The family environment was manifested in the language and affective behavior of the director toward the experts and the novices. She took on the role of a parent who cared enough to identify misbehavior and point out its effect on learning. She interacted extensively with the novices and the experts and cast them in responsible roles. These interventions, along with the continuing support of the family atmosphere, contributed to the success of the program.

Laosa (1978, 1980) writes of the impact such an environment can have on Latino children. He claims a family atmosphere bridges the abrupt discontinuity between the home and the school environments. Children are more at ease with interactions that most resemble those with which they are familiar. School practices that help link the home and the school are proving to be effective for Latino students (Moll and Diaz 1985; Moll, Amanti, and Gonzales 1992; De La Cruz 1996a; De La Cruz et al. 1995; Vasquez 1990).

The Roles of *Los Novatos* and *Los Expertos*

Although the experts shared the same social status in the program as the novices, there was a difference in their perceived roles. For example, one expert, Jackie, had been expelled from another after-school program for fighting. The principal encouraged Jackie to volunteer for the ASMT Program instead of punishing her by reporting the problem to her family.

The first day Jackie attended the ASMT Program, she fought with another tutor and was asked to talk to the director. The director reminded Jackie of her role as a model for the younger students and of the importance of modeling positive behavior. Jackie agreed to change her behavior and was allowed to stay in the program. She was encourage to set appropriate standards for the younger students to emulate. She was reminded that many of the younger students were having problems similar to hers in their own classrooms and needed to find more effective ways of dealing with those problems.

The experts had many opportunities to model appropriate behavior when faced with situations that required mediation among the novices. When a novice lost interest in working, an expert would be patient and react in a positive way to bring the novice's attention back to the task. These episodes played a very important part in creating a positive tutoring environment that benefited the novices. Active participation created an atmosphere of belonging among the novices. These experiences enabled them to advance in their cognitive understanding of mathematics and to develop their social skills as well.

THE STAGES IN THE GROWTH THROUGH LEARNING MODEL

The Growth through Learning Model in Figure 15.1 is described in stages to show the growth of the novices and the influence of the experts in the learning process. the novices perceived themselves, and were perceived by their regular teachers, as incapable of succeeding in mathematics or unwilling to do so. Although the novices had many limitations that impeded their learning, through their participation in the ASMT Program, they found that they were capable of learning and experienced intellectual growth in the caring hands of the experts.

Emergence

The first stage of the model, emergence, describes what occurred among the novices during the first several weeks in the program. The novices began to develop a positive self-image. They were treated with respect, which gave them support to try to learn. The novices were then able to risk sharing their feelings with the experts.

Thus, risk taking allowed the novices to learn in this supportive, "scaffold" tutoring situation. They began to believe in their self-worth after several successful experiences in learning mathematics. The novices realized they had the capacity to learn and began to accept this new self-image.

Quite often, the initial reason for many of the novices to attend the ASMT Program was not to learn more mathematics. Rather, they joined the program in order to get personal attention. Because they were behind in their schoolwork and they often were too shy or afraid to ask the teacher for help, they had accepted the idea that they were unsuccessful in mathematics and other subjects as well. During the program, the novices improved their knowledge of mathematics because of the personal attention and help they received. The experience made them aware that help was available when they needed it, and they became receptive to the academic assistance being offered to them. They began to experience success in understanding concepts that had been difficult for them and began to see their learning as important.

Prior to being in the program, the novices were reported to have become very upset when their teachers asked them to correct errors in their completed academic assignments. Instead of correcting the mistakes, they would throw the paper in the trash or claim that a younger sibling had destroyed their work. All the novices were reported to have had a low self-image and were unwilling to work effectively in small groups in the classroom. We observed that this low self-image had overpowering effects in the classroom similar to what Bennett (1990, p. 19) had found previously:

> When a student with low self-esteem enters a classroom, self-concept becomes one of the most challenging individual differences in how he or she will learn. Because students with a negative self-image are not fully able to learn, school becomes an arena for failure that prevents them from achieving the success needed for high self-esteem. A vicious cycle develops whereby the school itself, by providing experiences of failure, helps keep the student's self-image deflated.

In the emergence stage, however, the novices responded to the challenges in the tutoring program in a variety of ways. Several of the students who had had behavior problems prior to beginning the program found fewer reasons for misbehaving as they began to take their learning seriously. Several novices who had frequently found excuses to leave the tutoring sessions increasingly found less need to leave the sessions because the experts made it possible for them to experience success in their academic work. The experts countered the novices' misbehavior with patience and encouragement, which helped the novices accept the fact that they were not incapable of learning. The novices found they could do the work as long as they focused on the tasks. They increasingly found themselves willing to do precisely that; they began to concentrate more intensely on learning. Those personal triumphs resulted in the emergence of a desire to learn mathematics.

Several points must be made about the role of the experts in this first stage. As stated earlier, they did not possess extensive mathematics knowledge, but they were eager to help the younger students. This eagerness was reflected in the affect they demonstrated while working with the novices. According to their teachers, some experts had had behavior problems in their own classrooms and others had had other problems that resulted in frequent visits to the principal's office for disciplinary action. During the ASMT Program, these "problem" students became absorbed in their role as experts and were caring in dealing with disruptive behavior among the novices.

The experts found ways of motivating the novices by building on their self-confidence. One incident, between Carlitos (the novice) and Cristian (the expert), involved Carlitos's losing interest in a task and leaving his seat every few minutes to visit other students. Cristian assigned a problem that required Carlitos to explain the process of adding two-digit numbers. Carlitos had successfully explained the procedure the day before. Cristian openly expressed his surprise that Carlitos had lost interest in a task that he had already mastered. Carlitos listened attentively to Cristian and immediately began to work on the new set of two-digit addition problems. Cristian kept giving Carlitos words of encouragement that maintained Carlitos's interest in the work until he was successful. When this story was related to Cristian's teacher, she reacted with amazement because such an interaction would have resulted in a fight had Carlitos been a student in Cristian's classroom.

A similar occurrence happened with Mario (the expert) and Jermaine (the novice). Mario had been one of the low-achieving students who had received tutoring by teacher's aides earlier in the year. He volunteered to become a tutor because his teacher had encouraged him to help younger students in order to strengthen his own academic achievement. Indeed, Mario learned as he tutored.

He learned to have patience with the younger students. He also learned different teaching strategies, which helped the tutees see alternatives for learning and understanding new processes. Thus, when Jermaine wanted to give up, Mario acknowledged a similar feeling when he had not been able to understand something. Mario would focus Jermaine's interest on the work and proceed to search for new ways of communication.

These two examples are important because classroom teachers are generally unable to give such attention to students who are having problems. Mario was able to relate to Jermaine's frustrations and was successful in "scaffolding" ways to help Jermaine connect to the mathematics problems instead of giving up. Like Jermaine, many novices needed assistance in talking through frustrations to clarify their thinking and to be ready to focus on the assigned problems.

Partnership

In the second stage of the model, partnership, we saw the formation of supportive bonds created through an atmosphere of respect. This partnership allowed the novices to cast themselves in a new light as successful achievers and enabled them to develop an interest in learning. Although the ASMT Program places primary emphasis on the acquisition of knowledge, the novices are given opportunities to feel good about their contributions to their own learning. This attitude assists in self-reflection which in turn motivates the novice to seek ways to become more successful. The novices began to believe they could change their status of failure, and they were able to share their difficulties and successes in mathematics with the experts.

The supportive bonds between the tutor and the tutee encouraged the novices to become partners in their success. Nurturing self-esteem so as to heighten academic expectations was a focus in the ASMT Program. The experts were supportive of the novices' efforts and took a deep personal interest in their struggles to succeed. Each expert shared information with the novices about personal struggles in overcoming past failures. This sharing helped both experts and novices to begin to appreciate each other's efforts and commitments. The supportive bonds created in this relationship produced a willingness in the novices to attend the sessions and participate in their learning. They began to perceive and value their capacity to learn mathematics.

The time that the experts took to listen and to understand the needs of their tutees contributed to the success of the novices in this stage. After the expert got a sense of what the novices' needs were, the experts shifted the responsibility for learning to the novices themselves. The following is an example of this shifting of responsibility.

Carlitos failed to bring to the session the assignment Cristian had prepared for him. Carlitos claimed that his younger sister had spilled juice on the assignment and it was too wet to save. Carlitos had offered a similar excuse the day before. Instead of getting upset, Cristian put his arm around Carlitos's shoulder and recalled that he had had similar things happen to his assignments. He instructed Carlitos to find a quieter place at home where he could study and complete his assignments. Cristian told Carlitos that the assignments were to help him gain a better understanding by practicing at home. Cristian later revealed that Carlitos seldom forgot his assignments after this incident.

Sessions were held to allow the experts to share strategies that had been effective with each novice. The program director also shared scaffolding strategies with the experts. No experts wanted to leave the program because of problems they were having with their novice, even when the problems were difficult. Because they took their roles seriously, the experts were genuinely interested in seeking information that would assist them during the tutoring sessions.

The novices had come to the ASMT Program with insufficient knowledge of mathematics and poorly developed social skills. They were unhappy in school and were unable or unwilling to complete classroom assignments. Their continued attendance and commitment to the ASMT Program was the result of their positive experiences in learning mathematics in that supportive environment.

Consolidation

In the consolidation stage of the model, the tutees made adjustments to their old study habits. As a result of their academic accomplishments, the novices assumed more responsibility for their own learning. The connectedness created through the one-to-one tutoring in the partnership stage aided in creating the changes we saw in the consolidation stage. The partnership was consolidated to strengthen the academic success of each novice.

The novices were then able to concentrate on learning new material without becoming distracted. The affective and academic support the experts had given to them was evident in the new responsibilities undertaken by the novices. Their new success awakened their need to control the direction of their learning. The novices began to guide their own learning and to request help in areas where they needed it most, whereas earlier they had allowed the experts to select the work for the tutoring sessions. The novices began to choose some of the tasks for the sessions. The metacognitive foundation for this stage is the novices' recognizing their academic needs because they are aware of what they have previously learned in the ASMT Program.

The improvement in the affective domain during this stage manifested itself in an increase in the tutees' self-worth, which in turn became evident to the teachers in the classroom. For example, the novices began to volunteer answers to questions directed to the class at large. They also began to ask for help when they encountered difficulties with problems. They no longer lost interest or gave up when they were unsuccessful in understanding a new concept.

One expert, Jackie, commented that she was having to find more work for Juanita because the tutee had requested it. Juanita was a second grader who had fallen behind in her class and had often refused to do her homework. Juanita requested a second sheet of homework from her teacher, one to complete during tutoring and another to do for actual homework. Juanita had become comfortable with the work and was beginning to challenge herself while using Jackie as a resource to gain new understandings.

The ASMT Program director used one of the tutoring sessions to gain a better understanding of the scaffolding strategies used by the experts and the positive effects those strategies were having on the novices. Several novices stated that they liked the program because their concentration was interrupted less than in the classroom. Another offered that she liked the individual instruction because her teacher was always very busy and did not have the time to explain solutions in depth, as the expert did during the tutoring. The novices benefited from explaining their problem-solving strategies because doing so helped them retain something they might otherwise have forgotten. It also helped them see what they were understanding and where they still needed more help.

Another novice said the tutoring sessions allowed him to concentrate on what he was doing without worrying that the teacher would accuse him of wasting time. Juanita echoed that concern when she gave her fear of being misunderstood as one of the reasons she refused to do her classwork. According to her, the teacher thought she was lazy when she was actually thinking about her work and trying to figure out how to do it. Juanita often got upset when the teacher told her a problem was incorrect. Once she cried in the school bathroom because she thought she was the only one in her class who had trouble understanding the material being taught.

The experts described how they made decisions about what approaches to use with the novices. The successful strategies included (1) probing the novices to explain what they were doing so that the expert could understand where the learning gaps were, (2) asking the novices to draw a picture of a problem instead of becoming frustrated when they could not communicate the difficulty, (3) allowing the novices to review procedures in order to find additional gaps, and (4) giving the novices the responsibility of finding a way to communicate what they did and did not understand.

Responsibility motivated the novices to find strategies to communicate their problems so they could get the help they needed. Interpreting the novices' statements took entire sessions at times, but they and the experts found ways to communicate and move on together to other tasks.

Alignment

Alignment, the fourth stage of the model, showed the novices accepting their new status as capable learners. They made adjustments to their various situations with their personal resources and integrated the adjustments into their tutoring sessions as well as their regular classrooms. Their aspirations to improve in school were materializing. Because of their increased self-confidence in their ability to learn, they no longer feared new tasks, and they knew that help was available if they needed it. Teachers reported that the students in the ASMT Program showed a greater interest in class and participated more actively. Unacceptable behavior in the classroom was no longer a problem.

The novices' adjustment to their growing self-worth laid the foundation for the alignment stage. These changes in the affective domain gave them confidence that they could learn new ideas. The social and academic supports offered by each expert were essential to improving the academic achievement of each novice. The novices could make mistakes without being emotionally shaken. They knew that with practice, they would be successful in understanding new knowledge and in acquiring new learning strategies. Furthermore, they were accepting challenges and were open to demands for clarity in their explanations without feeling threatened or frustrated and giving up easily. They recognized the value of "taking a risk" to explain a process, even if they were not sure it was the correct one or even if they could not explain it with clarity. They knew that those risks usually resulted in positive learning experiences.

The following is an example of the effects of scaffolding as Mario and Jermaine worked on a two-digit addition problem. Jermaine had been using penny strips—long strips, each showing ten pennies—to find the answer to the problem 26 + 34 (see Fuson and Smith [1996] for a peer-tutoring case study using penny strips). Jermaine knew that 10 pennies made a penny strip, but he got confused about what to do when he added the 6 and the 4 and got 10 pennies. He quietly worked on the problem as Mario looked on silently. Jermaine laid out 2 penny strips and 6 loose pennies to represent the first number, 26. Then he laid out 3 penny strips and 4 loose pennies for the second number, 34. He counted the penny strips by tens to get 50 but did not know how to account for the 10 pennies. He repeated this procedure several times and gave the wrong answer of 50.

Mario watched as Jermaine struggled with the problem but did not offer any help. Jermaine began to get frustrated and was about to give up, but instead he turned to Mario and asked for help. Mario had Jermaine repeat the steps that he had just carried out. Jermaine tried to explain several times what he was doing and told Mario that he knew he was doing something wrong with the penny strips. Mario was unsure what was troubling Jermaine, so he asked Jermaine to explain the problem in his own words.

Jermaine again failed to explain the problem. After several more attempts to explain how he was using the penny strips, Jermaine instead drew a representation of what he was trying to communicate. Mario never showed impatience with Jermaine's inability to explain his difficulties. Mario empathized and told Jermaine that he had had difficulty with this type of problem when he was younger and that it had been hard for him as well. Mario pointed out what he thought the difficulty was.

Jermaine then clarified his explanation by making a drawing of his approach. He drew 2 long lines and 6 dots to present the first number then 3 long lines and 4 dots to represent the second number. Mario had him count all the dots, and Jermaine counted 10 dots. Mario asked Jermaine for the next step. Jermaine smiled and said, almost as if to himself, "I forgot to make a new ten from the ones." He then circled the 10 dots and drew an arrow pointing to the tens column.

In this episode, Mario's persistence in getting Jermaine to talk about the problem gave Mario an idea of where help was needed. This dialectical process helped Jermaine see that he had part of the problem correct but lacked a complete understanding of the procedure with the pennies.

That process allowed Jermaine to become an active participant in finding a solution. Mario was able to step back and allow Jermaine to struggle for a while with the problem in order to find an alternative approach, which afforded Jermaine another opportunity to clarify his misunderstandings through drawings and his explanation to Mario. Mario then reinforced Jermaine's understanding of what to do with the 10 dots, and Jermaine continued to finish the problem.

Reconstruction

In the fifth stage of the model, reconstruction, we witnessed the novices begin to take full responsibility for their behavior. They actively participated and directed their work both in the classroom and in the ASMT Program. At this stage the tutees willingly accepted the challenge and put out the effort necessary to acquire new knowledge. They were confident that their work would lead them to learning new concepts. They realized that the correct solution to a mathematical problem is not always immediately available. The novices knew how to navigate more difficult problems without giving up because they had learned many effective strategies to arrive at correct answers. They had discovered that they control their learning and were able to recognize their many accomplishments.

An important feature of this stage is that the novices no longer felt helpless when they had trouble understanding a new concept. They accepted the confusion as temporary when they encountered a difficult problem. In the past, they would have given up immediately, lost control of their behavior, and become angry with the novices who were successful. In this stage, however, they were accepting of those around them who learned at a faster pace and no longer became angry at the expert if they could not understand a new concept immediately. The novices no longer blamed others for their lack of understanding. They knew that they would eventually learn the concept if they tried.

This stage was important to the novices because (1) they became more responsible for their learning, (2) they listened more carefully to grasp the process, and (3) they tried solving the problem by themselves several times before they requested assistance.

Furthermore, their need for personal attention decreased. The foundation for this stage was the responsibility that the novices took for their learning and their increased level of self-confidence in their ability to succeed.

At this stage the tutees reported that they enjoyed choosing their own topics for the tutoring sessions. They also liked having the opportunity to express their own opinions because they believed that their thinking was important. This new role of assuming responsibility was reflected in their classrooms.

Teachers would observe the tutoring session to see their students work successfully with the experts. The number of teachers who dropped in on the sessions increased as they saw the performance of their "slow" students improve in the classroom.

Self-Nourishment

In the sixth stage of the model, self-nourishment, the novices were comfortable with their progress and valued their growing awareness of what they had gained from their hard work. They increasingly directed and managed their self-growth. Their new confidence was reflected in their social behavior and attitudes toward others around them. They showed their appreciation for the support that had been given to them, often by the small gifts that they brought to the experts. Learning was almost unscaffolded, and the novices continued to select the areas where they most needed help.

Summary of the Model

The novices were active in learning and enjoyed gaining new knowledge and making their own choices about their individual needs. The novices no longer blamed the teacher or anyone else for their lack of understanding.

Anger, frustration, embarrassment, and unwillingness to work subsided. The novices developed pride in being able to do the same academic work as the students they perceived to be more capable. The experts had allowed for slack periods among the novices in the beginning stages because they, too, had had similar experiences in school. However, they were able to use the lessons learned from those experiences to assist the novices in the tutoring sessions. The shared experiences created a bond that made it possible for the novices to open up and reveal conflicts that had prevented them from succeeding. The experts many times had to make on-the-spot judgments and decisions to bring the novices to a higher level of understanding.

Raising self-esteem was a planned aspect of the ASMT Program embedded in the attainment of mathematics knowledge. The experts created different learning environments that allowed the novices to see themselves as capable learners. In the classroom, the novices were easily frustrated because they missed many of the important steps required to learn mathematical concepts. In the ASMT Program, they were able to work at their own pace without the interruptions experienced in their classroom. Socially constructed learning helped the novices function in an environment that was familiar and nonthreatening.

These young, mostly Latino, children experienced intellectual and personal growth in an environment that gave them the opportunity to learn and to become successful. They acquired new knowledge, gained self-worth, and stopped blaming themselves and others for past failures. They were socialized into new learning communities that helped them succeed in the classroom. The tutoring environment provided them the necessary social space to begin to participate in, and eventually take control of, their own learning processes.

CONCLUSION

Students in grades 1–3 are young and so susceptible to external influences that they can be convinced that they are capable learners who can experience success in mathematics just as easily as they can be convinced otherwise. If older and younger students have had similar life experiences, such as frustration and failure, the older student can learn to be effective tutors for the younger, struggling ones. Their similar history as learners can bring about positive outcomes to both groups. The tutors in this ASMT Program became powerful and important resources that influenced the younger students and helped them develop partially understood mathematical procedures into more-meaningful understandings.

The use of a dialectical approach is effective for tutors who know how to probe to find areas where help is needed. These interactions can become a step in developing shared responsibility for the learning process. Active participation helps younger students see where gaps exist as they develop new competence in seeking the help they need.

The experiences of the ASMT Program suggest that alternatives are open to us to make mathematical learning a reality for all students. As described in this article, the affective and cognitive domains are intimately linked in the learning of mathematics. Investigators in mathematics education should devote more attention to the study of the relationship between these two domains. It seems that tutors can induce positive outcomes in the cognitive domain by operating on the affective domain. Mathematics educators in general, and mathematics teachers in particular, should not neglect the importance of this relationship.

REFERENCES

Bennett, Christine. *Comprehensive Multicultural Education: Theory and Practice.* 2nd ed. Boston: Allyn & Bacon, 1990.

D'Ambrosio, Ubiratan. "The Role of Mathematics Education in Building a Democratic and Just Society." *For the Learning of Mathematics* 10 (November 1990): 20–23.

De La Cruz, Yolanda. "The Beginning of a Dialogue: Issues for Latino Parents and Non-Latino Teachers." Paper presented at the annual meeting of the American Educational Research Association, San Francisco, April 1995a.

———. "A Case Study of Supporting Teachers with Mathematics Reform in Language Minority Classrooms." In *Proceedings of the North American Chapter of the International Group for the Psychology of Mathematics Education,* edited by Douglas T. Owens, Michelle K. Reed, and Gayle M. Millsaps, vol. 1, p. 331. Columbus, Ohio: ERIC Clearinghouse for Science, Mathematics and Environmental Education, 1995b.

———. "Learning/Teaching Practices That Build Conceptual Knowledge." Paper presented at the annual meeting of the American Educational Research Association, New York, April 1996a.

———. "The Process of Implementing Family Math in Non-Mainstream Families in South Africa." Doctoral dissertation. University of California at Berkeley, 1991.

———. "Supporting Reform Mathematics with Non-Latino Teachers of Latino Students." Paper presented at the annual meeting of the American Educational Research Association, San Francisco, April 1995c.

———. "Vygotskiian Perspectives Illuminating a Mathematics Tutoring Program for Inner-City Children." In *Proceedings of the North American Chapter of the International Group for the Psychology of Mathematics Education,* edited by Elizabeth Jakubowski, Dierdre Watkins, and Harry Biske, vol. 1, p. 178. Columbus, Ohio: ERIC Clearinghouse for Science, Mathematics and Environment Education, 1996b.

De La Cruz, Yolanda, Shelly Weber, and Kelli Jones. "Supporting Reform Mathematics Teaching with Non-Latino Teachers of Latino Students." Paper presented at the annual meeting of the American Educational Research Association, San Francisco, April 1995.

Erickson, Fredrick. "Transformation and School Success: The Politics and Culture of Educational Achievement." *Anthropology and Education Quarterly* 18 (1987): 335–56.

Fuson, Karen C., Ana María Lo Cicero, K. Hudson, and Steven Smith. "Snapshots across Two Years in the Life of an Urban Latino Classroom." In *Making Sense: Teaching and Learning Mathematics with Understanding,* edited by James Hiebert, Thomas J. Carpenter, Elizabeth Fennema, Karen C. Fuson, Diane Wearne, Hanlie Murray, Harry Olivier, and Piet Human. Portsmouth, N.H.: Heinemann, forthcoming.

Fuson, Karen C., and Yolanda De La Cruz. "Perspectives on Teaching Mathematics to Nonmainstream Learners." Unpublished manuscript.

Fuson, Karen C., Steven T. Smith, and Ana María Lo Cicero. "Supporting First Graders' Ten-Structured Thinking in Urban Classrooms." *Journal for Research in Mathematics Education* 28 (December 1997): 738–66.

Laosa, Luis M. "Maternal Teaching Strategies in Chicano and Anglo-American Families: The Influence of Culture and Education on Maternal Behavior." *Child Development* 51 (1978): 759–65.

———. "Maternal Teaching Strategies in Chicano Families of Varied Educational and Socioeconomic Levels." *Child Development* 49 (1978): 1129–35.

Mandler, G. *Mind and Body: Psychology of Emotion and Stress.* New York: Springer-Verlag, 1984.

Moll, Luis C., Cathy Amanti, Deborah Neff, and Norma González. "Funds of Knowledge for Teaching: Using a Qualitative Approach to Connect Homes and Classrooms." *Theory into Practice* 31, no. 2 (1992): 132–41.

Moll, Luis C., and Stephen Diaz. "Ethnographic Pedagogy: Promoting Effective Bilingual Instruction." In *Advances in Bilingual Education Research,* edited by Eugene Garcia and Ray V. Padilla, pp. 127–49. Tucson, Ariz.: University of Arizona Press, 1985.

Mullis, Ina V. S., Eugene H. Owen, and Gary W. Phillips. *Accelerating Academic Achievement: A Summary of Findings from Twenty Years of NAEP.* Princeton, N.J.: Educational Testing Service, 1990.

Oakes, Jeannie. "Opportunities, Achievement, and Choice: Women and Minority Students in Science and Mathematics." In *Review of Research in Education,* vol. 16, edited by Courtney B. Cazden, pp. 153–222. Washington, D.C.: American Educational Research Association, 1990.

Ogbu, John, and Maria Eugenia Matute-Bianchi. "Understanding Sociocultural Factors: Knowledge, Identity, and School Adjustment." In *Beyond Language: Social and Cultural Factors in Schooling Language Minority Students,* edited by Bilingual Education Office, California State Department of Education, pp. 73–142. Los Angeles: Evaluation, Dissemination and Assessment Center, California State University—Los Angeles, 1986.

Secada, Walter G. "Race, Ethnicity, Social Class, Languages, and Achievement in Mathematics." In *Handbook of Research on Mathematics Teaching and Learning,* edited by Douglas A. Grouws, pp. 623–60. New York: Macmillan Publishing Co., 1992.

Secada, Walter G., and Yolanda De La Cruz. "Teaching Mathematics for Understanding to Bilingual Students." In *Children of la Frontera,* edited by Judith LeBlanc Flores, pp. 285–308. Charleston, W.V.: ERIC Clearinghouse on Rural Education and Small Schools, 1996.

Vasquez, J. "Teaching to the Distinctive Traits of Minority Students." *Clearing House* 63, no. 7 (1990): 299–304.

There's More to Mathematics than Choosing the Letter *C*
The Limitations of Test-Driven Intervention

16

Milagros M. Seda
Carmen M. Seda

This study reports the action research of one teacher who discovered the limitations of a test-driven methodology. The teacher was responsible for an intervention mathematics course implemented by her campus to raise the scores of ELL (English-language learner) students on the state's mandated test, the Texas Assessment of Academic Skills (TAAS). Because of her limited knowledge and experience in teaching mathematics, she experienced an instructional crisis. She was also restricted by the methodology the school required for this particular class that involved drilling students by using right-or-wrong answer methods. She found that this type of regimented instructional process inhibited her ability to instruct the students adaquately. Thus she looked for methods to improve her instruction within these limitations. This report documents her efforts.

The second author of this study is the teacher of the intervention class, and the other author is the university graduate-studies mentor of the teacher, hereafter referred to as the teacher and the mentor, respectively.

BACKGROUND

The study describes three sessions in which twenty-four Latino middle school students were learning mathematics problem solving from a teacher, not certified in mathematics, in a class designed to facilitate students' success on a state-mandated test. Since the need was pressing, the district elected to assign all teachers to the intervention program, regardless of their subject-area specialization, in the hope that the teachers' classroom experience would compensate for their lack of content knowledge.

The authors theorized that mathematics teachers could apply the same principles of acquisition learning that are used in classrooms in which students learn English or Spanish as a second language. When language is learned according to a language-acquisition model, students use authentic, purposeful activities in order to make meaning through the new language. Some of the strategies commonly used in such classrooms include the use of pictures and modeling to communicate abstract ideas to students as their language evolves. Activities that are skills- or answer-focused are not usually used in language-acquisition models because such activities do not offer a meaningful context for acquiring language. It is difficult for teachers to implement these types of alternative instructional strategies, however, when the primary goal in mathematics curriculum in many schools is to select answers on multiple-choice worksheets. These types of worksheet activities may have some effect in preparing students for state-mandated multiple-choice tests but have questionable value in preparing students to thoroughly understand complex mathematics concepts.

The observations of the intervention teacher led her to recognize the limitations of the test-driven methodology and answer-focused mathematics instruction. Research supports the use of methods that lead students to understand underlying mathematics concepts. However, intervention programs continue to be designed on the basis of assembly-line learning and test-driven paradigms that may undermine students' success rather than facilitate it. The teacher questioned whether such programs were using methodologies supported by research.

The Supporting Research

The teacher and her mentor searched the literature for effective mathematics instructional strategies and language-acquisition methodologies for Latino learners. Since the intervention class was limited by the requirements of TAAS instruction, most of the information related to instructional practices was not useful. We found several articles on acquisition strategies for language-arts classrooms and on strategies for forming a bridge between language arts and mathematics. Chamot (1992) demonstrated that picture presentations of mathematics problems improved English-language learners' comprehension of the problems. Winograd and Higgins (1994–95, p. 312) showed how "the language arts and mathematics can be integrated as students write, solve, and discuss story problems." Newman (1995) demonstrated that just as there are a variety of learning styles, there are a variety of help-seeking styles. The teacher reflected on these matters in this study.

The Parameters of the Learning Environment

Community Information

The students were from a community that is 99 percent Latino and generally bilingual in Spanish and English. The area surrounding the school is classified by the state as middle to lower income. No information was available on the percent of recent immigrants in the community.

The Intervention Classroom

In 1994, more than 50 percent of the students in the district had failed the mathematics section of the TAAS, so the district implemented the intervention period to address a perceived deficit in test-taking and problem-solving skills. Although the intervention system was originally intended to serve "low performing" students—those who scored poorly on the TAAS—the district requires all students to be assigned to an intervention class, regardless of their level of success on the TAAS. The intervention system requires teachers of subjects other than mathematics to teach one daily forty-minute intervention class of twenty-five or fewer students. Mathematics teachers (hereafter referred to as *monitor teachers*) supervise the intervention teachers. Students are randomly assigned. No adjustments are made for learning levels, language, or special needs other than those covered by the state's regular requirements for special populations.

The Students

Twenty-four Latino students aged twelve to thirteen participated. The students represented a cross section of achievement levels. Of the twenty-four, ten had failed mathematics in the previous six weeks and twelve had failed the mathematics section of the mock TAAS, a practice trial of the state-mandated test. Nine had been in an ELL or academic-assistance class within the last three years. One student, who was in her first year of learning English, joined the English speakers only during the intervention period. The fourteen other students spoke English, usually without relying on Spanish to complete a sentence.

Teacher Preparation

No in-service instruction in teaching mathematics was given to the intervention teacher. Her own mathematics experience was limited to college algebra, a passing score on the Graduate Record Examination, and what she had learned from her monitoring teacher, Ms. Paulson. Once a month Ms. Paulson visited the class to assist in the areas of difficulty identified by the intervention teacher. Each intervention teacher uses her or his own strategies for determining the areas of weakness.

Procedural Requirements

The students in the intervention classes receive daily mathematics multiple-choice worksheets patterned after the state-mandated TAAS. The worksheets are numbered and coded. The students work on six to twelve multiple-choice word problems daily. The intervention teachers oversee the completion of the worksheets and devise reme-dial strategies. The intervention teachers may not set aside worksheets in favor of other activities. All instruction must relate to the TAAS objectives designated for the day.

THE STUDY

Since this segment of the study represents the intervention teacher's observations both as teacher and researcher, the remainder of the report will be given in her own words. *We* refers to the teacher and the mentor. *I* refers to the intervention teacher:

After consultation with my graduate mentor, we selected from the available research factors that could be considered in designing a small classroom study to improve my teaching skills. We looked first at my helping methods and realized that I was limiting my help to those who asked for it, thus overlooking students who were reluctant to ask for help. I also realized I had not incorporated strategies that help students focus on the process and content of mathematics. Although in my instruction I conveyed to them that it was important to understand the process and related concepts, I was still rewarding them for responding with correct answers without justifications.

With that in mind, I reflected on the strategies we had read about in the relevant research literature. I focused first on designing a minilesson, using pictures to depict the problem and the applicable parts of the related number sentence. To help the students understand how to solve word problems, I used a modeling technique some-times used in ELL classes. For example, whenever possible, I drew pictures to help them understand the principles involved. I used a method for solving a problem on the chalkboard wherein I would show, but not tell, them what to do. Instead of ver-bally explaining the procedures to them, I showed them how to solve the problems by drawing pictures. In this way they would acquire the information from observing my actions and choices. I kept track of my observations in a daily log that I brought to the graduate mentor for feedback. The information from my log forms the body of the following section of the study.

The Daily Procedure and Its Limitations

I was very surprised to find that prior to the study, students were scoring 100s on the TAAS worksheets and still doing poorly in their regular mathematics classes. The stu-dents received the worksheets and were to raise their hand when they had difficulty with a problem so I could focus on areas of need. We then went over the problems ver-bally while a group of students solved the problems on the chalkboard. Some students did not write out the solution but still scored 100 on the daily worksheets. I was puz-zled that the high-scoring students were regularly not on task during the lessons. After further observation I realized that the students were sharing answers among themselves. The stronger students were explaining their answers to the struggling students, but the struggling students were not attempting to understand the problem; they wanted only to know which letter to circle for the correct answer. *They were not learning anything.*

At this point, I pondered what I should do. I knew the stronger learners already had a process to search for a response. However, I wanted to give them a mechanism that alerted them to an error without giving them the answer. That mechanism would force them to analyze their work before redoing it. I also wanted a means of identi-fying the struggling learners. Finally, I wanted to find out what types of mathematics problems were particularly difficult for the whole class.

With these goals in mind, I devised a daily procedure to help the better learners find their own errors and also alert me to the struggling learners and their learning needs. I included the monitoring teacher's requirements that students must (*a*) read the entire quiz first, (*b*) read each word problem, (*c*) underline the question posed in each word problem, (*d*) circle the numbers relevant to the problem, and (*e*) cross out numbers not relevant to the problem. I subsequently incorporated strategies that would give me information on the students' progress. The whole procedure involved the following:

1. The students received the worksheets and had fifteen minutes to work out the problems, adhering to the steps demonstrated by the monitoring mathematics teacher.

2. The students then wrote the letters representing the answers in the margin of the test sheet.

3. I moved around the classroom with the answer key and circled incorrect answers.

4. The students reworked the problems they had answered incorrectly until they arrived at a correct answer or put a star by questions posing difficulty.

5. The students who were clearly unable to work out certain problems were placed in a tutoring circle for guided instruction or were assigned a student-mentor to assist them in solving the problem.

6. The students engaged in postlesson discussions and received oral feedback from fellow students on areas of difficulty or reflected on the process used to arrive at correct responses.

I implemented the new daily procedure for one week before beginning the information-gathering phase of the study. I was able to determine who the stronger learners were because they were the first ones to finish and usually had more than 80 percent of their answers correct on the first pass. The struggling students usually showed no work, had only circled answers, and were unable to tell me how they had arrived at the answer. The stronger students still felt obliged to help the struggling students and did so, but the struggling students were still not able to verbalize their understanding of the process during the postlesson discussion. I was beginning to get a more accurate picture of the disparity of abilities in the classroom and how it affected the students' behavior.

Initial Information Gathering

During the next few days of instruction, I decided I would involve the students in information gathering that would give them and me feedback on their progress. I informed the students that for that week, we were going to be changing some instructional procedures so that I could determine what were the most difficult aspects of problem solving for them. I also told them that I wanted to see if the adjustments were helping them understand the process and content of mathematics.

On the first day, the students received the designated worksheet for the day, Multiple Choice Review #3. The students were instructed to show an algebraic expression that represented the information that helped them solve the problem. Alternatively, they could put a star by the problem to indicate that they were not sure of their answer or that a problem was especially challenging for them. I told them that since putting a star by the question was an information-gathering procedure, wrong answers would not count against their daily grade. Since I needed an accurate assessment of their learning needs, I urged them not to share answers because, if they did, I would not have reliable information from which to design future interventions. Most of the stronger students understood mu instructions and kept their answers covered. Most of the struggling students still tried to get the answers from their classmates, but I reminded them to work out the problems by themselves and show their work.

I also restrained myself from helping the students. Several students were irritated that I would not help them that day. Telling them to put a star by questions they did not understand helped to appease them, but they often still looked around the room to find an answer to fill in the slot. The only assistance I offered was to circle their incorrect responses so that they could rework the problem on their own. I kept track of the areas posing challenges for the students so that the monitoring teacher could target those areas on her regular monthly visit, which was due that week.

The results of the students' efforts on Multiple Choice Review #3 were as follows. Fourteen of the students were able to complete at least seven of ten questions correctly without intervention, although they missed different questions. All fourteen students were able to find their own mistakes when informed that their answer was wrong. Eight of the remaining ten students had problems with at least two questions, even when alerted to their errors. The other two students made no attempt to answer the questions but had underlined the questions and circled the relevant numbers, as required by the daily procedure. I logged the number of problems missed on the first pass and after the students had had an opportunity to adjust their answers.

Finally, I polled the students about which problems were difficult. Even though I had logged their errors as I supervised them, I wanted to see if they were reluctant to acknowledge any difficulties. I also wanted to compare my findings with their perceptions of which problems were the most difficult. Almost none of the students were willing to admit their difficulties. I reminded them that this was a research project and honesty was essential to the outcome.

Then, I said "Please."

After my pleading, all the students participated in this portion of the project willingly. After the first day, the number of students who acknowledged difficulty on problems matched the number who actually answered those problems incorrectly.

Assessment of the First Day's Findings

From my observation of the first day, I determined that this class had difficulty with percents, fractions, and determining which operations to use in a given context. For example, on the first attempt 50 percent of the students missed the following question requiring them to determine the fraction that represents 1/9 of 2/3:

> Mr. Karly's class has been asked to paint 2/3 of the backdrop for the school play. How much of the backdrop will each of his 9 students paint if they each paint an equal amount? A) 1/18, B) 2/27, C) 2/9, D) 5/8, E) Not Here (Enselek and Griffin 1991)

More than 50 percent of the students also missed the following question requiring them to add mixed numbers:

> Mr. Craig used 45 1/2 gallons of beige paint to paint an apartment complex. He used 26 1/5 gallons of brown paint and 69 1/4 gallons of white paint. How many gallons of paint did he use? A)141, B) 140 19/20, C) 140 3/19, D) 139 19/20, E) Not Here (Enselek and Griffin 1991)

However, more than 75 percent of the class had little difficulty in answering questions involving simple arithmetic operations such as subtraction and addition.

The students were also reluctant to admit their limitations. The struggling students often wrote numbers down anywhere on the worksheet so that it would look as if they were accomplishing the task, and they were persuaded to admit areas of difficulty only when they saw other students raising their hand. One strong student tried to coax the struggling students to acknowledge their difficulties by convincing other strong students to raise their hand when they were polled about problems they found difficult. The students who were at first reluctant to acknowledge difficulty were more willing to participate after the strong students had set the example. The struggling students were also reluctant to hand in their work until they had hunted down and circled the correct letter for each answer, even though their errors had been recorded and they had acknowledged their difficulties.

Traditional Intervention

Ms. Paulson, the monitoring teacher, came to the classroom for her regular monthly visit on the second day. I told her about my project and current findings and asked her to intervene in a lesson on the problematic areas. I asked her to teach according to the traditional approach so that I could compare her intervention with something I wanted to try.

Ms. Paulson began with question 9, the question involving the addition of mixed numbers. She first created a question using tens, fives, and halves so that students could easily follow the procedure. She explained the steps as the students watched. Occasionally, she asked the class to suggest the next step in the process. Several of the students were inattentive and had to be asked to pay attention. The strongest students were alert and gave correct answers at the prompting of the teacher. One strong student, José, had to be disciplined for calling out the letter to the answers instead of answering the prompts. "It's *C, Miss!*" he would call out jubilantly. "The answer to number 9 is *C!*" Ms. Paulson reminded all the students not to call out answers while she was explaining the process of finding an answer, but José still seemed determined to be the first to get the correct answer.

The two students who had made no attempt to do their work the day before still made no attempt to follow the lesson, but they tried to look attentive. Four students were continuously off task and inattentive, and they began to irritate the other students. All four had scored less than 50 percent on Multiple Choice Review #3. The one ELL student, Nora, seemed determined to copy word for word everything the teacher wrote on the chalkboard. She sat beside a bilingual student who translated the explanations as the monitoring teacher wrote on the chalkboard. At one point, Nora called me over and asked me in Spanish to tell Ms. Paulson not to erase the chalkboard, since she had not finished copying the explanation. Nora had missed only question 9 on the Multiple Choice Review #3.

Assessment of the Traditional Intervention

According to Ms. Paulson, the four students who did not pay attention during her lesson continually fail to answer correctly or they copy other students' answers during regular mathematics classes. These same students were reluctant to admit difficulty in mathematics and covered their inadequacies by copying or calling out answers after someone else had given the correct answer.

Nora, in contrast, seemed to do better in the intervention class than in her regular mathematics class. I was not sure to what to attribute her success. Unlike the other students, Nora had performed every step of the daily procedure without fail. Despite her language limitations, she was able to analyze the word problem for the information needed to arrive at an answer. So something was going right, but I still was not certain how the students were processing concepts or which intervention strategies were effective.

The Results of a Non-Verbal Helping Strategy and a Picture Strategy

On the third day, I decided to implement one helping strategy: I wrote a problem on the chalkboard similar to the ones the students found difficult, but I substituted different numbers. I completed the operation silently, writing my answer line by line to show my work as I progressed. I did not give them any verbal cues, but I drew pictures where needed for clarity. As the students solved the problems in Multiple Choice Review #4 involving simple equations, I reminded them that they must either show an algebraic expression that demonstrated how they had arrived at their answer or put a star by the problem. I also told them that if I saw a pattern of difficulty, I would do a comparable problem on the chalkboard showing the work. On question 1, they were to subtract fractions.

Mrs. Whitley bought a certain stock on Monday for 37 1/8 dollars per share. On Friday she sold the stock for 35 5/8 dollars per share. How much did she lose per share of stock? A) 1 1/8 dollars, B) 1 1/2 dollars, C) 2 1/8 dollars, D) 2 1/2 dollars, E) Not Here (*TAAS Mathematics Workbook,* Education, Etc. 1991).

Ms. Paulson had demonstrated the procedure for solving the same problems the day before. During this class, however, only six students answered the questions correctly the first time. I set up a parallel problem on the chalkboard and drew stick figures handing each other money and stocks and set up a similar problem. After I modeled the problem, sixteen students answered the question correctly when they reworked the problem.

Earlier that day in the Texas history class, I had presented a problem on probability to each of my classes. (The students in the mathematics intervention class are also in my Texas history class.) I drew a picture of a bag with 100 grains in it. Of the grains, 45 were corn, 15 wheat, 25 barley, and 15 rice. The students were to determine for each kind of grain the probability of drawing a grain of that kind on the first try, with replacement. I did not use verbal cues as we went through the lesson. I drew pictures or used body language as the students called out the procedures to find the answer. The students seemed to follow easily, and they appeared comfortable with the procedure. Later that day, in the intervention class, 83 percent of the students responded correctly to a similar question on probability.

The class, however, did not do as well on subtraction of fractions as on probability. Fifty percent of the students missed the following two questions on estimating:

There are 11 students who have summer jobs as city lifeguards. They each work 39 1/2 hours per week. What is a good estimate for the number of hours they all work in 2 weeks? A) 200, B) 250, C) 400, D) 434, E) 800 (Enselek and Griffin 1991)

There are 79 boxes of chickens and 54 boxes of turkeys in the grocery freezer. Each box of chickens contains 34 chickens. What is a good estimate of the number of chickens in the freezer? A) 2200, B) 2400, C) 2800, D) 3200, E) Not Here (Enselek and Griffin 1991)

The students seemed to have trouble with the concept of estimation. Some used the strategy of rounding each number in the problem to arrive at an estimate. Others, however, confused estimating with rounding, so they actually computed the answer and then rounded. Still others simply circled the option "not here."

OBSERVATIONS

Six of the students who had had trouble during the first day of the study were still having problems with the same types of questions through the third day. Of those six, three improved somewhat on their own over the period of the study. These three did not receive special instructions but seemed to respond to my circling their incorrect responses and to the lesson I modeled.

On the first day of these observations, ten students did not attempt all the questions. However, on the third day, all but two of the students attempted all the questions. Nora, the ELL student, did as well on the third day as on the first.

Classroom Worksheets

Multiple Choice Reviews #3 and #4 covered the same topics. Those topics appeared in a different order on the two worksheets.

In addition, the questions in the reviews were phrased differently or were structured differently. When presented with alternative forms of the questions, the students seemed to have difficulty generalizing the concepts. The concepts had to be retaught whenever a problem was presented in a different form.

Students' Attitudes

Students' attitudes toward mathematics, informally assessed by observing the effort invested or the level of engagement on the assigned task, were a strong indicator of success. Six students exerted little effort and showed low levels of achievement. These students behaved as if they were not concerned with their own success, but they were still reluctant to admit their difficulties when they were polled about difficult questions. Two of these students had been held back by learning disabilities and were currently in pull-out assistance programs at other times of the day. Four of the reluctant students were bright, socially well-adjusted learners but consistently talked with other students during the lesson. When tested, they were embarrassed by their inability to solve a problem and would immediately look for help from friends. These four students appeared to believe they could overcome their limitations by merely getting a correct answer without having to invest time in actually learning the process for arriving at the solution. It appears that these students were more interested in cutting corners than in investing time to learn.

Perhaps the students' attitudes are related to prior experience in always succeeding at getting assistance from classmates. The classroom culture encourages students to be sympathetic with their classmates' struggles and to help one another, as when Nora needed and found a translator with relative ease and without my intervention. Unfortunately, the way they help often detracts from their learning. Rather than help their classmates understand the mathematical processes and solutions, they just gave them the answers. I believe that the four most reluctant students knew their friends would always be there for them and therefore were not interested in working their way through the questions. Whether they would have struggled any less if they *had* committed themselves to learning cannot be determined by these few observations.

ANALYSIS OF THE OBSERVATIONS

From my observations, I began to suspect that the students had learned to focus on finding correct answers and had not given proper attention to the learning process and the concepts that are necessary for success in problem solving. We teachers often assume that students understand when they give correct answers, and we don't require them to demonstrate or explain the process that leads to the correct solution.

I also suspect that we teach procedures to students instead of providing examples from which they can abstract general concepts. For example, when Ms. Paulson showed the students how to subtract fractions, several of them followed dutifully but still could not solve similar problems correctly on their first try because the new problems involved different procedures, which Ms. Paulson had not covered (in other words, students learn what they are taught). However, when they were shown various examples of subtracting fractions similar to the problem they were solving, they were able to adjust their responses accordingly because all the procedures had been reviewed.

Furthermore, after I presented the probability question in the Texas history lesson by drawing pictures and demonstrating the process and the solution, 83 percent of the students were able to solve a comparable problem on the first try. Only 50 percent of them had been able to answer the probability question on the first day without instruction or without my using pictures and demonstrating the process. Drawing pictures along with presenting the solution appears to facilitate the learning and retention of concepts for this particular group. This approach may be particularly beneficial for students who are learning English as a second language.

Finally, requiring students to underline the questions and circle the relevant numbers in the problem appears to have some positive effect on their success but does not indicate that they understand the process. Even after instruction, some students were still unable to understand some problems or the nature of their solution. For example, in attempting to find the cost of a $560 stereo "after a 35% discount has been applied," some students gave the correct answer, $364.00. Others, however, gave $196 as the answer, which shows that many students did not know which percent—65% or 35%—to use in calculating the cost of the stereo after the discount was taken.

Furthermore, the wording of several of the estimation questions was confusing, which leads me to believe that in multiple-choice tests, the assessment of mathematics skills may be confounded by inadequate language skills. In the example above, the wording confused some students who thought *applied* meant "added." The students understood how to calculate a percentage, but their answers were incorrect because they misunderstood the vocabulary in the problem. Therefore, we need to recognize the limitations of standardized tests in evaluating students' true comprehension of mathematics problem solving.

RECOMMENDATIONS

I believe that I now have a better understanding of some of my weaknesses as a teacher of mathematics besides my lack of training in that discipline. Even trained mathematics teachers may be poorly prepared to deal with the gap that exists between the strongest and weakest mathematics students. Having teachers who are not certified to teach mathematics does little to meet the state's expressed goals for students' learning in mathematics.

My experience as an English teacher has taught me that emphasizing the process in teaching writing helps students understand and analyze their ideas more clearly. Similarly, teaching mathematics through a process approach can help students analyze and understand the concepts and principles involved in mathematics problem solving. Moreover, writing in mathematics can also assist the teacher and learner in connecting writing and thinking. For example, stronger students can be taught to help struggling students in meaningful ways through written feedback and help in understanding the process. If students who are both receiving and giving help write their thoughts about a mathematical procedure that has just been taught and learned, they can collaborate in finding a solution instead of focusing on the meaningless circling of letters on a multiple-choice test.

On the basis of my observations of the teaching and learning process described in this article, I can conclude that the students in my intervention class might be more visual than auditory in their learning style. Thus, talking to them about problems may hinder rather than help their learning. Furthermore, it appears that mathematics teaching needs to change from a product-oriented approach to a process-oriented one so that students can learn to value mathematics processes. Certainly, problem solving must be more meaningful than having students calling out, "The answer is *C.*"

CONCLUSION

The intervention teacher's limited experience with teaching mathematics initially led to students' copying and sharing answers, which was devoid of meaningful learning. The two interventions that yielded success for this particular group of students were presenting material visually and providing models, cues, and prompts. The teacher was limited both by her lack of experience and by the test-driven approach to teaching. Even though the intervention teacher was not certified in mathematics, through her experiences in this project, she learned to appreciate the value of a process-oriented approach in mathematics teaching, of modeling solutions, and of visual presentations. Although we did not examine any social variables related to the Latino students in this article, it is possible that economic or sociopolitical conditions affect their learning environments in ways we could not identify.

The study was action research and was limited to three days of observations. Therefore, the observations and insights gleaned from the study and discussed by the teacher cannot be generalized to a larger population without the use of an appropriate quantitative research design. However, the study did suggest important areas of investigation that include, but are not limited to, the following: What are the effects on Latino students of a test-driven, worksheet style of instructional program? How much training of what sort should a teacher have before being assigned to instruct students in mathematics, or what kind of emergency training should be available for districts facing a similar crisis?

Mathematics intervention programs must allow teachers to explore their instructional options, in order to assist them in improving the effectiveness of their teaching. Creating intervention programs is only the first step.

REFERENCES

Chamot, Anna Uhl. "Learning and Problem Solving Strategies of ESL Students." *Bilingual Research Journal* 16 (Summer-Fall 1992): 1–34.

Enselek, Patricia, and Susan Griffin. *8th Grade Mathematics TAAS Instruction Packet,* pp. 52–69. Baytown, Tex.: Education, Etc., 1991.

Newman, Richard S. "Students' Help Seeking during Problem Solving: Effects of Grade, Goal, and Prior Achievement." *American Educational Research Journal* 32 (Summer 1995): 352–76.

Winograd, Ken, and Karen M. Higgins. "Writing, Reading, and Talking Mathematics: One Interdisciplinary Possibility." *Reading Instructor* 48 (December 1994–January 1995): 310–18.